Parking Management Best Practices

By

Todd Litman

AMERICAN PLANNING ASSOCIATION
Chicago, Illinois
Washington, D.C.

ISBN (paperback edition): 1-932364-04-8 and 978-1-932364-04-0
ISBN (hardcover edition): 1-932364-05-6 and 978-1-932364-05-7
Library of Congress Control Number: 2005935930

Printed in the United States of America

Interior composition and copyediting by Joanne Shwed, Backspace Ink
Cover design by Susan Deegan

Contents

Acknowledgements

This book could not have been produced without the help of many people. I would like to thank them all, particularly my family—Suzanne, Graham, and Raviv—for putting up with a husband and father who has unusual interests.

I would specifically like to thank Ron Allan, Kathy Anderson, Rudolf Anner, Alex Beck, Dan Benson, George Brown, Mark Chase, Deborah Curran, Teun de Wit, Marcus Enoch, Erik Ferguson, Bern Grush, Jan Usterud Hanssen, Dave Holladay, Nick Lester, Herb Levinson, Randy McCourt, Gabriel Metcalf, Adam Millard-Ball, Hayat Muhammed, John A. Nawn, Warwick Pattinson, Paul Pinsker, Steve Reddish, John Renne, Mohsen Salehi, Steve Sinclair, Mary Smith, MaryCatherine Snyder, Howard Strassner, Al Swanson, Peter Swift, and JoAnn Woodhall.

Preface

Years ago, singer Joni Mitchell lamented, "They've paved paradise and put up a parking lot." The song resonates because there is much to dislike about parking facilities. They tend to be expensive, unattractive, and harmful to the environment. Cherished, old buildings and lovely greenfields are often replaced by brutal pavement that is hot during summer, cold and icy during winter, and ugly at any time. A parking lot is generally considered the least glamorous, least interesting, and least attractive type of land use. Parking facilities are an unpleasant necessity.

Yet, the same people who complain about them often travel by automobile and require parking at their destinations. We dislike parking facilities until we need one, at which time we want them to be abundant, convenient, and free. The tension between our dislike for parking facilities and our desire to have them on demand creates conflicts for individuals, businesses, and communities.

This book identifies ways to help reconcile this conflict. It describes various management strategies that can reduce the amount of parking required at a location and address many of their undesirable impacts. This is a practical and effective way to save money and land, create more attractive communities, increase user convenience, and support other planning objectives.

Most parking management strategies have modest individual impacts—a 5 percent reduction here, a 10 percent reduction there—but together they can significantly reduce the number of parking spaces needed to serve a particular location. This can represent the difference between a successful or an unsuccessful development, an ugly or a beautiful streetscape, or a walkable or an automobile-dependent community.

Our challenge is noble but formidable. There are many obstacles to the implementation of innovative parking management programs, so arm yourself before you proceed. Be sure that you are familiar with all possible parking management strategies. Identify and publicize benefits. Develop contingency plans. Treat your allies with kindness and your foes with respect. Ultimately, you will succeed because the strategies described in this book make the world a better place. Parking management helps restore paradise.

List of Figures

List of Tables

1

Introduction

Parking is an essential component of the transportation system. Vehicles need to park at each destination. A typical automobile is parked 23 hours each day and uses several parking spaces each week. Parking facilities are a major type of land use; their location and design affect the kind of development that occurs as well as how we view a building or use a street. Parking is generally the first and last interaction that visitors have with a destination, and so has a major impact on their experience.

In the past, parking planning activities were primarily concerned with providing a generous amount of free parking at each destination. If the supply was ever inadequate, governments and businesses were expected to add more. However, there is a growing realization that this approach can be harmful. In many situations, there are better ways to satisfy our parking demands.

Parking management includes a variety of specific strategies that, when appropriately applied, can significantly reduce the number of parking spaces required in a particular situation and provide a variety of additional benefits by:

- Improving user quality of service.
- Creating more accessible land-use patterns.
- Reducing motor vehicle traffic.
- Reducing congestion, accidents, and pollution.
- Creating more attractive communities.
- Improving mobility for nondrivers.

For these reasons, improved management is often the best solution to parking problems. For more information on these benefits, see the sidebar entitled "Summary of Parking Management Benefits and Costs."

Below is a list of the types of parking management strategies described in this book:

I. Strategies That Increase Parking Facility Efficiency
- Share parking.
- Regulate parking.
- Establish more accurate and flexible standards.
- Establish parking maximums.
- Provide remote parking and shuttle services.
- Implement smart growth policies.
- Improve walking and cycling conditions.
- Increase capacity of existing parking facilities.

II. Strategies That Reduce Parking Demand
- Implement mobility management.
- Price parking.
- Improve pricing methods.
- Provide financial incentives.
- Unbundle parking.
- Reform parking taxes.
- Provide bicycle facilities.

III. Support Strategies
- Improve user information and marketing.
- Improve enforcement and control.
- Establish transportation management associations and parking brokerage.
- Establish overflow parking plans.
- Address spillover problems.
- Improve parking facility design and operation.

This book provides guidance for evaluating and implementing these strategies and developing an integrated parking plan, plus examples, and resources for more information. Most of these strategies have been described previously, but no existing publication describes all of them or how to plan and implement a comprehensive parking management program.

Parking management is an art as well as a science. It is not usually possible to predict exactly how effective a particular parking management strategy will be or what combination of strategies is most appropriate in a particular situation. It requires creativity, judgment, and a little bit of courage. Over time, parking management becomes easier as planners, operators, and users gain experience. (The sidebar entitled "Parking Management Principles" describes general principles that can help guide you in developing an effective and acceptable parking management program.)

Parking management is particularly appropriate in locations with the following attributes:
- Perception of a parking problem.
- Rapid population, business activity, or traffic growth.
- Compact land-use patterns, such as a commercial district.

Parking Management Principles

These 10 general principles can help guide planning decisions to support parking management:

1. **Consumer choice:** People should have a variety of parking and travel options from which to choose.
2. **User information:** Motorists should have information on their parking and travel options.
3. **Sharing:** Parking facilities should serve multiple users and destinations.
4. **Efficient utilization:** Parking facilities should be sized and managed so spaces are frequently occupied.
5. **Flexibility:** Parking plans should accommodate uncertainty and change.
6. **Prioritization:** The most desirable spaces should be managed to favor higher-priority uses.
7. **Pricing:** As much as possible, users should pay directly for the parking facilities they use.
8. **Peak management:** Special efforts should be made to deal with peak demand.
9. **Quality versus quantity:** Parking facility quality should be considered as important as quantity, including convenience, comfort, aesthetics, and security.
10. **Comprehensive analysis:** All significant costs and benefits should be considered in parking planning.

- Efforts to redevelop and infill urban areas.
- High levels of walking and public transit use or a desire to encourage these modes.
- Perception that parking problems are a constraint to economic development.
- High land values.
- Concerns about equity, including fairness to nondrivers.
- Environmental concerns.
- A desire to preserve unique landscapes, historic districts, or building design features.

PARADIGM SHIFT

Parking management represents a paradigm shift (a fundamental change in how a problem is perceived and how solutions are evaluated). The current paradigm assumes that, when it comes to parking, more is usually better. This reflects "predict and provide" planning where past trends are extrapolated to predict future demand, which planners then try to satisfy. This often creates a self-fulfilling prophesy, since abundant parking supply increases vehicle use

Summary of Parking Management Benefits and Costs

BENEFITS

- **Facility cost savings:** These savings reduce costs to governments, businesses, developers, and consumers.
- **Improved quality of service:** Many strategies improve user quality of service by providing better information, increasing consumer options, and reducing congestion, and by creating more attractive facilities.
- **More flexible facility location and design:** Parking management gives architects, designers, and planners more ways to address parking requirements.
- **Revenue generation:** Some management strategies generate revenues that can fund parking facilities, transportation improvements, or other important projects.
- **Reduction of land consumption:** Parking management can reduce land requirements and help preserve greenspace and other valuable ecological, historic, and cultural resources.
- **Mobility management support:** Parking management can help encourage more efficient use of the transportation system, which helps reduce traffic congestion, roadway costs, pollution emissions, energy consumption, and traffic accidents.
- **Smart growth support:** Parking management helps create more accessible and efficient land-use patterns, and supports other strategic land-use planning objectives.
- **Improved walkability:** By allowing more compact development, and more flexible site design, parking management helps create more walkable communities.

and urban sprawl, causing parking demand and parking supply to ratchet further upward, resulting in automobile dependency (see Figure 1-1).

Table 1-1 compares the old and new parking paradigms. Under the old paradigm, "parking problem" meant that there was insufficient free parking available at each destination; it strived to maximize supply and minimize price. The new paradigm strives to provide *optimal* parking supply and price; it considers too much supply to be as harmful as too little supply, and prices that are too low to be as harmful as prices that are too high.

The old paradigm assumes that a parking lot should almost never fill and that every destination should satisfy its own parking needs. The new paradigm strives to use parking facilities efficiently. It emphasizes sharing of parking facilities among multiple destinations. It considers full lots acceptable,

Summary of Parking Management Benefits and Costs (cont.)

- **Transit support:** Parking management supports transit-oriented development and transit use.
- **Reduced stormwater management costs, water pollution, and heat island effects:** Parking management can reduce total paved area and incorporate design features, such as landscaping and shading, which reduce stormwater flow, water pollution, and solar heat gain.
- **Support of equity objectives:** Management strategies can reduce the need to subsidize parking facilities, improve travel options for nondrivers, provide financial savings to lower-income households, and increase housing affordability.
- **More livable communities:** Parking management can help create more attractive and efficient urban environments by reducing total paved areas, allowing more flexible building design, increasing walkability, and improving parking facility design.

COSTS

- **Additional costs:** Parking management may require additional planning, construction, and administrative costs.
- **Reduced motorist convenience:** Some parking management strategies increase the distance that motorists must walk from a parking facility to their destination.
- **Spillover impacts:** Parking management may increase spillover parking problems and resulting conflicts between neighbors.
- **Uncertainty:** When first introduced, parking management may introduce additional uncertainty into the planning process.

provided that additional parking is available nearby, and that any spillover problems are addressed.

The old paradigm assumes that "transportation" means "automobile travel." The new paradigm recognizes the value of multimodalism, that is, a transportation system or facility designed for and used by more than one mode, including walking, cycling, ridesharing, and public transit. This is important because parking management supports and is supported by efforts to accommodate and encourage alternative modes.

The old paradigm assumes that buildings generate parking demand, so parking costs should be incorporated into building costs. The new paradigm recognizes that motorists generate parking demand, so it is most efficient and fair to charge users directly, so people only pay for the parking they actually use.

Figure 1-1
Cycle of Automobile Dependency

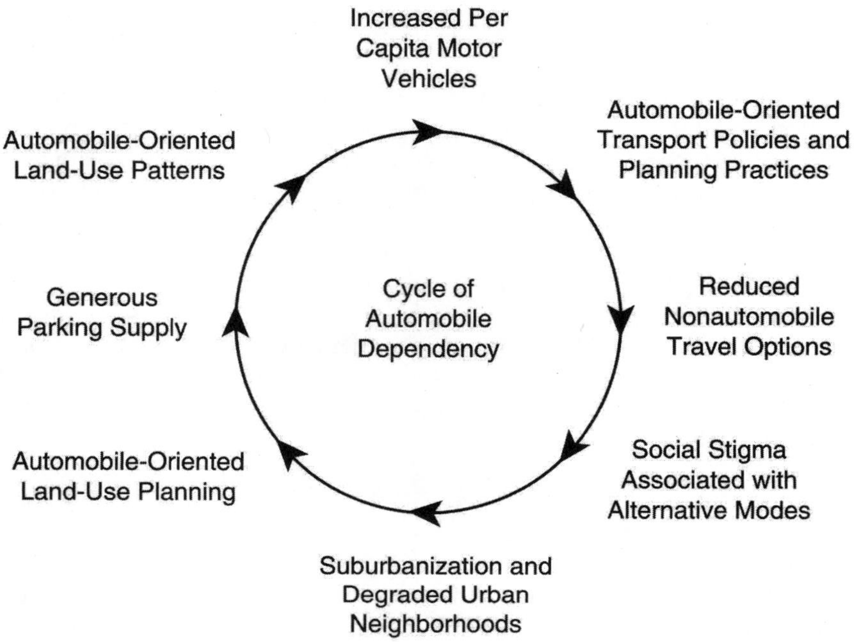

Increased Per
Capita Motor
Vehicles

Automobile-Oriented
Land-Use Patterns

Automobile-Oriented
Transport Policies and
Planning Practices

Generous
Parking Supply

Cycle of
Automobile
Dependency

Reduced
Nonautomobile
Travel Options

Automobile-Oriented
Land-Use Planning

Social Stigma
Associated with
Alternative Modes

Suburbanization and
Degraded Urban
Neighborhoods

Generous parking supply is part of a cycle that leads to increased automobile dependency. Parking management can help break this cycle.

The old paradigm tends to resist change. It places a heavy burden of proof on innovative solutions. The new paradigm recognizes that transport and land-use conditions evolve, and parking planning and management practices need frequent adjustment. It shifts the burden of proof, allowing new approaches to be tried until their effectiveness (or lack thereof) is proven.

REDEFINING PARKING PROBLEMS

It is important to define parking problems carefully. For example, if people complain about a parking problem, it is important to determine the type of problem, the location, the time, and to whom the problem occurs.

As previously described, people often assume that the term "parking problem" simply means that motorists cannot always find a convenient and free parking space at every time and place. However, there are other types of parking problems that may be equally important:

- To motorists, parking problems can consist of inadequate information about parking availability and price options, inconvenient pricing methods, or poorly designed parking facilities.

Table 1-1
Comparison of Old and New Parking Paradigms

Old Parking Paradigm	New Parking Paradigm
"Parking problem" means inadequate parking supply.	"Parking problem" can mean inadequate supply, inefficient management, inadequate user information, and other types of problems associated with parking facilities and activities.
More parking is better.	Too much parking is as harmful as too little.
Parking should generally be free. Whenever possible, parking facilities should be funded indirectly through building rents or taxes.	As much as possible, users should pay directly for parking facilities.
Parking should be available on a first-come basis.	Parking should be managed to favor higher-priority uses and encourage efficiency.
Parking requirements should be applied consistently, without exception or variation.	Parking requirements should reflect each situation and should be applied flexibly.
Traditional solutions should be favored. New approaches should be discouraged since they are unproven and not widely accepted.	Innovations should be encouraged, since even unsuccessful experiments often provide useful information.
Parking management should only be applied as a last resort where it would be too costly to increase supply.	Parking management programs should be widely applied to increase efficiency and prevent problems.
Transportation consists of driving. Dispersion of destinations (urban sprawl) is acceptable or even desirable.	Driving is just one of many transport modes. Dispersed, automobile-dependent land-use patterns may be undesirable.

Parking management requires changing the way we think about parking problems and solutions.

- To developers, parking problems may consist of the financial costs of satisfying generous parking requirements and the constraints these requirements impose on building design.
- To nearby residents, parking problems may include the aesthetic impacts of parking facilities.
- To local officials, parking problems may consist of numerous conflicts among different interest groups, including motorists, residents, visitors, businesses, and taxpayers.

In fact, there are many different parking problems, and a solution to one often exacerbates others.

Table 1-2 lists various parking problems and compares the impacts of increasing parking supply with management solutions. Increasing supply helps reduce parking congestion and spillover impacts but increases most other problems. Management solutions tend to reduce most problems and so tend to provide the most total benefits (see the sidebar entitled "Parking Management Solutions").

Table 1-2
Comparing Increased Supply and Management Solutions

Problem	Increased Supply	Management Solutions
Parking congestion: too many vehicles trying to use available parking facilities.	Positive.	Positive.
Spillover: problems from motorists parking where they are not wanted.	Positive.	Mixed (some management strategies increase spillover problems; others reduce them).
Development costs: increased costs to developers to provide generous, subsidized parking.	Negative.	Positive (reduces parking requirements).
Traffic congestion: too many vehicles for existing road capacity.	Negative (generous, free parking increases vehicle use).	Positive (many management strategies reduce vehicle use).
Inequity: nondrivers forced to pay for parking they do not use.	Negative.	Positive (reduces parking requirements and charges users).
Tax costs: increased tax burden required to subsidize parking facilities.	Negative.	Positive (reduces parking requirements and charges users).
Environmental impacts: loss of greenspace, stormwater management costs, air pollution, and unattractive landscapes.	Negative.	Positive (reduces total parking requirements and vehicle use).
Sprawl: dispersed, automobile-dependent development.	Negative (contributes to sprawl; discourages multimodel, compact development).	Positive (encourages smart growth development patterns).

Comparison of the effects of increasing parking supply and implementing parking management solutions. Parking management helps achieve more planning objectives and so tends to provide more total benefits.

Parking Management Solutions

While I was drinking coffee one morning at a popular café, I overheard a customer complain about her difficulty in finding a parking space there. Yet, a quick survey of the area showed plenty of unoccupied parking spaces nearby, several at a bank that was not yet opened, a dozen spaces behind a pub that are only used during weekend evenings, and many unoccupied spaces in the parking lots of nearby apartments. Behind several of the buildings were parking spaces that were seldom used because few customers know about them, or because they are unattractive and unpleasant. Subsequent surveys indicated that any time of the day or week, at least a third of the parking spaces in the area are unoccupied. There is not really a lack of parking, but many parking facilities have regulations that limit their use, and motorists are often unaware of all the parking options available.

According to conventional thinking, that neighborhood has a parking problem because, during peak periods, motorists sometimes have difficulty finding a free parking space at their destination. The conventional response is to increase the minimum parking requirements at new developments, or to demand that local governments subsidize the construction of additional public parking facilities. However, this is costly and would make the area less attractive. Instead, existing parking facilities could be managed more efficiently. For example, the café could arrange for its customers to use the bank's parking lot during weekends and to lease unoccupied parking spaces from nearby apartments for their employees. Regulations and pricing of the most convenient spaces can be used to increase parking turnover, so they better serve customers. Signs and maps could provide better information to motorists about nearby parking options, and improved maintenance, security, and pedestrian access could increase the number of parking spaces available. These management solutions are generally more cost effective and beneficial overall.

2

How Much
is Optimal?

How much parking should be provided at a particular location? The answer can vary significantly depending on planning objectives, assumptions, and perspective. Optimal supply depends on the number and type of trips to a destination, the range of travel and parking options available there, how parking facilities are managed, the severity of problems that result if parking is unavailable, the cost of providing parking facilities, and the cost of implementing parking management strategies.

According to economic theory, optimal parking supply is the amount consumers would purchase in an efficient market (if they are charged the full cost of providing parking facilities and have a reasonable range of options from which to choose) ("Market Principles," VTPI, 2005; Shoup, 2005). For example, the optimal downtown parking supply is the amount that is commercially profitable if travelers have various travel and parking options. Similarly, the optimal supply of employee parking is the amount commuters would choose if they pay directly for parking or are able to cash out their parking subsidy (e.g., they can choose cash instead of a parking space) and have various commuting options available, such as ridesharing and public transit services.

However, parking supply decisions are not often determined by consumers' willingness to pay. Instead, planners rely on recommended minimum standards published by professional organizations (see the sidebar entitled "Examples of Conventional Parking Standards"). Although these standards may seem rational and efficient, the process used to develop them contains various biases that tend to result in economically excessive parking supply. The next section describes the process by which these standards are developed and their biases.

Examples of Conventional Parking Standards

The following are a few examples of conventional minimum parking requirements. Note the wide range of definitions and standards often applied to a given land-use category.

BOWLING ALLEY

- 1 space for every 3 persons of maximum capacity permitted by fire regulations, plus 1 space per 200 square feet of gross floor area used in a manner not susceptible to such calculations (Yavapai County, Arizona)
- 2 spaces for each alley, plus 1 additional space for each 2 employees, plus 1 space for each 100 square feet of gross floor space used for amusement or assembly (Canton, Georgia)

BEACH COMMUNITY

- 1 space for each 100 square feet of beach (Anne Arundel County, Maryland)

DAIRY

- 1 space per 2 employees on maximum working shift (Biloxi, Mississippi)
- 2.5 spaces per 1,000 square feet of gross floor area (Naperville, Illinois)

MINIATURE GOLF COURSE

- 1 space per tee, plus 1 space per 75 square feet of gross floor area (Las Cruces, New Mexico)
- 1 space per hole (Columbia, Missouri)
- 1 space per employee on the maximum shift (Coconino County, Arizona)
- 3 spaces per hole (Aventura, Florida)

POOL HALL

- 1 space per billiard table (North Ogden, Utah)
- 1 space per 300 square feet (Columbia, Missouri)
- 1 space per 3 persons based on maximum occupancy, plus 1 space per employee on the major shift (Smithfield, Virginia)
- 1 space per 2 persons who may be legally admitted at one time, based on the occupancy load established by local codes, plus 1 space per employee, or 1 space per 100 square feet of usable floor area, whichever is greater (Canton, Michigan)
- 1 space per 2 billiard tables, plus 1 space per 2 employees (Humboldt County, Nevada)
- 4 spaces for each table (Platte County, Missouri)

Source: Davidson and Dolnick, 2002.

CONVENTIONAL PARKING STANDARDS

Various professional organizations, such as the Institute of Transportation Engineers and the American Planning Association, publish recommended minimum parking standards such as those shown in Table 2-1. This provides an index or parking ratio value (a reference value used to calculate the number of parking spaces required at a particular location) based on some reference unit, such as dwelling units, employees, or building floor area.

These values are unconstrained (they assume that parking is cheap to supply) and unadjusted (they are not adjusted to reflect specific conditions), and so generally reflect the highest level of parking supply that may be required. In most situations, these standards are excessive and can be adjusted down-

Table 2-1
Typical Minimum Parking Standards

Land-Use Category	Unit	Index (85th Percentile)	Peak Parking Period
Single-family housing	Dwelling unit	2.0	Evening
Multifamily housing	Dwelling unit	1.5	Evening
Elderly housing	Dwelling unit	0.5	Weekday
Hotel	Guest room	1.0	Weekday-evening
Hospital	100 square miles per bed	5/2.6	Weekday-day
Health spa	100 square miles GLA	6.8	Weekday
Retail/shopping center	100 square miles GLA	5.0	Saturday-day
Office building	100 square miles GFA per employee	3.3/0.9	Weekday-day
Light industry	100 square miles GFA per employee	2.2/1.0	Weekday-day
Heavy industry	100 square miles GFA per employee	1.7/0.6	Weekday-day
Fast food restaurant	Seat	0.85	Weekday
Church/synagogue/ mosque	Seat	0.2	Sunday/Saturday/Friday
Movie theater	Seat	0.25	Saturday-evening

GLA = gross leasable area; GFA = gross floor area.

Illustration of typical minimal parking standards developed by planning organizations. The index is used to calculate the number of parking spaces that should be supplied at a particular location. These "unadjusted" values reflect the maximum amount of parking that is usually required and can often be reduced based on various factors and management strategies described in this book.

Sources: Davidson and Dolnick, 2002; Stover and Koepke, 2002.

ward, often by a significant amount. To understand why, it is helpful to know a little about how these parking standards are developed.

Conventional parking standards are based on numerous parking demand surveys, the results of which are collected and published in technical reports, such as the *Parking Generation Informational Report* (ITE, 1987 and 2004). These surveys involve counting the number of parking spaces occupied at a particular site during its peak period, that is, the time period when parking demand is greatest.

Figure 2-1 illustrates one set of surveys—in this case, land-use category 836, "Fast Food Restaurant with Drive-In Window." Each dot shows the building size and number of parking spaces occupied at one particular site. This information is used to calculate an 85th percentile demand curve, which represents the parking supply needed to insure that only 15 percent of sites would be completely filled during their peak period.

This process implies a higher degree of accuracy than the data actually justify (Shoup, 2005) (see the sidebar entitled "Accuracy Versus Precision"). Despite considerable effort by transportation professionals, the supply of quality parking demand data is often inadequate. Fewer than a dozen surveys are used to set standards for many land-use categories. Survey data often provide little or no information on geographic, demographic, and economic factors that affect parking demand, such as whether sites are urban or suburban and whether parking is free or priced. It is therefore impossible to know how representative and transferable the information is to other situations.

Accuracy Versus Precision

Statisticians make a distinction between accuracy and precision. "Accurate" means truthful or correct; "precise" means measured in small units. Data can be very precise but inaccurate. It can be a mistake to focus too much on precision and not enough on accuracy.

For example, a standard bathroom scale can measure a person's weight within about 1 pound. More expensive scales are more precise, but knowing that you weigh "exactly 168.38 pounds" rather than "about 170 pounds" is not very useful for assessing your health. A more accurate assessment considers other factors that may be more difficult to measure, such as whether you eat a balanced diet, get sufficient exercise, or have hereditary health risks.

Similarly, minimum parking standards are often published with two, three, or even four significant figures, indicating a great deal of precision. Yet, the underlying assumptions used to calculate these requirements may be highly inaccurate because they fail to account for significant geographic, demographic, and economic factors that affect the amount of parking supply required in a particular situation.

Figure 2-1
Example of Parking Demand Survey Data

FAST FOOD RESTAURANT WITH DRIVE-IN WINDOW (836)

Peak Parking Spaces Occupied vs: **1,000 GROSS SQUARE FEET LEASABLE AREA**
On a: **WEEKDAY**

PARKING GENERATION RATES

Average Rate	Range of Rates	Standard Deviation	Number of Studies	Average 1,000 GSF Leasable Area
9.95	3.55–15.92	3.41	18	3

DATA PLOT AND EQUATION

CAUTION—USE CAREFULLY—LOW R².

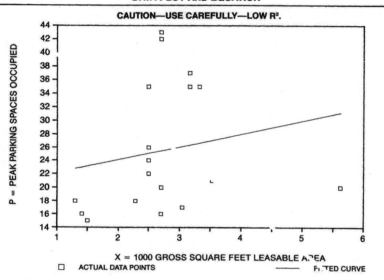

X = 1000 GROSS SQUARE FEET LEASABLE AREA

☐   ACTUAL DATA POINTS   ———   FITTED CURVE

Fitted Curve Equation: $P = 1.95(X) + 20.0$
$R^2 = 0.038$

Summary of demand survey results used to establish parking standards for this land-use category.

Source: Copyright © 1987 Institute of Transportation Engineers. Used by permission.

Figure 2-2
Automobile-Dependent Land Use
Increases Parking Requirements

Conventional parking standards are based on parking demand surveys performed at isolated, automobile-dependent sites, such as those illustrated above. Less parking supply is needed where parking can be shared, or at locations where more people rely on alternative modes such as walking, cycling, ridesharing, and public transit.

Source: Alex Maclean.

Note the high degree of scatter in Figure 2-1. For example, sites of approximately 2,500 square feet have from 16 to 43 spaces occupied. If all of these sites had 25 spaces, reflecting average demand, those in the lowest range would have about 10 unoccupied spaces during peak periods, while some would be nearly 20 spaces short of what they need. If all sites had 35 parking spaces, reflecting the 85th percentile demand curve, more than half of the spaces would be unoccupied during peak periods at some sites.

These standards err toward oversupply in various ways. Most data used to calculate parking standards come from automobile-dependent, suburban locations where parking demand is relatively high. This occurs because single-use sites are easiest to survey. For example, if a barber shop, store, and theater share a parking lot, it is difficult to determine which business attracts which vehicles. It is easier to survey isolated barber shops, stores, and theaters, such as those often located in suburban areas. As a result, conventional parking standards are excessive where parking is shared or priced, in areas with more diverse transportation systems, where land costs are high, if overflow parking facilities are available nearby, and where mobility management programs could be implemented (see Figure 2-2).

The units used to measure parking are somewhat arbitrary. For example, "light industry," "office," and "retail" buildings can contain diverse activities with different parking demands, and some categories can be measured in various ways (e.g., floor area, employees, or seats) that give different conclusions as to how much parking should be supplied. When multiple options exist, zoning codes often state "whichever is greater," even if a lower requirement would be more accurate.

Conventional standards are based on an 85th percentile curve, which means that 85 out of 100 sites will have more parking than is actually needed, even during peak periods. This assumes that it is better to have eight or nine sites with excess parking supply than to have one or two sites with insufficient parking. A peak period is usually based on the 10th to 20th design hour (the number of annual hours that parking demand is allowed to exceed supply at a particular location). For retail, this is often defined as the middle of the holiday shopping season (around December 12th), which means that most destinations will have more parking than is needed 350 days a year. A parking facility is considered full if it has 85 to 90 percent occupancy, which may be justified for facilities with high turnover, so motorists can easily find an unoccupied space; however, those serving longer-term users, such as employees and residents, can generally be sized for 95 to 100 percent occupancy.

This process is said to measure parking demand, but "demand" actually refers to the quantity of goods a consumer would purchase at a given price. Most parking surveys are performed where parking is free, which is equivalent to asking how much food a grocery store could give away. To truly measure demand, surveys must determine how much parking motorists would use under various prices and conditions. For example, rather than saying, "This site requires 100 parking spaces," a planner should be able to say, "This site requires 100 parking spaces if parking is free, 80 spaces if priced at $2 per day, and 60 spaces if priced at $5 per day."

Most parking facilities have significantly more spaces than is normally needed and many are never fully occupied. This is inefficient by any measure, particularly where land costs are higher or when a community wants to encourage more compact development and the use of alternative modes.

The sidebar entitled "Factors That Contribute to Excessive Parking Supply" summarizes various technical and political factors that contribute to economically excessive standards and parking supply. Transportation professionals are increasingly aware of these problems (Shoup, 1999; Kuzmyak et al., 2003; ITE, 2004). However, the use of unadjusted parking standards is well established and is often codified in zoning laws, creating obstacles to more efficient management.

In addition to these factors that increase parking supply, several factors increase parking demand (the number of parking spaces that could be occupied at a particular location, time, and price) by reducing parking prices and

Factors That Contribute to Excessive Parking Supply

- Most parking demand studies are performed at single-use, suburban sites where parking is unpriced. The resulting standards tend to be excessive for other conditions.
- Parking standards are not usually adjusted to reflect geographic, demographic, and economic factors that affect parking demand (discussed in Chapter 3).
- Standards are often based on an 85th percentile demand curve, the 10th or 20th annual design hour, and 85 to 90 percent occupancy, resulting in excessive supply under most conditions.
- When demand can be calculated in various ways, zoning codes require use of the highest value regardless of which is most accurate.
- A heavy burden of proof is often placed on reductions from these standards.
- Excessive parking requirements are often imposed on new developments to remedy deficiencies at existing sites, rather than sharing the burden with existing facilities or implementing parking management programs.
- Parking standards are often designed to accommodate the highest level of demand the site may encounter over its entire operating life.
- Transportation professionals and public officials who set parking standards may perceive little incentive to choose a lower standard since they do not bear any direct costs.
- Project evaluation often overlooks many indirect costs that result from excessive parking supply, such as increased automobile traffic, sprawled land use, stormwater management costs, and other environmental impacts. This underestimates the full costs of increasing parking supply and the full benefits from parking management alternatives.
- Some municipal codes prohibit charging for parking.
- In many areas, generous parking standards were created when land costs were lower and there was less concern about sprawl and other negative impacts of automobile dependency.
- Per capita vehicle ownership and trip rates increased steadily until the 1980s, leading many officials to assume that parking demand will continue to grow. However, in recent years, per capita rates have stabilized and some have even declined, justifying lower parking requirements (see Figure 2-3).
- Older pricing methods (e.g., parking meters and passes) tend to be inconvenient and expensive to operate, reinforcing opposition to priced parking.
- Zoning laws and development practices often discourage shared parking, forcing each site to supply its own parking facilities.
- Parking facilities are not generally included when calculating a development's floor area ratio, which encourages developers to favor parking over other building amenities.

Factors That Contribute to Excessive Parking Supply (cont.)

- More resources (e.g., municipal funds, private building money, and land) tend to be available for building parking facilities than for parking management programs, even if management solutions are the most cost effective and provide the greatest total benefits.
- Property assessments often treat land devoted to parking as having less value than if it were devoted to other uses, which favor increasing parking supply over management solutions.
- Commercial developments often have a "honeymoon" period of high activity when they first open, particularly if they introduce new services to a market. Surveys performed under such conditions may indicate higher parking demand than what normally occurs.

Source: Shoup, 2005.

Figure 2-3
U.S. Vehicle Ownership Growth

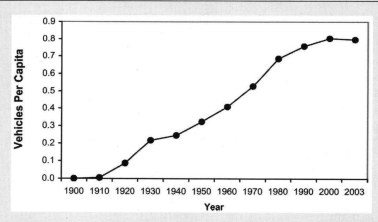

U.S. vehicle ownership rates increased during most of the 20th century, reaching about 0.8 vehicles per capita in the year 2000. This rate has since started to decline. Other developed countries also appear to be experiencing saturation and perhaps even declines in per capita vehicle ownership.

Source: FHWA, annual reports for various years.

stimulating vehicle ownership and use beyond what is economically optimal (see the sidebar entitled "Factors That Contribute to Economically Excessive Parking Demand").

Current planning practices result in excess parking supply because they do not take into account other planning objectives, such as a desire to minimize development costs, create more compact and accessible land-use patterns, or encourage alternative forms of transportation in order to reduce traffic problems. Excessive parking requirements reduce the incentive to implement transportation and parking management programs because, if they are successful in reducing parking demand, the excess spaces will be unoccupied and wasted. Changing the planning process to place more emphasis on management allows parking solutions that better reconcile parking planning decisions with other community goals.

Current parking planning practices tend to focus primarily on *quantity* and less on parking facility *quality*. Motorists may sometimes prefer having fewer but larger spaces, awnings to protect cars against sun and rain, safer walkways, and better landscaping to create more pleasant parking lots. Excessive parking standards leave little flexibility to make such trade-offs.

Unfortunately, many decision-makers apply parking standards with little understanding of the biases and errors they contain and of the problems resulting from excessive parking supply. The use of generous and inflexible parking standards is often defended as being *conservative,* implying that it is cautious and responsible. Use of this word in this context is confusing because it often results in the opposite of what is implied. Excessive parking requirements waste resources: directly, by increasing the money and land devoted to parking facilities; and indirectly, by leveraging an increase in automobile use and sprawl. Parking management is actually a more conservative approach to dealing with parking problems.

Although individually these various planning and market distortions may seem modest and reasonable, their impacts are cumulative and synergistic (total impacts are greater than the sum of their individual impacts). A public official or developer may assume that a few extra parking spaces at a particular site impose modest costs. Similarly, a business manager might consider employee parking subsidies normal and convenient, while subsidies for other travel modes not worth the bother. However, when all economic, social, and environmental impacts are considered, the total costs of excessive automobile parking are often large.

Excessive parking demand tends to be self-fulfilling: generous supply leads to more automobile-dependent land-use patterns. Where parking supply is abundant, there is little incentive for efficient management. Abundant supply discourages parking pricing, which encourages automobile ownership and use, and ultimately increases demand. Where supply is more constrained, decision-makers are more likely to implement the strategies described in this

Factors That Contribute to Economically Excessive Parking Demand

- Generous minimum parking standards result in abundant parking supply, which discourages owners from charging for parking.
- Parking is bundled with buildings, so buyers and renters are forced to pay for parking whether or not they want it.
- Governments often provide unpriced or low-priced parking on streets and in municipal lots, which discourages businesses from charging for parking at their sites.
- Tax policies make parking subsidies an attractive employee benefit.
- Zoning codes and development policies limit density and encourage dispersed development, creating automobile-oriented land-use patterns.
- Businesses often reimburse customer parking costs and subsidize employee parking, but not other travel modes.
- Many motor vehicle costs are fixed or are external, so driving seems relatively cheap.
- Many communities make limited investments in travel alternatives (e.g., walking, cycling, ridesharing, and public transit services), leading to automobile dependency.

Table 2-2
Northwest Connecticut Parking Utilization Survey

Land Use	Average Occupancy	Highest Observed Occupancy
Bank	36.1%	59.1%
Big-box retail	24.3%	35.7%
Drive-thru restaurant	55.1%	100.0%
Retail	47.1%	100.0%
Office building	54.0%	94.7%
Industrial plant	42.3%	92.1%
Medical office building	46.6%	68.8%
Nursing homes	58.1%	96.1%
Restaurants	54.4%	100.0%
Small shopping plaza	56.1%	78.6%
Averages	**47.4%**	**82.5%**

Summary of the results of 42 parking utilization studies performed during the holiday shopping season, which indicate excessive parking supply at most sites.

Source: Gould, 2003.

book, resulting in more efficient use of parking facilities and more efficient transportation and land-use patterns. The best way to describe how much parking to supply is often a qualified statement: "As many as 100 spaces may be needed, but this can be reduced to 50 spaces with better management."

EVIDENCE OF EXCESSIVE PARKING SUPPLY

Many parking studies show that existing supply is frequently underutilized (Kuzmyak et al., 2003; Shoup, 2005). For example, a parking demand study at suburban office sites in southern California found that conventional standards are nearly twice as high as needed, and their oversupply will increase if efforts to encourage alternative commute modes are successful (Willson, 1995). A study at The University of Iowa found that parking supply exceeded peak-period demand by 16 to 63 percent at various commercial centers (Shaw, 1997). Parking surveys in 26 Seattle, Washington, neighborhoods found that most had only 40 to 70 percent peak-period occupancy (City of Seattle, 2000). A parking demand study at several shopping centers in St. Paul, Minnesota, found that peak-hour occupancy averaged 31 percent, and so recommended reducing municipal parking requirements to about half of conventional standards, from 3.6 to 2.0 spaces per 1,000 square feet (TLC, 2003).

Table 2-2 summarizes the results of parking surveys performed during the holiday shopping season at 42 parking lots associated with 10 land-use categories in 13 towns and rural communities in northwest Connecticut. This study concluded that current parking supply, and the minimum parking standards and zoning code requirements they reflect, are economically excessive and environmentally harmful.

Table 2-3 shows the parking supply and utilization rates at various suburban business parks, indicating wide variation from one region to another. The results shown in Table 2-3 are particularly dramatic because many of these sites have less parking than current standards require and none have parking management programs. If built to current standards, many sites would have less than 50 percent peak-period utilization. Parking management programs typically reduce parking requirements by 20 to 40 percent, further increasing oversupply.

This does not suggest that these areas never have parking problems. Even areas with economically excessive parking supply may experience parking congestion simply because motorists lack information on where parking is available or they face barriers to walking between parking facilities and destinations. In these situations, management improvements are often more effective at addressing parking congestion problems than increasing parking supply.

Table 2-3
Suburban Business Park Parking Utilization Survey

Size, Age, and Location	Percent Floor Area Occupied	Parking Supply (Spaces Per 1,000 Square Feet GFA)	Percent Parking Occupancy During Peak Periods	Peak Space Utilization Per 1,000 Square Feet Occupied GLA)
Large, old, east	96.0%	1.2	47.6%	0.6
Small, old, east	96.3%	1.9	53.2%	1.0
Small, old, west	82.6%	2.1	28.0%	0.7
Medium, new, west	86.7%	2.3	34.0%	0.9
Large, new, east	84.2%	2.5	60.6%	1.8
Large, old, west	83.6%	3.1	43.6%	1.6
Large, new, west	88.4%	3.2	49.1%	1.8
Small, new, west	71.7%	5.8	56.1%	4.5
Averages	**86.9%**	**2.6**	**46.8%**	**1.4**

GFA = gross floor area; GLA = gross leasable area.

Level of parking supply and utilization at various suburban business parks. Less than half of all spaces are occupied during peak periods.

Sources: ULI, 1986; cited in Kuzmyak et al., 2003.

BETTER WAYS TO DETERMINE
HOW MUCH PARKING TO SUPPLY

There are better ways to determine how much parking to supply at a particular site. One approach is to use efficiency-based standards, which means that parking supply decisions are based on the specific needs of each location and take into account geographic, demographic, and economic factors. With such standards, parking facilities are sized so that they may fill up, with management strategies used to ensure user convenience and address any overflow problems when this occurs. For example, parking facilities at a store can be sized to be fully occupied frequently as long as overflow parking is available nearby, motorists have information about available parking options, regulations are adequately enforced, and additional management strategies (e.g., commute trip reduction programs and shuttle services) are implemented as needed.

Management solutions should be used whenever they are more cost effective than adding more parking supply. Less parking is supplied where parking facilities are more expensive to build, where management programs are easy to implement, and where reduced parking supply supports other planning objectives. In many situations, parking management solutions can be justified even if increasing parking supply has a lower direct cost, because they support strategic objectives, such as a desire for more compact development or reduced vehicle traffic in an area.

A common method for determining parking requirements at a particular location is to study comparable sites, provided there is detailed information on geographic, demographic, and management factors that affect parking demand. For example, to predict parking demand at a proposed housing or office development, it may be appropriate to perform detailed surveys of parking generation rates for similar facilities located in similar areas, taking into account factors such as the type of development, the demographics of users, proximity to transit services, and other factors that could affect vehicle ownership and trips.

Because it is not possible to predict exactly how much parking will be needed at a particular location and how effective management programs will be, efficiency-based standards use contingency-based planning, a planning strategy that deals with uncertainty by implementing some solutions immediately and others on an as-needed basis. This means that a relatively small supply of parking is built initially and planners identify specific solutions that can be deployed if needed in the future. For example, if a new building is predicted to need 60 to 100 parking spaces, the conventional approach is to supply either the average (80 spaces) or the higher-bound value (100 spaces) to be "conservative." With contingency-based planning, the lower-bound value (60 spaces) is initially supplied, conditions are monitored, and various strategies are identified for deployment if needed. This may include banking land for building additional parking and implementing additional parking management strategies. This approach gives decision-makers the confidence they need to use reduced and more flexible parking requirements and to try new parking management solutions.

Contingency-based planning requires a monitoring process to alert managers to possible problems. For example, the plan might include specific indicators that will determine whether additional supply or management strategies should be deployed (see the sidebar entitled "Indications of Parking Problems").

Parking management is not really a new idea. In fact, most communities have areas where parking is managed and parking requirements are reduced, but this is often limited to central business districts. Increased emphasis on efficiency expands where, when, and how much these strategies are applied (see Figure 2-4).

Justifications for higher and lower parking supply requirements are summarized in Table 2-4. All of these factors should be considered when choosing between increased parking supply and improved parking management.

Indications of Parking Problems

The following indicators can be used to determine if parking problems exist at a particular location that may require mitigation.

- More than 90 percent of short-term parking (parking spaces intended for 2 hours or less duration, for use by delivery vehicles, customers, and other visitors) is occupied during peak periods.
- Motorists often have difficulty finding a suitable parking space.
- Vehicles often cruise streets while searching for parking.
- All spaces within view of a destination are frequently occupied.
- Vehicles frequently park illegally, such as parking in no-parking areas or double parking to load and unload.
- Motorists are frequently cited for parking violations.

Figure 2-4
Parking Management Expands with Greater Appreciation of Benefits

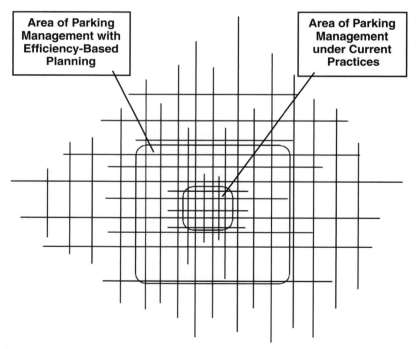

With current practices, parking management solutions are generally implemented only in central business districts. With greater emphasis on efficiency, parking management is applied over a greater area.

Source: Peter Apanel

Example of Conventional Parking Planning

Downtown Pomona, an older city in southern California, has approximately 4,800 parking spaces. There is currently no evidence of inadequate parking supply. Weekday occupancy averages 42 percent and motorists seldom have trouble finding a space.

As part of a downtown planning process, future parking demand was projected by applying conventional parking standards (four parking spaces per 1,000 square feet of commercial floor area), assuming all downtown land was developed to its maximum floor area. This indicated that 3,000 to 4,500 additional parking spaces will be needed, nearly doubling current parking supply, which would require 24 to 36 acres if provided on surface lots. Meeting this requirement with surface lots would result in about three-quarters of downtown land being devoted to roads and parking facilities. Only 6 to 9 acres are needed if parking is provided in four-story garages, but this adds $30 million to $65 million in construction costs.

Applying conventional parking requirements is misguided in this situation because downtown areas have many features that reduce the amount of parking required, including shared parking, a low automobile mode split, regulation and pricing of parking, and the ability to implement other parking management strategies if needed to address parking problems. It also fails to consider the high cost of providing generous parking supply in a commercial center, including financial costs and undesirable impacts on the downtown environment. For these reasons, downtown Pomona should continue to grow with little or no additional parking supply for the foreseeable future and instead rely on management solutions to address parking problems.

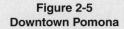

Figure 2-5
Downtown Pomona

Source: Peter Apanel.

Table 2-4
Justifications for More and Less Parking Supply

Justifications for More Parking Supply	Justifications for Less Parking Supply
• Increases motorists' convenience. • Helps businesses attract customers who drive. • Avoids spillover impacts.	• Reduces construction costs. • Helps create more efficient land-use patterns. • Improves facility design flexibility. • Reduces vehicle travel and therefore traffic problems. • Increases parking pricing revenues. • Reduces subsidies borne by nondrivers. • Supports environmental objectives.

Summary of factors to consider when determining how much parking to supply at a location.

CHAPTER 2
REFERENCES AND INFORMATION RESOURCES

Alexander, Christopher et al. (1977), *A Pattern Language*, Oxford University Press (Oxford, UK) (www.oup.co.uk).

Campoli, Julie, Elizabeth Humstone, and Alex Maclean (2001), *Above and Beyond*, American Planning Association (Chicago, IL) (www.planning.org).

City of Seattle (2000), *Seattle Comprehensive Neighborhood Parking Study* (Seattle, WA) (www.cityofseattle.net); available online (www.cityofseattle.net/transportation/pdf/CNPS.pdf).

Davidson, Michael and Fay Dolnick (2002), *Parking Standards*, Planning Advisory Service Report 510/511, American Planning Association (Chicago, IL) (www.planning.org).

Federal Highway Administration (FHWA) (annual reports for various years), *Highway Statistics,* U.S. Department of Transportation (www.fhwa.dot.gov/policy/ohpi/hss/index.htm).

Gould, Carol (2003), "Parking: When Less is More," *Transportation Planning*, Vol. 28, No. 1, Transportation Planning Division, American Planning Association (Chicago, IL) (www.planning.org), Winter 2003, pp. 3-11.

Institute of Transportation Engineers (ITE) (1987 and 2004), *Parking Generation Informational Report*, ITE (Washington, DC) (www.ite.org).

Kuzmyak, J. Richard, Rachel Weinberger, Richard H. Pratt, and Herbert S. Levinson (2003), *Parking Management and Supply: Traveler Response to Transport System Changes*, Chapter 18, Report 95, Transit Cooperative Research Program; Transportation Research Board (www.trb.org); available online (http://gulliver.trb.org/publications/tcrp/tcrp_rpt_95c18.pdf).

Litman, Todd (1999), *Socially Optimal Transport Prices and Markets: Principles, Strategies and Impacts*, Victoria Transport Policy Institute (www.vtpi.org); available online (www.vtpi.org/opprice.pdf).

Shaw, John (1997), *Planning for Parking*, Public Policy Center, The University of Iowa (Iowa City, IA) (www.uiowa.edu).

Shoup, Donald (1999), "The Trouble With Minimum Parking Requirements," *Transportation Research A*, Vol. 33, No. 7/8, Sept./Nov. 1999, pp. 549-574; available online (www.vtpi.org/shoup.pdf).

Shoup, Donald (2005), *The High Cost of Free Parking*, American Planning Association (Chicago, IL) (www.planning.org).

Stover, Vergil G. and Frank J. Koepke (2002), "Parking Design," *Transportation and Land Development, Second Edition*, Institute of Transportation Engineers (Washington, DC) (www.ite.org).

Transit for Livable Communities (TLC) (2003), *The Myth of Free Parking*, TLC (www.tlcminnesota.org); available online (www.tlcminnesota.org/parking/mythoffreeparking/mythoffreeparking.pdf).

Urban Land Institute (ULI) (1986), *Employment and Parking in Suburban Business Parks: A Pilot Study*, ULI (Washington, DC) (www.uli.org).

Victoria Transport Policy Institute (VTPI) (2005), *Online TDM Encyclopedia*, VTPI (www.vtpi.org); available online ("Market Principles" (www.vtpi.org/tdm/tdm60.htm)).

Willson, Richard (1995), "Suburban Parking Requirements; A Tacit Policy for Automobile Use and Sprawl," *Journal of the American Planning Association*, Vol. 61, No. 1, Winter 1995, pp. 29-42.

3

Factors Affecting Parking Demand and Requirements

This chapter discusses various factors that affect parking demand (the number of parking spaces that could be occupied at a particular location, time, and price) and parking requirements (the number of parking spaces considered necessary at a particular location). Many parking management strategies make use of these factors to increase efficiency and reduce the supply of parking needed at a particular location.

In general, changes in vehicle ownership rates affect residential parking demand, while changes in vehicle trip rates affect demand at other destinations. For example, if a particular demographic group has vehicle ownership rates 20 percent lower than average, their residential parking requirements can be reduced by that amount compared with conventional standards. Similarly, if automobile commute mode split is 30 percent lower than average at a worksite or a commercial district, employee parking requirements can be reduced by that amount.

Multiple adjustment factors may apply in a particular situation. For example, a site may have both demographic (serves lower-income people) and geographic (located close to a transit station) factors that affect parking demand. More detailed statistical methods, such as regression analysis, can be used to determine how each factor affects vehicle ownership or trip generation rates. Additional techniques for calculating the total effects of multiple adjustment factors are discussed at the end of this chapter.

Factors that affect parking demand and parking requirements at a particular location are discussed in detail below.

PARKING FACILITY LOCATION, TYPE, AND DESIGN

Parking demand is affected by a facility's location, type, and design, and by how this compares with other nearby options. Demand is highest for the most convenient and visible spaces. For example, motorists tend to use parking spaces in front of a building first; spaces behind a building second; more distant, surface lots third; and structured parking last. Demand also depends on the number of destinations a particular facility serves, its location, and whether it is available for use by the general public.

Here are some general guidelines indicating the relative demand for various types of parking:

- On-street parking is convenient and visible, is available to the general public, serves multiple destinations, and therefore tends to have the highest demand.
- Off-street public parking, such as a downtown municipal lot, is available to the general public, serves multiple destinations, and therefore tends to have high demand.
- Commercial parking (parking provided by a for-profit business for which users pay a direct fee) is available to the general public and serves multiple destinations.
- Surface parking (parking facilities built directly on the ground) tends to have more demand than structured parking, and the ground floor of a parking structure tends to have more demand than upper stories.
- Single-destination parking (a parking facility that only serves one destination and may not be used by motorists going elsewhere) has demand patterns that reflect activities at that destination.

Public parking facilities serving multiple destinations are often occupied 100 or more hours a week, while private spaces serving a single destination are generally occupied just 20 to 40 hours per week. As a result, a centrally located public parking space can often substitute for two to three private, single-destination spaces. For example, if a restaurant, a shop, and an office building each need more parking, adding 15 public spaces in a convenient central location may provide the same benefit as 30 single-destination spaces (10 at each destination).

Certain design features can make a particular space relatively attractive and can increase its demand:

- Larger parking spaces are easier to use, particularly with larger vehicles; small-car spaces will have less demand than full-size spaces.
- Some locations may be considered less secure from vandalism or personal assault and will therefore have less demand.
- Spaces that provide protection from sun, rain, and snow may have greater demand.
- Aesthetic and comfort improvements (such as walkways, lighting, and cleanliness) can increase demand.

These factors should be considered when evaluating parking problems and designing management programs. Parking problems often consist of conflicts over the most convenient, high-demand spaces, even if less convenient parking is available nearby. Increasing the supply of less convenient parking may do little to solve parking problems, while regulation and price incentives that shift demand from more to less convenient locations can be an effective way to reduce parking problems without increasing supply. For this reason, if somebody complains that parking is unavailable, be sure to determine the exact location and time, and identify the type of parking for which they are looking. Parking inventories and demand surveys should evaluate each location and type of facility (e.g., in front/behind buildings, central/fringe location, public/private, priced/unpriced, on-street/off-street, and surface/structured). This can help identify opportunities for solving parking problems by shifting demand to less utilized locations.

GEOGRAPHY

Parking demand varies from one geographic area to another. Residents of communities with more diverse transportation systems tend to own fewer cars and take fewer vehicle trips than in more automobile-dependent areas, and people working in such areas commute more by alternative modes. Average per capita and per-household vehicle ownership varies from one city to another. Even greater variations can exist between different neighborhoods and districts within a city (e.g., between a central location with good transit service and a suburban location where almost all trips are made by automobile).

Density (number of people or jobs in an area), clustering (major trip generators located close together), land-use mix (different land-use types, such as residential and commercial, located close together) and transportation diversity (a range of available transportation options) tend to reduce per capita vehicle ownership and use. As cities grow in size and density, parking demand *per capita* (e.g., per resident, employee, and customer) tends to decrease due to rising land costs and an increasing portion of travel by alternative modes. However, parking demand *per acre* tends to increase with density due to increased people per acre.

Figure 3-1 shows how household vehicle ownership tends to decline with density. Figure 3-2 indicates that residents of higher-density urban areas make about 25 percent fewer motor vehicle trips than the national average.

Table 3-1 summarizes an estimate of the elasticity of per capita vehicle trips and vehicle mileage with respect to various land-use factors. For example, it indicates that doubling neighborhood density reduces per capita automobile travel by 5 percent. Similarly, doubling land-use mix or improving land-use design to support alternative modes also reduces per capita vehicle travel 5 percent.

Figure 3-1
Vehicles Per Household by Population Density

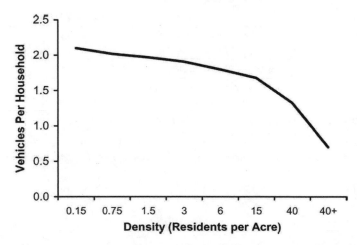

Vehicle ownership declines with density. Households in medium-density urban neighborhoods (10 to 30 residents per acre) typically own 20 percent fewer vehicles than those in suburban locations; much greater reductions occur in high-density areas (with more than 30 residents per acre).

Source: BTS, 1995.

Figure 3-2
Daily Motor Vehicle Trips Per Resident

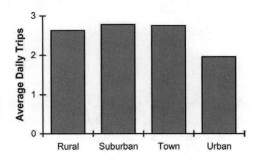

Urban residents make fewer automobile trips than people living in other geographic locations.

Source: BTS, 1995.

Table 3-1
Built Environment Travel Elasticities

Factor	Description	Vehicle Trips	Vehicle Miles Traveled
Local density	Residents and employees divided by land area	−0.05	−0.05
Local diversity (mix)	Jobs/residential population	−0.03	−0.05
Local design	Sidewalk and street network connectivity and density	−0.05	−0.03
Regional accessibility	Distance to other activity centers in the region	—	−0.20

Elasticity values of vehicle trips and vehicle miles traveled with respect to various land-use factors.

Source: Ewing and Cervero, 2002.

Household Vehicle Ownership and Use By Land-Use Formula

Household Vehicle Ownership = $2.702 \times (\text{Density})^{-0.25}$

Household Annual Vehicle Miles Traveled
= $34{,}270 \times (\text{Density})^{-0.25} \times (\text{TAI})^{-0.076}$

Density = households per residential acre
TAI (Transit Accessibility Index) = 50 transit vehicle seats per hour (about one bus) within one-quarter mile (one-half mile for rail and ferries) averaged over 24 hours

Source: Holtzclaw, 1994.

The sidebar entitled "Household Vehicle Ownership and Use by Land-Use Formula" summarizes the model used in the *This View of Density Calculator* (SFLCV, 2002) for predicting how density and transit-service availability affect vehicle ownership and use.

A survey of parking demand around the SkyTrain stations in Vancouver, British Columbia, found that nearly a quarter of households living near transit stations own no vehicles, and average household vehicle ownership is 31 percent lower within the SkyTrain corridor than at suburban locations a few miles away (Bunt and Joyce, 1998).

Carsharing (automobile rental services located in residential areas that substitute for private vehicle ownership) tends to reduce vehicle ownership and parking demand. User surveys have found that nearly one-third of carshare organization members reduce their household vehicle ownership, each car-share vehicle serves 5 to 10 users, and members drive 40 to 60 percent fewer average annual miles (Steininger et al., 1996; Cervero and Tsai, 2003).

One study found that residents in a pedestrian-friendly community walked, bicycled, or rode transit for 49 percent of work trips and 15 percent of nonwork trips, which is 18 and 11 percentage points more than residents of more automobile-oriented communities (Cervero and Radisch, 1995). Pedestrian improvements also reduce parking requirements by expanding the range of parking facilities serving a destination. This suggests that parking requirements can often be reduced 15 to 25 percent in pedestrian-friendly areas. Other studies show that significant walking and cycling improvements typically reduce automobile travel 5 to 10 percent and more if implemented with driving disincentives (Macket, 2000).

Employment density has even greater impacts than residential density on commute mode split (the portion of commuters who use a particular travel mode). Automobile commuting declines significantly when workplace densities reach 50 to 75 employees per gross acre (Frank and Pivo, 1995). As commercial centers grow beyond about 5,000 employees, it becomes increasingly difficult to provide surface parking for all commuters. Additional parking must be structured, which significantly increases costs, so fewer employees receive free parking. As commercial centers increase in size, an increasing portion of parking is priced and a declining portion of commute trips are made by automobile. Worksites in automobile-dependent areas (e.g., isolated suburban office parks) may require one parking space per employee, while large city central business districts (major commercial centers of a city, which usually contain high-value business activity, including banking, insurance, real estate, and related services) often have just one parking space per four employees. Figure 3-3 illustrates how parking demand varies by type of commercial center.

Some communities use a formula to adjust parking requirements to reflect geographic factors. Table 3-2 shows trip reduction factors used in Portland, Oregon. For example, if development has a floor area ratio of 1.0, and is located in a commercial area near a light rail transit station, parking requirements can be reduced by 5 percent.

In addition:

- Trips are reduced an additional 5 percent at a mixed-use development with at least 24 dwelling units per gross acre and 15 percent or more of floor area devoted to commercial or light industry uses.
- Trips are reduced 2 percent if 41 to 60 percent of buildings in a zone are oriented toward the street.
- Trips are reduced 5 percent if 60 to 100 percent of buildings in a zone are oriented toward the street.

Figure 3-3
Parking Spaces Per Employee

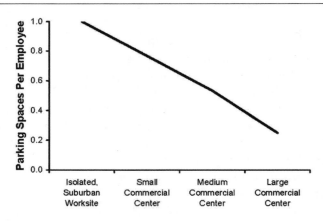

Commute parking demand declines with employment center density and size. In automobile-dependent suburban areas, nearly every employee requires a parking space; in large commercial centers, only about 0.25 parking spaces per employee are needed, since most use other commute modes. Of course, actual parking demand will vary depending on specific conditions.

Table 3-2
Trip Reduction Factors

Minimum FAR	Mixed Use	Commercial Near Bus	Commercial Near LRT Station	Mixed Use Near Bus	Mixed Use Near LRT
No minimum	—	1.0%	2.0%	—	—
0.5	1.9%	1.9%	2.9%	2.7%	3.9%
0.75	2.4%	2.4%	3.7%	3.4%	4.9%
1.0	3.0%	3.0%	5.0%	4.3%	6.7%
1.25	3.6%	3.6%	6.7%	5.1%	8.9%
1.5	4.2%	4.2%	8.9%	6.0%	11.9%
1.75	5.0%	5.0%	11.6%	7.1%	15.5%
2.0	7.0%	7.0%	15.0%	10.0%	20.0%

FAR = floor area ratio, or ratio of floor space to land area; LRT = light rail transit.

"Mixed Use" means commercial, restaurants, and light industry with 30 percent or more floor area devoted to residential. "Near Bus" or "Near LRT" means location within one-quarter mile of a bus corridor or LRT station.

Source: City of Portland, 1995.

Figure 3-4
Household Travel by Neighborhood Type

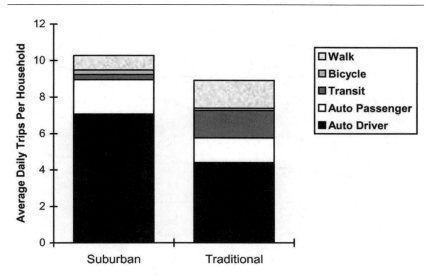

Vehicle trips per household are significantly higher in automobile-dependent suburban communities due to lower densities and fewer travel choices.

Source: Friedman et al., 1995.

- Trips are reduced 3 percent if Pedestrian Environmental Factor (an index that indicates the quality of walking conditions in urban areas) equals 9-12.
- Trips are reduced 1 percent if it is adjacent to a bicycle path and secure bicycle storage is provided.
- In a central business district, trips are reduced 40 percent, plus 12 percent if Pedestrian Environmental Factor is 9 to 11, and 14 percent if Pedestrian Environmental Factor is 12.

Although these impacts may individually seem small, they are cumulative. Neighborhoods with favorable density, mix, street design, and regional accessibility features typically have 20 to 40 percent fewer vehicles and vehicle trips per capita than otherwise comparable automobile-dependent communities (see Figure 3-4; also see Hess, 2001 and Hess and Ong, 2001). Since conventional parking standards are based on suburban parking demand, conventional parking requirements are 20 to 40 percent higher than actually required in more accessible, multimodal neighborhoods, even without parking management programs. These various land-use factors that affect travel behavior are incorporated in the *Smart Growth Index (SGI) Model* (USEPA, 2001), which can be used to predict vehicle travel, and therefore parking demand, in an area.

Figure 3-5
Vehicle Ownership by Household Income

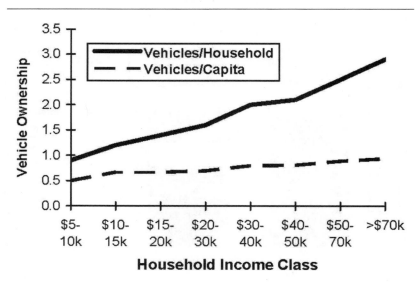

Lower-income households own fewer automobiles than wealthier households.

Source: BLS, 2002.

Parking management can be effective in suburban as well as urban conditions, since suburban areas tend to start with the most excessive parking supply and so have greater potential for change. For example, parking cash-out (offering commuters a cash benefit as an alternative to a free parking space) causes similar reductions in automobile commute trips in urban and suburban work locations: in urban locations, commuters tend to shift from driving to walking and transit; in suburban locations, they tend to shift to cycling and ridesharing (Shoup, 1997). Many suburban communities are becoming more urbanized, developing from low-density sprawl into compact, mixed-use towns (see the section entitled "Implement Smart Growth Policies" on page 103). Parking management supports and is supported by these trends.

DEMOGRAPHICS

Demographic factors (e.g., income, age, and housing type) affect vehicle ownership and use. For example, college students, renters, elderly people, people with disabilities, and residents of group homes all tend to own fewer than average vehicles. Figure 3-5 shows how income affects average vehicle ownership. The lowest income category owns about one-quarter as many vehicles per household as the highest income quintile. Applying inflexible parking standards

Figure 3-6
Vehicles Per Household by Income Class

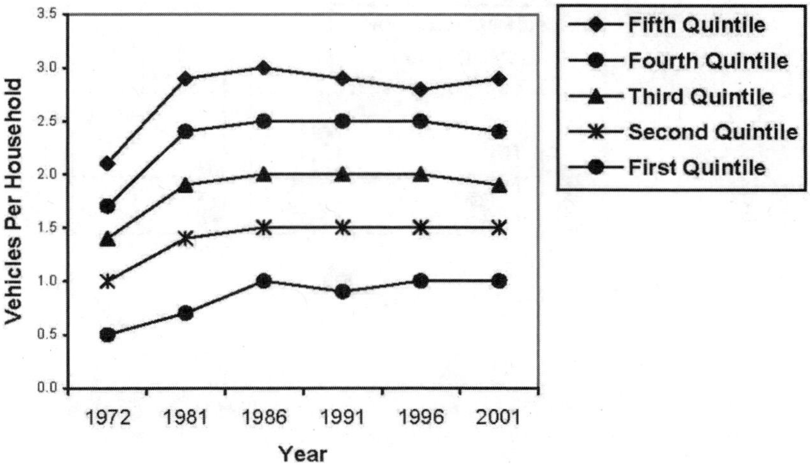

Average vehicles per household by income quintile, which increased significantly during the 1970s but leveled off, and even declined, for some groups during the 1990s.

Source: BLS, 2002.

forces lower-income households to pay for parking they don't really need and makes housing less affordable, particularly in areas with higher land costs.

Figure 3-6 illustrates how per-household vehicle ownership changed between 1972 and 2001. Vehicle ownership increased significantly during the 1970s and for lower-income households during the 1980s, but ownership rates flattened and even declined for some groups during the 1990s (also see Figure 2-3 on page 18). Average vehicle ownership per household is likely to decline somewhat as Baby Boomers age. Until the 1980s, transportation professionals could justify relatively high parking requirements on the grounds that it anticipated future growth in vehicle ownership rates, but this is no longer appropriate. Parking requirements based on studies performed in the 1980s may be excessive in the future.

Figure 3-7 illustrates how home tenure, location, and age affect vehicle ownership. For example, renters own about half as many vehicles per household as homeowners; vehicle ownership is low for urban residents, and for households headed by people who are young (under 30). Smaller households tend to own fewer vehicles and therefore need less parking (see Figure 3-8). Local transportation surveys, census data, and the Bureau of Labor Statistics' annual *Consumer Expenditure Survey* can help determine vehicle ownership rates for specific groups (BLS, 2002).

Figure 3-7
Vehicles Per Household

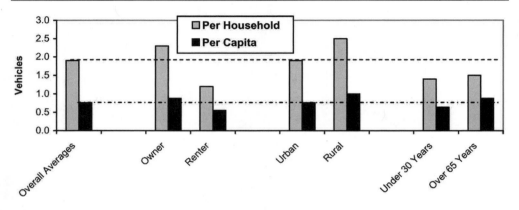

Vehicle ownership varies depending on factors such as home tenure, geographic location, and resident age. Dashed lines indicate average values.

Source: BLS, 2002.

Figure 3-8
Vehicle Ownership by Household Size

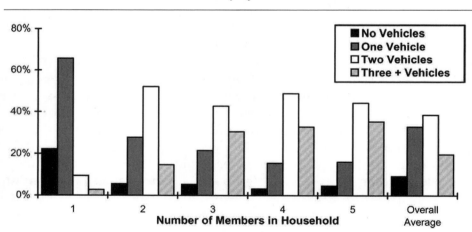

Smaller households tend to own fewer vehicles than larger households.

Source: BTS, 1995.

PRICING AND REGULATION

Consumers can respond to parking pricing and regulation in various ways (see Table 3-3). Some of these responses provide more benefits to society than others and deserve more public support. For example, shifting travel to alternative modes reduces traffic congestion, roadway costs, and pollution emissions, and so tends to provide more total benefits than shifting parking to an alternative location.

Economists measure pricing impacts in terms of elasticities, the percentage of change in consumption of a good in response to a percentage change in its price. The elasticity of vehicle *ownership* with respect to price is typically –0.4 to –1.0, which means that a 10 percent increase in total vehicle costs reduces vehicle ownership 4 to 10 percent (Jansson, 1989). Table 3-4 indicates the reduction in vehicle ownership that can be expected from various residential parking fees. For example, a $600 annual residential parking fee is likely to reduce vehicle ownership by 8 to 15 percent, and a $1,200 annual fee reduces vehicle ownership by 15 to 30 percent. Households often shed their second or third vehicle, which tend to have relatively low annual mileage. In a typical case, a two-driver household eliminates a second car that was previously driven 9,000 annual miles (two-thirds the overall average) and adds 1,000 annual miles to their existing vehicle, to carshare or rental vehicles, and to

Table 3-3
Potential Responses to Parking Pricing and Regulation

Consumer Response	Community Impact
No change; pay fee or citation.	Provides revenue.
Reduce vehicle ownership.	Reduces parking demand and supports mobility management objectives.
Shift to an alternative parking location nearby.	Desirable if it makes convenient parking spaces available to priority uses; undesirable if it causes spillover parking problems.
Travel to an alternative destination.	Has mixed impacts; undesirable to businesses that lose customers but beneficial to those that gain.
Shift mode (walking, cycling, or transit).	Reduces parking demand and supports mobility management objectives.
Reduce trips (consolidate errands, telecommute, or forgo trips).	Reduces parking demand and supports mobility management objectives.
Reduce parking duration (length of stay).	Desirable if it reduces peak-period parking congestion; undesirable to businesses that lose customers.
Replace one vehicle trip with two chauffeured vehicle trips.	Generally undesirable since it increases total vehicle traffic.

Summary of potential consumer responses to parking pricing and regulations. Some provide more benefits to society than others.

Table 3-4
Vehicle Ownership Reductions from Residential Parking

Annual (Monthly) Fee	−0.4 Elasticity	−0.7 Elasticity	−1.0 Elasticity
$300 ($25)	4%	6%	8%
$600 ($50)	8%	11%	15%
$900 ($75)	11%	17%	23%
$1,200 ($100)	15%	23%	30%
$1,500 ($125)	19%	28%	38%

Reductions in vehicle ownership that may be expected from various residential parking fees, assuming that free parking is unavailable nearby.

Table 3-5
Vehicle Trips Reduced by Daily Parking Fees

Worksite Setting	$1.35	$2.70	$4.00	$5.40
Low-density suburb	6.5%	15.1%	25.3%	36.1%
Activity center	12.3%	25.1%	37.0%	46.8%
Regional central business district/corridor	17.5%	31.8%	42.6%	50.0%

Reductions in vehicle trips that result from daily parking fees (in 2005 U.S. dollars) in various geographic locations. (See VTPI (2005) for additional tables and information.)

Sources: "Trip Reduction Tables," VTPI, 2005; based on Comsis Corporation, 1993.

vehicle travel by friends who make additional chauffeured trips, resulting in a net 8,000 vehicle-mile reduction for the household, or 4,000 vehicle miles per driver. Exact impacts will vary depending on specific circumstances.

The elasticity of vehicle *trips* with respect to parking price is typically found to be −0.1 to −0.3, which means a 10 percent parking fee increase reduces vehicle use by 1 to 3 percent (Pratt, 2000; Kuzmyak et al., 2003; "Transportation Elasticities," VTPI, 2005). Higher elasticities are often recorded for a specific location (because motorists shift where they park), when measured over longer time periods (impacts tend to increase over time), and for pricing implemented with other travel management strategies (such as transit improvements).

Pratt (2000, pp. 13-40) finds significantly higher elasticities (−0.9 to −1.2) of parking price with regard to commercial parking gross revenues, since motorists can respond to higher prices by reducing their parking duration or changing to cheaper locations and times, as well as reducing total vehicle trips. Similarly, in a study of downtown parking meter price increases, Clinch and Kelly (2004) find that the elasticity of parking frequency is smaller (−0.11) than the elasticity of vehicle duration (−0.20), indicating that higher prices cause some motorists to reduce how long they stay.

Table 3-6
Parking Price Elasticities

Term/Purpose	Car Driver	Car Passenger	Public Transport	Slow Modes*
Commuting	−0.08	+0.02	+0.02	+0.02
Business	−0.02	+0.01	+0.01	+0.01
Education	−0.10	+0.00	+0.00	+0.00
Other	−0.30	+0.04	+0.04	+0.05
Total	**−0.16**	**+0.03**	**+0.02**	**+0.03**

* Slow modes include walking and cycling.

Typical changes in various types of travel for each 1 percent change in parking prices in an automobile-oriented urban area.

Source: TRACE, 1999, Tables 32 and 33.

Shifting from free to cost-recovery parking (prices that reflect the cost of providing parking facilities) typically reduces automobile commuting 10 to 30 percent (Comsis Corporation, 1993). Hess (2001) finds that shifting from free parking to a $6 daily parking fee in downtown Portland, Oregon, reduces automobile commutes 21 percent. Nearly 35 percent of automobile commuters surveyed would consider shifting to another mode if required to pay daily parking fees of $1 to $3 in suburban locations and $3 to $8 in urban locations (Kuppam et al., 1998). Table 3-5 shows the typical reduction in automobile commute trips that result from various parking fees.

TRACE (1999) provides detailed estimates of parking pricing impacts on various types of travel (e.g., car trips, car kilometers, transit travel, walking/cycling, commuting, and business trips) under various conditions. Table 3-6 summarizes long-term elasticities for relatively automobile-oriented urban regions.

Of course, the effects of pricing on parking and travel demand in a particular situation depend on the exact price structure, the quality of parking and travel alternatives at that location, user demographics, enforcement practices, and numerous other factors. For example, a $1 per hour parking fee may have different impacts on vehicle travel and parking demand for lower-income suburban employees than for higher-income downtown shoppers. Similarly, charging for residential parking may have little impact on vehicle ownership if free parking is available on the street nearby.

PARKING AND MOBILITY MANAGEMENT PROGRAMS

"Mobility management" (also called "transportation demand management") is a general term for various strategies and programs that result in more efficient use of transportation resources, by changing travel timing, route, mode, destination, and frequency. (Chapter 5 discusses mobility management in more detail.) There are many different mobility management strategies, including the following:

- Improvements to alternative modes (e.g., walking, cycling, ridesharing, transit, and telework).
- Incentives to change modes (e.g., high-occupant vehicle priority, transit fare discounts, road pricing, parking pricing, and marketing programs).
- More accessible land use (e.g., more compact, mixed land use, and more connected road and path networks).
- Encouragement and support programs (e.g., commute trip reduction, school and campus transport management, and tourist transport management).

A comprehensive parking and mobility management program can often reduce parking requirements by 20 to 40 percent. A 20 percent reduction is usually feasible with cost-effective, short-term strategies, such as shared parking (a parking lot that serves multiple destinations and parking spaces shared by more than one user) and commute trip reduction programs that promote alternative modes, while 40 percent reductions are feasible with more comprehensive, long-term programs that include financial incentives, such as pricing or cashing out currently free parking, and improved transit services

Figure 3-9
Employee Parking Requirements by Geographic Area

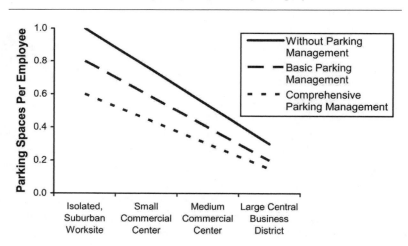

Parking requirements per employee decline as commercial areas become more compact and multimodal. An isolated suburban worksite typically requires one parking space per employee; a central business district requires only a quarter as many spaces (0.25 spaces per employee). Cost-effective parking and transport management programs can typically reduce parking demand 20 to 40 percent compared with what would otherwise occur, depending on the extent of the program.

(see Figure 3-9). Similarly, residential parking requirements can often be reduced by 10 to 40 percent with various management strategies, such as sharing parking spaces (rather than assigning reserved spaces), unbundling parking (so residents only rent the number of parking spaces they actually want), and carsharing services located in residential areas. The more strategies that are applied, the more parking requirements can be reduced.

TIME PERIOD

Parking demand has daily, weekly, and annual cycles, plus long-term trends. Analysis of parking requirements is therefore affected by the hour, day, and month when demand is measured, and how average values are calculated. Many locations have adequate parking supply except during occasional peak periods, such as holiday shopping periods or special events. As described in Chapter 2, conventional parking standards are often based on the 20th annual design hour (parking facilities are sized to be fully occupied less than 20 hours a year). In some cases, generous parking supply is provided to accommodate possible future demand increases.

This has several implications for parking evaluation and management:

- Parking demand analysis and evaluation of parking problems are sensitive to the time period used for analysis and how peak periods are defined. For example, simply shifting from a 10th to 20th design hour may reduce parking requirements by 10 percent or more.
- Parking management strategies that reduce peak-period parking demand also provide the greatest congestion reduction benefits, and congestion management strategies can provide significant parking cost savings. For example, employee trip reduction programs that encourage commuters to use alternative modes, and shuttle services between major destinations and more distant parking facilities provided during busy periods, can reduce both local traffic congestion and parking problems. This is another reason to coordinate parking and mobility management activities.
- It is not generally desirable to try to accommodate the maximum peak demand that may occur during a facility's lifetime. It is better to supply less parking and use contingency-based planning to address potential future parking problems that might develop.

SUMMARY OF FACTORS AFFECTING
PARKING DEMAND AND REQUIREMENTS

Table 3-7 summarizes factors affecting parking demand and parking requirements. As described earlier, conventional, minimum parking standards reflect the upper range of demand, so these factors generally allow parking standards to be adjusted downward. Of course, professional judgment must be used when determining whether to apply the "typical adjustment" factors provided.

Table 3-7
Factors Affecting Parking Demand and Requirements

Factor	Description	Analysis Method	Typical Adjustment
Geographic location	Vehicle ownership and trip generation rates in an area.	Population and travel data to identify variations.	Adjust parking requirements to reflect variations in vehicle ownership and trip rates in an area.
Residential density	Number of residents or housing units per acre/hectare.	Models, such as Holtzclaw (1994), can be used to determine how density affects vehicle ownership and use.	Reduce parking requirements 1% for each resident per acre: reduce requirements 15% where there are 15 residents per acre, and 30% where there are 30 residents per acre.
Employment density	Number of employees per acre.	Adjust employee parking requirements to reflect automobile commute mode split.	Reduce requirements 10% to 15% in areas with 50 or more employees per gross acre.
Land-use mix	Range of land uses located within convenient walking distance.	Apply trip and parking demand reduction factors, such as Portland (City of Portland, 1995). Apply shared parking factors.	Reduce requirements 5% to 10% in mixed-use developments; additional reductions if parking facilities are shared.
Transit accessibility	Nearby transit service frequency and quality.	Adjust worksite parking to reflect transit commute mode split. Models, such as Holtzclaw (1994), can predict how transit service quality affects vehicle ownership and use.	Reduce requirements 10% for housing and employment within one-quarter mile of frequent bus service, and 20% for housing and employment within one-quarter mile of a rail transit station.
Carsharing	Whether a carsharing service is located within or near a residential development.	Based on experience with comparable programs.	Reduce residential requirements 5% to 10% if a carsharing service is located within one-quarter mile, or reduce 5 to 10 parking spaces for each carshare vehicle located in a building.

Table 3-7 (cont.)
Factors Affecting Parking Demand and Requirements

Factor	Description	Analysis Method	Typical Adjustment
Walkability	Quality of walking environment.	Pedestrian Environmental Factor and pedestrian level of service ("Evaluating Nonmotorized Transport," VTPI, 2005).	Reduce requirements 5% to 15% in walkable communities, with additional reductions if walking improvements allow more shared and off-site parking.
Demographics	Age and physical ability of residents or commuters.	Census and other surveys with information on age, physical ability, and vehicle ownership.	Reduce requirements 20% to 40% for housing for young (under 30), elderly (over 65), or disabled people.
Income	Average income of residents or commuters.	Census and other surveys with income and vehicle ownership information.	Reduce requirements 10% to 20% for the 20% lowest income households, and 20% to 30% for the lowest 10% income households.
Housing tenure	Whether housing is owned or rented.	Census and surveys with information on vehicle ownership by housing tenure.	Reduce requirements 20% to 40% for rental versus owner-occupied housing.
Pricing	Parking that is priced or cashed out.	Price elasticity models ("Transportation Elasticities," VTPI, 2005; Pratt, 2000).	Reduce requirements 10% to 30% for cost-recovery pricing (parking priced to pay the full cost of parking facilities).
Unbundled parking	Parking sold or rented separately from building space.	Price elasticity models.	Reduce requirements 10 to 30% where parking is unbundled.
Parking and mobility management	Parking and mobility management programs are implemented at a site.	Methodologies described in this book, VTPI (2005), and experience with comparable programs.	Reduce requirements 10% to 40% at worksites with well-planned parking and mobility management programs.

Table 3-7 (cont.)
Factors Affecting Parking Demand and Requirements

Factor	Description	Analysis Method	Typical Adjustment
Design hour	Number of allowable annual hours a parking facility may fill.	Parking generation data and experience with comparable sites.	Reduce requirements 10% to 20% if a 10th annual design hour is replaced by a 30th annual peak hour; this requires an overflow parking plan.
Contingency-based planning	Use lower-bound requirements, as long as additional parking management strategies can be implemented if needed.	Develop a contingency-based parking plan as described in this book.	Reduce requirements based on the projected effectiveness of parking management strategies available for implementation.

Summary of various factors that affect parking demand and how they can be applied to adjust parking supply requirements.

EVALUATION OF MULTIPLE FACTORS

Multiple adjustment factors often apply in a particular situation. For example, a particular apartment building or worksite may have a variety of demographic, geographic, and management factors that reduce parking demand relative to conventional standards, such as being located near transit stations, serving lower-income people, and having shared parking facilities. Care is needed when calculating their cumulative impacts. Some factors overlap. For example, the lower parking demand for rental housing partly reflects the lower average incomes of their residents, and the lower parking demand in dense, urban areas reflects, at least in part, the increased land-use mix, walkability, and transit service in such areas. When evaluating the impacts of factors that overlap, use professional judgment to determine how much of each to apply.

Total impacts are multiplicative and not additive because each additional factor applies to a smaller base. For example, if one factor reduces demand 20 percent, and a second factor reduces demand an additional 15 percent, their combined effect is calculated as 80 percent × 85 percent = 68 percent, a 32-point total reduction, rather than adding 20 percent + 15 percent = 35 percent. This occurs because the 15 percent reduction applies to a base that is already reduced 20 percent. If a third factor reduces demand by another 10 percent, the total reduction provided by the three factors together is 38.8 percent (which is calculated as (100 percent – [80 percent × 85 percent × 90 percent]) = (100 percent – 61.2 percent) = 38.8 percent), not 45 percent (20 percent + 15 percent + 10 percent).

However, some strategies have synergistic effects (total impacts are greater than the sum of their individual impacts). For example, by itself, providing off-site parking information may reduce demand at a particular location by just 5 percent, and by itself a parking fee may reduce demand by just 10 percent, but together they may reduce demand by 20 percent because they provide complementary incentives to change parking location.

CHAPTER 3
REFERENCES AND INFORMATION RESOURCES

Bunt, Paul and Peter Joyce (1998), *Car Ownership Patterns Near Rapid Transit Stations*, Canadian Institute of Transportation Engineers; available online (www.citebc.ca/Feb98_Ownership.html).

Bureau of Labor Statistics (BLS) (2002), *Consumer Expenditure Survey*, BLS (www.bls.gov); available online (www.bls.gov/cex/home.htm).

Bureau of Transportation Statistics (BTS) (1995), *National Personal Transportation Survey*, BTS, Oak Ridge National Laboratory (http://nhts.ornl.gov/2001/index.shtml).

Cervero, Robert and Carolyn Radisch (1995), *Travel Choices in Pedestrian Versus Automobile Oriented Neighborhoods*, UCTC No. 281, The University of California Transportation Center (www.uctc.net); available online (www.uctc.net/papers/281.pdf).

Cervero, Robert and Yu-Hsin Tsai (2003), *San Francisco City CarShare: Travel-Demand Trends and Second-Year Impacts*, Working Paper 2003-05, Institute of Urban & Regional Development, University of California Berkeley (www-iurd.ced.berkeley.edu), August 2003; available online (www-iurd.ced.berkeley.edu/pub/abstract_wp200305.htm).

City of Portland (1995), *Parking Ratio Rule Checklist; Self-Enforcing Strategies* (Portland, OR), Office of Transportation (www.trans.ci.portland.or.us).

Clinch, J. Peter and J. Andrew Kelly (2004), *Temporal Variance of Revealed Preference On-Street Parking Price Elasticity*, Department of Planning and Environmental Policy, University College Dublin (www.environmentaleconomics.net).

Community Research & Development Information Service (2001), *COST 342: Parking Policy Measures and their Effects on Mobility and the Economy*, European Commission; available online (www.cordis.lu/cost-transport/src/cost-342.htm).

Comsis Corporation (1993), *Implementing Effective Travel Demand Management Measures: Inventory of Measures and Synthesis of Experience*, U.S. Department of Transportation (www.dot.gov) and Institute of Transportation Engineers (www.ite.org); available online (www.bts.gov/ntl/DOCS/474.html).

Ewing, Reid and Robert Cervero (2002), "Travel and the Built Environment—Synthesis," *Transportation Research Record 1780*, Transportation Research Board (Washington, DC) (www.trb.org).

Frank, Lawrence and Gary Pivo (1995), "Impacts of Mixed Use and Density on Utilization of Three Modes of Travel: SOV, Transit and Walking" *Transportation Research Record 1466*, Transportation Research Board (Washington, DC) (www.trb.org), pp. 44-55.

Friedman, Bruce, Stephen Gordon, and John Peers (1995), "Effect of Neotraditional Neighborhood Design on Travel Characteristics," *Transportation Research Record 1466*, Transportation Research Board (Washington, DC) (www.trb.org), pp. 63-70.

Gould, Carol (2003), "Parking: When Less is More," *Transportation Planning*, Vol. 28, No. 1, Transportation Planning Division, American Planning Association (Chicago, IL) (www.planning.org), Winter 2003, pp. 3-11.

Hess, Daniel B. (2001), *The Effects of Free Parking on Commuter Mode Choice: Evidence from Travel Diary Data*, The Ralph & Goldy Lewis Center for Regional Policy Studies, University of California, Los Angeles (http://lewis.sppsr.ucla.edu/index.cfm), April 2001.

Hess, Daniel Baldwin, and Paul M. Ong (2001), *Traditional Neighborhoods and Auto Ownership*, The Ralph & Goldy Lewis Center for Regional Policy Studies, University of California, Los Angeles (www.sppsr.ucla.edu/lewis/WorkingPapers.html), July 2001; available online (http://lewis.sppsr.ucla.edu/publications/workingpapers/Hess2.pdf).

Holtzclaw, John (1994), *Using Residential Patterns and Transit To Decrease Auto Dependence and Costs*, Natural Resources Defense Council (www.nrdc.org), June 1994; available online (www.smartgrowth.org/library/cheers.html).

Holtzclaw, John, Robert Clear, Hank Dittmar, David Goldstein, and Peter Haas (2002), "Location Efficiency: Neighborhood and Socio-Economic Characteristics Determine Auto Ownership and Use?" *Transportation Planning and Technology* (www.tandf.co.uk/journals/online/0308-1060.html).

ICF Incorporated (1997), *Opportunities to Improve Air Quality through Transportation Pricing Programs*, U.S. Environmental Protection Agency (www.epa.gov); available online (www.epa.gov/otaq/transp/publicat/pub_mrkt.htm).

Jansson, J.O. (1989), "Car Demand Modeling and Forecasting," *Journal of Transport Economics and Policy*, May 1989, pp. 125-129.

Kolozsvari, Douglas and Donald Shoup (2003), *Turning Small Change Into Big Changes*, ACCESS No. 23, University of California Transportation Center (www.uctc.net), Fall 2003, pp. 2-7; available online (www.uctc.net/access/23/Access%2023%20-%2002%20-%20Small%20Change%20into%20Big%20Change.pdf).

Kuppam, Arun R., Ram M. Pendyala, and Mohan A.V. Gollakoti (1998), "Stated Response Analysis of the Effectiveness of Parking Pricing Strategies for Transportation Control," *Transportation Research Record 1649*, Transportation Research Board (Washington, DC) (www.trb.org), pp. 39-46.

Kuzmyak, J. Richard and Richard H. Pratt (2003), *Land Use and Site Design: Traveler Response to Transportation System Changes*, Chapter 15, Report 95, Transit Cooperative Research Program; Transportation Research Board (www.trb.org); available online (http://gulliver.trb.org/publications/tcrp/tcrp_rpt_95c15.pdf).

Kuzmyak, J. Richard, Rachel Weinberger, Richard H. Pratt, and Herbert S. Levinson (2003), *Parking Management and Supply: Traveler Response to Transport System Changes,* Chapter 18, Report 95, Transit Cooperative Research Program; Transportation Research Board (www.trb.org); available online (http://gulliver.trb.org/publications/tcrp/tcrp_rpt_95c18.pdf).

Mackett, Roger (2000), *How to Reduce the Number of Short Trips by Car,* European Transport Conference, Centre for Transport Studies, University College London (www.ucl.ac.uk/transport-studies); summary reports available online (www.ucl.ac.uk/transport-studies/shtrp.htm).

Nelson/Nygaard Consulting (2002), *Housing Shortage/Parking Surplus,* Transportation and Land Use Coalition (www.transcoalition.org); available online (www.transcoalition.org/reports/housing_s/housing_shortage_home.html).

Pratt, Richard H. (2000), *Traveler Response to Transportation System Changes, Interim Handbook,* Transit Cooperative Research Program Web Document 12, Transportation Research Board (www.trb.org); available online (http://gulliver.trb.org/publications/tcrp/tcrp_webdoc_12.pdf).

San Francisco League of Conservation Voters (SFLCV) (2002), *This View of Density Calculator,* SFLCV (www.sflcv.org); available online (www.sflcv.org/density).

Shoup, Donald (1997), "Evaluating the Effects of California's Parking Cash-out Law: Eight Case Studies," *Transport Policy,* Vol. 4, No. 4, pp. 201-216.

Shoup, Donald C. (2003), "Truth in Transportation Planning," *Journal of Transportation and Statistics,* Vol. 6, No. 1, U.S. Department of Transportation Bureau of Transportation Statistics (www.bts.gov), pp. 1-12; available online (www.bts.gov/publications/journal_of_transportation_and_statistics/volume_06_number_01/pdf/entire.pdf).

Steininger, K., C. Vogl, and R. Zettl (1996), "Car Sharing Organizations," *Transport Policy,* Vol. 3, No. 4, pp. 177-185.

TRACE (1999), *Elasticity Handbook: Elasticities for Prototypical Contexts,* TRACE, European Commission, Directorate-General for Transport, No: RO-97-SC.2035, Community Research and Development Information Service (www.cordis.lu); available online (www.cordis.lu/transport/src/tracerep.htm).

U.S. Environmental Protection Agency (USEPA) (2001), *Smart Growth Index (SGI) Model,* Smart Growth Program, USEPA (www.epa.gov/smartgrowth); available online (www.epa.gov/dced/topics/sg_index.htm).

Victoria Transport Policy Institute (VTPI) (2005), *Online TDM Encyclopedia,* VTPI (www.vtpi.org); available online ("Evaluating Nonmotorized Transport" (www.vtpi.org/tdm/tdm63.htm), "Transportation Elasticities" (www.vtpi.org/tdm/tdm11.htm), and "Trip Reduction Tables" (www.vtpi.org/tdm/tdm41.htm)).

4

Parking Facility Costs

A major benefit of parking management is its ability to reduce various parking costs. The magnitude of these savings is an important factor in parking management evaluation. Most parking facility costs are paid indirectly through rents and taxes and as a component of retail goods. Consumers almost never purchase a parking space as an individual item and so have little idea of the full costs incurred in producing them. This chapter examines the full costs of parking and therefore the economic savings that can result from parking management strategies that reduce parking supply requirements. Various components of parking costs are described below.

LAND

Because parking must be located near destinations, parking facilities occupy prime real estate with high land costs. A typical parking space is 8 to 10 feet (2.4 to 3.0 meters) wide and 18 to 20 feet (5.5 to 6.0 meters) deep, totaling 144 to 200 square feet (13 to 19 square meters). Off-street parking requires driveways (connecting the parking lot to a road) and access lanes (for circulation within a parking lot), and therefore typically requires 300 to 400 square feet (28 to 37 square meters) per space, resulting in 100 to 150 spaces per acre (250 to 370 per hectare). On-street parking is usually 7 to 8 feet wide (2.1 to 2.4 meters) and requires 20 to 22 feet (6.1 to 6.7 meters) of curb. Figure 4-1 compares the land used for parking facilities under various conditions.

The amount of land required per parking space varies depending on type and location. On-street parking requires the least amount of land because it does not need access lanes and driveways. Structured parking reduces land requirements per space. For example, compared with surface parking, a two-story parking structure uses about half the land per space, and a four-story parking structure uses about a quarter as much land. Underground parking (parking facilities located under a building) requires no additional land. As a

Figure 4-1
Typical Parking Facility Land Requirements

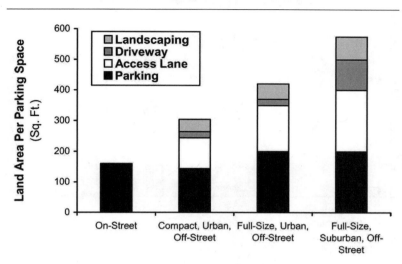

Land requirements per parking space vary depending on type and size.
Off-street spaces require driveways and access lanes. Landscaping
typically adds 10 to 15 percent to a parking lot area.

Sources: Arnold and Gibbons, 1996; Litman, 2004c; Shoup, 2005.

result, there is a trade-off between land costs and construction costs. Structured or underground parking tends to become cost effective where land costs are relatively high.

The portion of total land devoted to parking varies depending on conditions (see Figure 4-2). In commercial and industrial areas, such as a downtown or retail mall, streets often cover 5 to 15 percent of land, while driveways and off-street parking cover 30 to 50 percent of land.

Often, more land is devoted to parking than to the buildings it serves. For example, at three spaces per 1,000 square feet of gross floor area, the building/parking footprint (the outline of a structure viewed from above) ratio is approximately 1:1 for a single-story building, 1:2 for a two-story building, and 1:4 for a four-story building. As a result, parking is a dominant component of the urban landscape and is often an overriding concern in building location and design (see Figure 4-3).

Parking requirements can have a significant impact on land-use patterns and be a constraint on economic development. For example, in a commercial district where buildings average four stories, an acre of land can only accommodate about 100 employees if each needs a surface parking space, but more than 500 employees if no surface parking is required (see Figure 4-4). Structured or underground parking allows higher densities, but it is expensive and

Figure 4-2
Surface Coverage

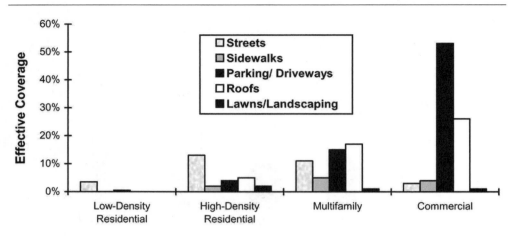

Land coverage in various urban conditions.

Source: Arnold and Gibbons, 1996.

Figure 4-3
Surface Parking Area for Various Parking Requirements

In commercial areas, parking is a dominant land use, often covering more than half of all land.

Figure 4-4
Employees Per Acre

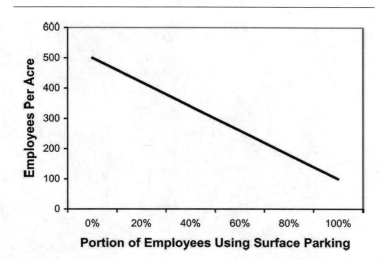

Vehicle parking requirements can constrain growth in major
business districts. As more employees use surface parking, the
number of employees per acre declines (assumes 300 square feet
gross floor area per employee, four-story buildings, and 350 square
feet per surface parking space).

so cannot usually be provided for free to all potential users. In many circumstances, parking costs limit the growth of a commercial district, activity center, or public event.

The opportunity cost of land used for parking is often overlooked in conventional accounting and planning. For example, property owners sometimes only consider construction and administrative expenses when evaluating their parking facility costs. Similarly, local governments often overlook rent or taxes foregone when calculating the cost of devoting public land to parking facilities.

CURB SPACE

On-street parking uses less land per space than off-street parking because it requires no driveway, but the land it uses often has a high opportunity cost. Using curb space for parking displaces traffic lanes, bicycle lanes, sidewalks, and landscaping. A driveway requires about the same amount of curb space as a parked car, so a driveway for two parking spaces provides a net gain of just one space due to lost curb parking (see Figure 4-5).

Figure 4-5
Driveways Displace On-Street Parking

These driveways displace on-street parking.

CONSTRUCTION

Table 4-1 indicates typical construction costs for aboveground parking facilities under optimal conditions; costs are about double for underground parking. Actual costs are often higher due to poor soil conditions and steep or irregularly shaped lots, or for amenities such as washrooms, elevators, or significant landscaping. In addition to these *hard* costs, there are *soft* costs for project planning, design, permits, and financing, which typically increase costs by 30 to 40 percent for a stand-alone project.

OPERATION AND MAINTENANCE

Operation and maintenance costs include cleaning, lighting, maintenance, repairs, security services, landscaping, snow removal, access control (e.g., entrance gates), fee collection (for priced parking), enforcement, insurance, labor, and administration. Parking facilities need periodic resurfacing and repaving. Parking structures typically have an operating life of 20 to 40 years, after which they require major reconstruction or replacement. Structured parking may require additional costs for fire control equipment and elevators, and underground parking may require mechanical ventilation. Private parking facilities must pay taxes and provide profits. Typical annual operating costs range from $200 per space for basic maintenance of a surface lot up to $800 or more for a facility with high service quality (Dorsett, 1998; ITE, 1999).

Table 4-1
Typical Parking Construction Costs Per Space

Area Per Space	Small Site (30,000 Square Feet)	Medium Site (60,000 Square Feet)	Large Site (90,000 Square Feet)
	350 Square Feet	325 Square Feet	315 Square Feet
Surface parking	$1,838	$1,706	$1,654
Ground + 1 level	$7,258	$6,143	$5,705
Ground + 2 level	$8,085	$6,767	$6,284
Ground + 3 level	$8,407	$6,996	$6,491
Ground + 4 level	$8,747	$7,269	$6,747
Ground + 5 level	$8,973	$7,451	$6,918
Ground + 6 level	$9,135	$7,581	$7,040
Ground + 7 level	$9,256	$7,678	$7,132
Ground + 8 level	$9,351	$7,754	$7,203

These figures (in 2000 U.S. dollars) assume a rectangular site, good soil conditions, quality finish, and no special amenities included in a parking facility.

Source: PT, 2000.

Figure 4-6
Commercial Parking Operating Costs

Commercial parking facilities have additional costs for collecting fees, taxes, and profits.

TRANSACTION COSTS

Transaction costs are any incremental costs required for regulations and pricing, including costs for equipment (signs, parking meters, ticket printers, and access gates), attendants, land (such as sidewalk space used by parking meters), administration, and enforcement. The incremental cost of pricing parking ranges from less than $50 annually per vehicle (for a basic pass system with minimal enforcement) to more than $500 per space (for facilities with attendants or automated control systems). Regulations and pricing also impose incremental time and inconvenience costs on motorists.

OTHER COSTS

There is sometimes a specific opportunity cost associated with constructing or maintaining a parking facility. For example, a resident may want to convert a garage into a bedroom or studio, or a business may want to use land currently devoted to parking for a new building or other productive activity.

Paving land for parking imposes environmental costs, including loss of greenspace, increased impervious surfaces and related stormwater management costs, heat island effects (higher local temperatures due to solar gain from dark-colored surfaces, such as pavement and building roofs), and aesthetic degradation.

In addition, generous and free parking tends to increase vehicle ownership and use, and creates more dispersed land-use patterns and more automobile-dependent transportation systems. This increases problems such as traffic congestion, traffic accidents, pollution emissions, and reduced travel options for nondrivers. Put another way, to the degree that parking management reduces vehicle traffic and creates a more accessible land-use pattern, it provides additional benefits, such as reduced traffic congestion, accidents, and pollution (see the sidebar entitled "Transportation Trade-Offs Involving Parking").

TOTAL PARKING COST

Table 4-2 and Figure 4-7 indicate typical parking facility financial costs. These estimates do not include indirect and nonmarket costs, such as stormwater management, aesthetic degradation, and reduced accessibility. These costs vary from about $250 annually per space (when construction costs are minimal and otherwise unused land is available) up to more than $2,250 for structured parking with attendants. On-street parking requires less land per space than off-street parking, but its opportunity costs are often high if space is needed for traffic lanes or sidewalks. The *Parking Cost, Pricing and Revenue Calculator* (VTPI, 2003) can be used to calculate these costs for a particular situation.

In addition to these direct financial savings, more efficient parking management can provide the following indirect benefits:

Transportation Trade-Offs Involving Parking

Planning decisions often involve trade-offs between different forms of transportation. For example, using road space for parking reduces the space available for traffic lanes and sidewalks. In some situations, converting parking lanes to bus or bicycle lanes can be justified if this reduces automobile trips to an area and therefore parking demand. For example, converting 1 mile of on-street parking to transit or bicycle lanes might reduce parking supply by 100 spaces; this loss may be offset if the improved transit service or cycling conditions reduces 100 daily automobile trips to that area.

Parking planning decisions can also involve trade-offs between mobility (the movement of people or goods) and land-use accessibility (the ease of reaching activities and destinations). Generous parking requirements tend to create more dispersed land-use patterns, which require more vehicle travel; parking management tends to support more compact, multimodal land-use patterns where less automobile travel is needed to reach destinations. For example, with commercial strip development, businesses are scattered along a highway. To run a dozen errands, it may be necessary to take a dozen individual automobile trips from one business to another. A downtown or other urban center has narrower streets and less parking supply, which reduce mobility but improve accessibility. Running a dozen errands downtown generally takes only one or two car trips, with most destinations accessible by walking.

Site design often involves trade-offs between parking convenience and other design objectives. Locating parking in front of a building increases convenience for motorists but tends to be unattractive and less convenient for pedestrian access (and therefore transit access) compared with a building located at the sidewalk. Similarly, the area around a transit station can be developed as a Park & Ride lot or as transit-oriented development, with a mix of residential and commercial land uses. Park & Ride facilities tend to increase mobility, allowing suburban commuters to use public transit; transit-oriented development increases accessibility and therefore helps reduce total per capita vehicle travel. Effective parking management can help balance these conflicting objectives, allowing more Park & Ride parking capacity within a transit-oriented center.

- Increased productive activity per land area, which will increase profits, property values, and tax revenues within a community.
- Improved accessibility and walkability between destinations.
- Reduced impervious surfaces, which reduces stormwater management costs and heat island impacts.
- Improved design flexibility, which can increase the aesthetic quality and functionality of buildings and streetscapes.
- Increased efficiency of alternative modes (e.g., walking, ridesharing, and public transit use) and reduced vehicle traffic problems.

Table 4-2
Typical Parking Facility Financial Costs

| Type of Facility | Land Costs | | Construction Costs | O & M Costs | Total Cost | Daily Cost |
	Per Acre	Per Space	Per Space	Annual, Per Space	Annual, Per Space	Per Space
Suburban, on-street	$50,000	$200	$2,000	$200	$408	$1.36
Suburban, surface, free land	$0	$0	$2,000	$200	$389	$1.62
Suburban, surface	$50,000	$455	$2,000	$200	$432	$1.80
Suburban, 2-level structure	$50,000	$227	$10,000	$300	$1,265	$5.27
Urban, on-street	$250,000	$1,000	$3,000	$200	$578	$1.93
Urban, surface	$250,000	$2,083	$3,000	$300	$780	$3.25
Urban, 3-level structure	$250,000	$694	$12,000	$400	$1,598	$6.66
Urban, underground	$250,000	$0	$20,000	$400	$2,288	$9.53
CBD, on-street	$2,000,000	$8,000	$3,000	$300	$1,338	$4.46
CBD, surface	$2,000,000	$15,385	$3,000	$300	$2,035	$6.78
CBD, 4-level structure	$2,000,000	$3,846	$15,000	$400	$2,179	$7.26
CBD, underground	$2,000,000	$0	$25,000	$500	$2,645	$8.82

O & M = operations and maintenance; CBD = central business district.

Direct financial parking facility costs under various conditions. Assumes 7 percent annual interest rate, amortized over 20 years.

Sources: "Parking Evaluation," VTPI, 2005; citing VTPI, 2003.

Figure 4-7
Typical Parking Facility Annualized Costs

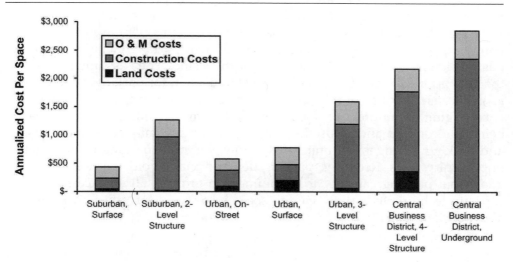

Direct financial costs of building and operating various types of parking facilities.

Sources: "Parking Evaluation," VTPI, 2005; citing VTPI, 2003.

Figure 4-8
Land-Use Impacts of Parking Requirements

Generous parking requirements often result in prime city-center land being paved over for parking lots.

Source: Alex Maclean.

SUNK COSTS

Existing parking facilities are often considered sunk costs (costs incurred in the past that are irretrievable and therefore do not affect current decisions). For example, building managers may only consider operating and maintenance expenses when calculating the cost of their parking facilities, ignoring past capital investments and the value of their land. They assume that, since the land is already owned, there is no cost to using it for parking. Where there is generous parking supply, reducing parking demand, for example, by encouraging commuters to use other modes, may result in parking spaces being unoccupied and unused. As a result, parking may seem inexpensive and parking management unjustified. However, most parking facilities have opportunity costs. Reducing parking demand may avoid the need to build additional parking capacity to accommodate growth, allow excess parking capacity to be rented, allow garage space to be used for other purposes, or allow parking facility land to be converted to other uses.

For example, with conventional parking requirements, a quarter of a parcel is devoted to buildings and half to parking (the rest is used for landscaping and sidewalks). Reducing parking requirements by 50 percent allows twice as many buildings to be constructed on that parcel (see Figure 4-9). This reduces building costs, increases productivity, and allows more compact development.

Figure 4-9
Reducing Parking Requirements

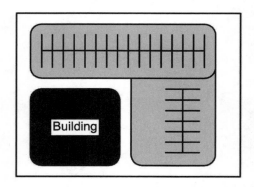 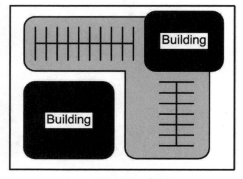

Conventional Parking Requirements   **With Improved Parking Management**

With conventional parking requirements, more than half of land is devoted to parking facilities. With improved parking management, nearly twice as much building can occur on a given parcel, increasing productivity, improving accessibility (particularly people's ability to walk between destinations), reducing automobile travel, and reducing total impervious surface in an area.

Various strategies can accelerate the speed with which reductions in parking demand provide economic savings. Regulations can be more flexible, procedures can be defined to allow excess parking supply to be decommissioned and converted to other uses, and parking brokerage services can help property owners share, trade, lease, and sell excess parking. These strategies are described in Chapter 5.

PARKING COMPARED WITH TOTAL DEVELOPMENT COSTS

Parking typically represents about 10 percent of building development costs, and more where land values are high. Since developers typically earn 10 percent return on investments, each unit of reduced parking requirements can provide a comparable increase in profits. For example, a 20 percent reduction in parking requirements can increase profits about 20 percent, and even more in situations where parking costs are higher than average.

Excessive parking requirements reduce housing affordability and shift lower-priced housing to urban fringe locations where land prices are lower but transport costs are higher (Jia and Wachs, 1998; Litman, 2004b). Figure 4-10 illustrates the portion of housing costs devoted to parking. For higher-priced housing in suburban areas with lower land costs, supplying two parking spaces per unit adds just 10 percent to development costs; for lower-priced res-

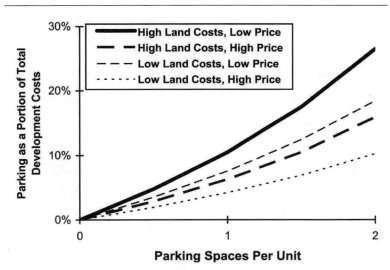

Figure 4-10
Parking Costs as a Portion of Total Development Cost

Parking costs as a percentage of housing development costs for different land costs and retail prices. Generous parking requirements tend to make housing unaffordable in areas with high land prices.

Source: Litman, 2004b.

idential buildings in urban areas with higher land costs, providing two parking spaces increases costs more than 20 percent. Many urban redevelopment and affordable housing projects are only financially feasible if parking requirements are reduced from conventional standards. This makes sense because residents of affordable urban housing tend to own fewer than average vehicles.

Generous and inflexible minimum parking requirements often constrain other types of development. For example, plans to reuse an otherwise empty building or redevelop an older urban neighborhood are often limited by conventional parking standards. This occurs even when planners know that such standards are higher than justified by actual demand. The result is higher development costs, reduced urban redevelopment, increased sprawl, and reduced building quality.

PARKING COSTS COMPARED WITH OTHER TRANSPORTATION COSTS

Parking costs represent a major portion of total transportation system costs, although they are often ignored in transportation planning and economic evaluation. There are estimated to be two on-street and three off-street spaces (one residential and two nonresidential) per motor vehicle in a typical urban area, with an average annualized cost of $400 per on-street space, $600 per residential space, and $800 per nonresidential space, totaling $3,000 annually per vehicle (Litman, 2004a; Shoup, 2005). Costs per space are lower in suburban and rural areas due to lower land costs, but there tend to be more spaces per vehicle in such areas, so per-vehicle parking costs are probably about the same. Estimates by KPMG (1995) and Delucchi (1997), updated to account for inflation and vehicle ownership growth, indicate that the annualized economic value of all U.S. parking facilities totals approximately $500 billion in 2000—more than three times the total expenditures on public roads and more than half the total expenditures on private vehicles (see Figure 4-11). For every dollar motorists spend directly on their car, somebody spends an additional $.50 on parking facilities.

Most parking costs are borne indirectly through rents, taxes, and higher prices for retail goods. A typical motorist would need to spend hundreds of dollars annually if they paid directly for all of the parking they use. Similarly, a commuter who uses employer-supplied parking would usually need to earn an additional $1,500 to $2,500 in taxable wages to pay for it out of their own pocket. Indirect parking costs average approximately $.15 per vehicle-mile—more than what a typical motorist pays in vehicle operating expenses.

IMPLICATIONS OF UNDERPRICED PARKING

There is some debate among economists whether parking paid indirectly should be considered a subsidy (a payment to reduce the price of a particular

Figure 4-11
Comparing Vehicle and Parking Costs

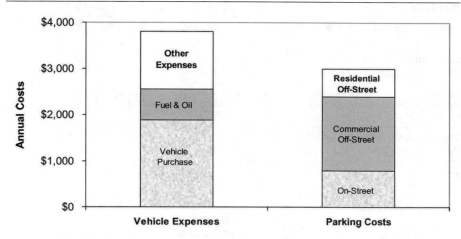

Motorists spend about $4,000 annually per vehicle directly on each automobile. There are an estimated five parking spaces per vehicle with a total annualized value of approximately $3,000.

Sources: Delucchi, 1997; Litman, 2004a.

product) or a bundled good (goods included at no extra cost with a purchase). Regardless of what it is called, unpriced parking is a market distortion that violates basic principles of economic efficiency, which require that consumers should be able to decide whether or not to purchase a particular good, and that prices reflect full marginal costs ("Market Principles," VTPI, 2005). Paying for parking facilities indirectly is unfair and inefficient because it fails to reward consumers who reduce the parking costs they impose. For example, if parking is bundled with housing, residents must pay regardless of whether or not they use it and receive no savings if they reduce their parking demand by reducing their vehicle ownership. Similarly, if employees are given free parking, they do not receive the parking cost savings that result when they use an alternative commute mode. Charging directly rather than indirectly for parking gives consumers a new opportunity to save money.

Many of the management strategies described in this book reflect market principles and so tend to increase economic efficiency and equity (see Table 4-3).

Although their individual impacts may seem modest, these market distortions have significant cumulative effects. The combination of lower-density development and underpriced parking increases parking demand and vehicle travel 15 to 25 percent over what would occur if parking requirements were more accurate, motorists paid directly for parking, and land development were more compact (Litman, 1999). This increases parking

Table 4-3
Market Requirements and Parking Management Corrections

Market Requirement	Parking Management Corrections
Choice: Consumers need viable options from which to choose.	Many management strategies improve parking and transport options.
Information: Consumers need information on their parking and travel options.	Many management strategies give consumers better information on parking availability and price and their travel options.
Cost-based pricing: Prices should reflect costs as much as possible.	Many management strategies involve more efficient pricing.
Economic neutrality: Public policies (e.g., laws, taxes, subsidies, and investment policies) should apply equally to comparable goods.	Parking management includes tax, investment, and pricing reforms that reduce existing distortions, which result in economically excessive parking supply.
Land use: Land-use policies should not favor lower-density development.	Parking management includes strategies that reduce excessive parking requirements and correct other market distortions that result in more dispersed land-use patterns.

Summary of the requirements for an efficient market and examples of how parking management can help correct existing market distortions.

Source: Based on "Market Principles," VTPI, 2005.

costs and exacerbates many other transportation problems, including congestion, accidents, pollution, and inferior transportation options for non-drivers, and suggests that about a fifth of current traffic problems result from economically inefficient parking policies. Put more positively, correcting parking-related market distortions helps solve a variety of economic, social, and environmental problems, providing significant overall benefits to society.

CHAPTER 4
REFERENCES AND INFORMATION RESOURCES

Arnold, Chester and James Gibbons (1996), "Impervious Surface Coverage: Emergence of a Key Environmental Indicator," *American Planning Association Journal*, Vol. 62, No. 2, Spring 1996, pp. 243-258.

Campoli, Julie, Elizabeth Humstone, and Alex Maclean (2001), *Above and Beyond*, American Planning Association (Chicago, IL) (www.planning.org).

Delucchi, Mark (1997), *Annualized Social Cost of Motor-Vehicle Use in the U.S., 1990-1991*, Vol. 6, University of California Davis Institute of Transportation Studies (www.its.ucdavis.edu), UCD-ITS-RR-96-3 (6).

Dorsett, John (1998), "The Price Tag of Parking," *Urban Land*, Urban Land Institute (Washington, DC) (www.uli.org), May 1998, pp. 66-70.

Ewing, Reid, Rolf Pendall, and Don Chen (2002), *Measuring Sprawl and Its Impacts*, Smart Growth America (Washington, DC) (www.smartgrowthamerica.org).

Institute of Transportation Engineers (1987 and 2004), *Parking Generation Informational Report*, Institute of Transportation Engineers (Washington, DC) (www.ite.org).

Institute of Transportation Engineers (ITE) (1999), *Transportation Planning Handbook*, ITE (Washington, DC) (www.ite.org).

Jia, Wenyu and Martin Wachs (1998), *Parking Requirements and Housing Affordability: A Case Study of San Francisco*, Research Paper 380, The University of California Transportation Center (www.uctc.net); available online (www.uctc.net/scripts/countdown.pl?380.pdf).

KPMG (1995), *Commuter Choice Initiative: Weighted Survey Results*, prepared for the Internal Revenue Service; cited in Kuzmyak, J. Richard, Rachel Weinberger, Richard H. Pratt, and Herbert S. Levinson (2003), *Parking Management and Supply: Traveler Response to Transport System Changes*, Chapter 18, Report 95, Transit Cooperative Research Program; Transportation Research Board (Washington, DC) (www.trb.org).

Litman, Todd (1999), *Socially Optimal Transport Prices and Markets: Principles, Strategies and Impacts*, Victoria Transport Policy Institute (www.vtpi.org); available online (www.vtpi.org/opprice.pdf).

Litman, Todd (2004a), *Transportation Cost and Benefit Analysis; Techniques, Estimates and Implications*, Victoria Transport Policy Institute (www.vtip.org); available online (www.vtpi.org/tca).

Litman, Todd (2004b), *Parking Requirement Impacts on Housing Affordability*, Victoria Transport Policy Institute (www.vtpi.org); available online (www.vtpi.org/park-hou.pdf).

Litman, Todd (2004c), *Evaluating Transportation Land Use Impacts*, Victoria Transport Policy Institute (www.vtpi.org); available online (www.vtpi.org/landuse.pdf).

Nonpoint Education for Municipal Officials (NEMO) (http://nemo.uconn.edu) is a University of Connecticut educational program that supports reduced impervious surface.

Parking Today (PT) (2000), "Determining the Cost of an Above-Grade Parking Structure," *Parking Today* (www.parkingtoday.com), May 2000, pp. 27-28.

Russo, Ryan (2001), *Costs: Assessing and Communicating the Costs of Parking*, The Non-Profit Housing Association of Northern California (www.nonprofithousing.org); available online (http://dcrp.ced.berkeley.edu/students/rrusso/parking/Developer%20Manual/Costs).

Shoup, Donald (2005), *The High Cost of Free Parking*, American Planning Association (Chicago, IL) (www.planning.org).

Victoria Transport Policy Institute (VTPI) (2003), *Parking Cost, Pricing and Revenue Calculator*, VTPI (www.vtpi.org); available online (www.vtpi.org/parking.xls).

Victoria Transport Policy Institute (VTPI) (2005), *Online TDM Encyclopedia*, VTPI (www.vtpi.org); available online ("Land Use Evaluation" (www.vtpi.org/tdm/tdm104.htm), "Market Principles" (www.vtpi.org/tdm/tdm60.htm), and "Parking Evaluation" (www.vtpi.org/tdm/tdm73.htm)).

CHAPTER

5

Parking
Management
Strategies

This chapter describes and evaluates specific parking management strategies. The following information is provided for each one:

- *Description* includes a general description of this strategy and any variations.
- *Impacts on Parking Demand and Requirements* discusses how this strategy affects parking demand (number of spaces that would be used at a particular location, time, and price) and parking requirements (number of spaces considered necessary at a particular location).
- *Benefits, Costs, and Consumer Impacts* discusses the incremental benefits and costs of the strategy and how it affects consumers.
- *Suitable Applications* describes the conditions in which this strategy is best applied.
- *Implementation* discusses how this strategy is implemented.
- *Examples and Case Studies* describes examples of this strategy's implementation.
- *References and Information Resources* lists references cited in that section and sources of additional information.

These strategies are grouped into the following categories (see Table 5-23 for a summary of the parking management strategies in this book):

I. STRATEGIES THAT INCREASE PARKING FACILITY EFFICIENCY

SHARE PARKING

Description

"Share parking" means that a parking facility serves multiple users or destinations. There are several ways to do this ("Shared Parking," VTPI, 2005).

Shared Rather Than Reserved Spaces within a Parking Facility

Motorists share parking spaces rather than being assigned a reserved space (a parking space that may only be used by a particular motorist). For example, 100 employees can usually share 60 to 80 parking spaces since, at any particular time, some are on leave, some are commuting by an alternative mode, some are in the field, and some are working another shift. Similarly, a hotel, apartment, condominium, or dormitory can share parking spaces among residents rather than assigning spaces to each unit, since the number of vehicles per unit varies over time. Sharing can be optional (e.g., motorists could choose between $60 per month for a shared space or $100 for a reserved space).

Share Parking among Destinations

Parking can be shared among multiple destinations. For example, an office building can share parking with a restaurant or theater, since peak demand for offices occurs during weekdays and on weekend evenings for restaurants and theaters (see Table 5-1). This is most effective if diverse activities are clustered together into an activity center, mall, or campus.

Public Parking Facilities

Public parking (parking facilities that may be used by the general public) generally serves multiple destinations. Converting from single destination to public parking allows more sharing.

Table 5-1
Typical Peak Parking Periods for Various Land Uses

Weekday	Evening	Weekend
• Banks and public services • Offices and other employment centers • Park & Ride facilities • Schools, daycare centers, and colleges • Factories and distribution centers • Medical clinics • Professional services	• Auditoriums • Bars and dance halls • Meeting halls • Quality restaurants • Theaters • Hotels	• Religious institutions • Parks • Shops and malls

Peak parking demand for different land-use types. Parking can be shared efficiently by land uses with different peaks.

In-Lieu Fees and Assessments

"In-lieu fees" means that developers fund public parking facilities instead of private, single-destination facilities. This tends to be more cost effective and efficient because it leads to shared parking. It can be mandated or optional.

Businesses can be assessed a special tax or levy to fund parking facilities in their area as an alternative to each supplying its own facilities. This is often implemented through a downtown business improvement district.

Clustered Development

Buildings and businesses can be clustered into activity centers, such as shopping malls, research campuses, and industrial parks, where parking is shared, rather than each providing its own separate parking.

Support of Sharing

Parking facility sharing and trading can be supported in various ways. For example, apartment and condominium managers can maintain a list of residents who want to rent parking spaces in their buildings, and business associations can provide parking brokerage services.

More Efficient Use of On-Street Parking

On-street parking spaces can be carefully managed to efficiently serve multiple destinations (see the sidebar entitled "On-Street Parking").

The feasibility of shared parking depends on the types of destinations, their proximity, and the quality of walking conditions between parking facilities and destinations (see the section entitled "Improve Walking and Cycling Conditions" on page 111). Some shared parking occurs naturally. For example, if a shop or restaurant is located near a large employment center, workers will often walk rather than drive for errands and meals, so parking requirements can be lower than at more isolated sites. On the other hand, some developments that claim to be mixed use may actually be too dispersed or otherwise unsuited for significant shared parking.

Sharing is most successful if destinations have different peak hours. Figure 5-1 illustrates typical weekly demand cycles for four land-use categories.

To calculate shared parking requirements, create a weekly demand graph and stack the results (see Figure 5-2). In this example, an office, a retail center, a restaurant, and a tavern/bar would require 250 spaces if each provided its own parking, but only 180 spaces if parking is shared. In this case, maximum demand occurs on weekday afternoons.

On-Street Parking

On-street (curb) parking tends to be shared efficiently since it is convenient to use and serves multiple destinations. An on-street parking space can usually substitute for two or three off-street parking spaces. On-street parking uses less land per space than off-street parking since it does not require access lanes. As a result, on-street spaces typically use a quarter of the land that would be needed to provide the same amount of service with off-street parking serving a single destination. On-street parking therefore supports more compact development and deserves careful management, particularly in busy commercial districts.

On-street parking can be considered part of a destination's supply. For example, if a store requires a total of 75 parking spaces, and 100 on-street spaces are located within 300 feet, a quarter of these can be counted toward the store's requirements, reducing on-site requirements to 50. This is appropriate even if the on-street spaces are priced, since motorists are often willing to pay for short-term parking.

In the past, some traffic engineers opposed the provision of on-street parking on the grounds that streets should be used to accommodate traffic and parking should be provided off street by property owners. However, planners increasingly recommend providing on-street parking because it is efficient and it creates a buffer between street traffic and pedestrians. On-street parking can also be a traffic-calming device, reducing vehicle traffic speeds. For these reasons, on-street parking is a feature of new urbanist design principles.

People sometimes oppose the use of curb lanes for parking on the grounds that it reduces traffic flow, but this is not usually true. Since surface street traffic flow is generally limited by intersection capacity, dedicating midblock curb lanes to parking does not usually reduce overall traffic capacity. Even if mid-block capacity is needed during peak periods, on-street parking can be allowed at other times.

Some studies suggest that vehicles entering and exiting on-street parking spaces have high accident rates. However, off-street parking requires additional driveways, which also impose risks on motorists, cyclists, and pedestrians. Many accidents that occur in driveways and parking lots are not recorded; as a result, statistics indicating that on-street parking is more hazardous than off-street parking may simply reflect biased data.

Figure 5-1
Parking Demand Cycles

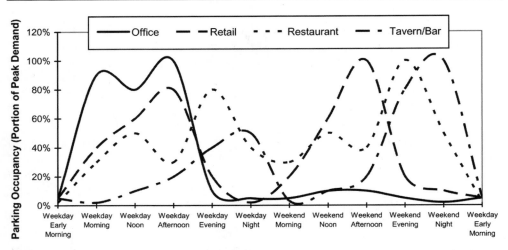

Typical demand cycles for various land uses. Because their peaks differ, parking can be shared efficiently among them. This example is illustrative; actual demand cycles will depend on specific conditions.

Figure 5-2
Stacked Parking Demand Cycle

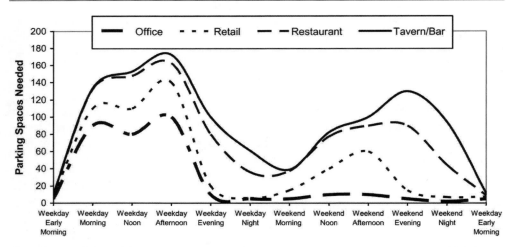

Stacking weekly parking demand curves shows when maximum demand occurs. This is lower than the sum of each peak, allowing parking requirements to be reduced.

Impacts on Parking Demand and Requirements

Shifting from reserved to shared parking within a facility (e.g., 80 spaces serve 100 employees at a worksite or residents at an apartment complex) typically reduces parking requirements 10 to 30 percent, reflecting the maximum portion of users likely to park at one time. Actual reductions depend on demand patterns and the severity of problems that result if demand occasionally exceeds the parking facility's capacity.

Sharing parking among multiple destinations can typically reduce parking requirements by an additional 10 to 30 percent, depending on specific conditions. Various guides describe how to determine suitable reductions (Barton-Aschman, 1982; ITE, 1995; ITE, 1999; Stein Engineering, 1997). Kuzmyak et al., (2003) describe successful shared parking examples. Of 17 projects evaluated, reductions compared with conventional standards ranged from 5 to 49 percent. Some jurisdictions limit reductions from shared parking to 10 or 20 percent, but this is arbitrary and unnecessarily restrictive.

Benefits, Costs, and Consumer Impacts

Shared parking reduces parking facility costs, allows greater flexibility in facility location and site design, and creates more compact land use. By encouraging park-once trips (the practice of motorists parking in one location and walking to various nearby destinations, rather than driving to and parking at each destination), shared parking can reduce vehicle traffic, particularly in congested commercial centers. In-lieu fees can provide cost savings compared with developers supplying their own parking facilities.

Sharing parking can increase administrative and enforcement costs. It may reduce user convenience and prestige (a reserved parking space is considered a status symbol). Parking facilities may need to be redesigned to provide better pedestrian connections to destinations, which may impose costs but also provide user benefits by expanding parking options and allowing park-once trips.

Suitable Applications

Shared parking can be applied in a wide variety of conditions. Most worksites and many multifamily residential buildings can share parking rather than assign reserved spaces. Sharing among different destinations is appropriate where they have different peak demand periods or have the same patrons and are located within reasonable walking distance. It tends to be most effective where land use is compact and mixed, with good pedestrian connections, and is particularly appropriate where parking facility costs are high.

Implementation

Shared parking is a well-known and widely accepted concept that can be implemented in a variety of ways. Some sharing strategies, such as shared rather than assigned spaces within a lot, can be implemented by individual facility managers, but others require coordination among different managers, which can be facilitated by a third party, such as a parking brokerage service. The best approach for implementing shared parking is often to contract with an independent parking operations company (a person or organization that provides day-to-day parking facility operations) to manage and enforce facilities that serve multiple users and destinations.

Shared parking is often constrained by inflexible rules and inadequate institutional support and may require changing management practices and zoning codes. Several model shared parking regulations and agreements are available (ITE, 1995; Stein Engineering, 1997). Some of these are unnecessarily restrictive (e.g., limiting shared parking to destinations located within 500 feet of each other, prescribing a single method for calculating supply reductions, or limiting reductions to 10 to 20 percent of supply). A more flexible and comprehensive approach allows greater parking supply reductions, making sharing more feasible and rewarding.

Shared parking requires effective enforcement to ensure that only qualified vehicles use a facility. For example, if an office and retail business share parking facilities, it may be necessary to identify employee commute vehicles that are allowed to park any time, and monitor other vehicles to ensure that they belong to legitimate retail business customers. This can be done using enforcement technologies that track vehicles' parking activity by their license plate numbers (see the section entitled "Improve Enforcement and Control" on page 178).

There are many specific ways to implement and encourage shared parking:

- A municipal government or business association can inventory parking supply and develop an area parking plan, which provides support and incentives for sharing parking. Maintain parking inventory data in a Geographic Information System format to help identify the location of parking supply near a particular location.
- Specify in zoning codes that shared parking is allowed and define methods for determining parking requirement reductions. For example, offer a standard 20 percent reduction for mixed land uses, and define methodologies that may be used to calculate additional reductions. Detailed traffic engineering analysis is generally preferred, but its cost may deter use for smaller projects, so it may be appropriate to offer several options.
- Shift from reserved to shared spaces at apartment complexes, worksites, and commercial parking lots. Reserved spaces should only be provided when essential or as an option to motorists who pay a premium.
- Allow or require developers to pay in-lieu fees to fund public parking facilities instead of building private, single-destination parking at each site.
- Encourage compact, mixed-use development, which increases shared parking opportunities (see the section entitled "Implement Smart

Growth Policies" on page 103). For example, implement policies and encourage compact infill development and mixed-use projects.

- Improve walking conditions between parking facilities and destinations (see the section entitled "Improve Walking and Cycling Conditions" on page 111).
- Provide information, encouragement, parking brokerage, and other support services for shared parking (see the section entitled "Establish Transportation Management Associations and Parking Brokerage" on page 182).
- Develop enforcement programs and overflow parking plans to prevent potential problems with shared parking (see the sections entitled "Establish Overflow Parking Plans" on page 186 and "Improve Enforcement and Control" on page 178).
- Establish agreements among property owners who share parking facilities that identify:
  - How conflicts will be avoided and addressed (e.g., a parking sharing agreement between an office and a restaurant might require some office workers to use off-site parking if they have evening events that would otherwise fill the parking lot during the restaurant's peak demand period).
  - Responsibilities for maintenance, cleaning, and lighting costs.
  - Liability requirements (standard property liability insurance is usually adequate for sharing parking facilities).
- Governments can promote shared parking by:
  - Maximizing on-street parking supply and managing it efficiently.
  - Providing public, off-street parking.
  - Rewarding businesses that share parking with reduced parking requirements and density bonuses.
  - Improving pedestrian connections among parking facilities and destinations.
  - Encouraging more compact development.
  - Allowing or requiring in-lieu fees and assessments instead of private, off-street parking.

Examples and Case Studies

Monrovia Downtown Parking Management

Monrovia, a southern California suburb, allowed developers to build a 12-screen, 2,400-seat movie theater in the middle of downtown without providing additional parking. Monrovia's Old Town business district is compact (six blocks long and two wide) and is abutted by residential neighborhoods on three sides. Medium- and high-density housing (mainly for senior citizens) had been developed immediately adjacent to the commercial properties.

A shared parking plan seemed feasible. There are more than 1,200 public parking spaces in the area, which were never more than 80 percent occupied. A Family Festival street fair—running weekly from March through Christmas—drew as many as 8,000 people on a typical summer night with little parking spillover into residential neighborhoods. Most downtown offices with employees that rely on public parking closed at 5 PM and a few stores stayed open past 7 PM.

The theater was built on one of the public parking lots, so those spaces were replaced by expanding another city-owned lot and reconfiguring an adjacent side street. When the theater opened, there were more spaces than before the project began. Since it was completed, the theater has attracted good crowds and inadequate parking has yet to be a problem. The available public parking is sufficient to handle the demand and convenient enough that movie-goers happily walk two to three blocks between their cars and the theater, providing additional business to shops and restaurants (Singer, 2004).

Shared Parking at Transit Stations

The TriMet (Portland, Oregon, area) *Park & Ride Policy* encourages shared parking near transit stations as a way to provide parking with minimum land consumption. More than three dozen Park & Ride lots are shared with various land uses, including apartment complexes, a regional justice center, churches, and movie theaters (Tri-Met, 2001).

Commercial Center Shared Parking

Figure 5-3 illustrates a 50-stall parking lot at a small commercial center. Approximately 20 of those spaces are reserved, during the daytime for employees at an office and during the evening for patrons at a restaurant. The remaining 30 spaces are rented to the general public by the hour or by the month. A combination of signs and pavement markings indicates who may use each space. The facility is managed by a commercial operator who collects fees and enforces regulations at this and dozens of other parking facilities in the area. It has a high utilization rate (most spaces are used most days) and serves multiple destinations and users.

In-Lieu Parking Fees

Some cities allow developers to pay in-lieu fees rather than building private, on-site parking (Shoup, 1999; Gray, 2004). This is attractive to developers because these fees are lower than developers' cost of building parking.

- *Coconut Grove*

Coconut Grove, Florida, adopted an in-lieu fee program in 1993, which has experienced considerable success. The fee is a one-time payment of $10,000 or monthly payments of $50 per space. Developers have chosen this option for

Figure 5-3
Shared Parking at a Commercial Center

This parking lot serves a variety of destinations and users. Some spaces are reserved for office employees during the day and restaurant patrons at night; other spaces are rented to the general public.

938 spaces, generating $3 million in revenues. The majority of the funds were used to develop a 416-space public parking structure with ground-floor retail. The fund also paid for a $250,000 study for a downtown circulator bus and $100,000 for a parking mitigation project, which included landscaping changes and installation of traffic-control devices to improve parking and pedestrian access (Gray, 2004).

- *Lake Forest*

Lake Forest, Illinois, has had an in-lieu fee policy for about 15 years. All generated funds must pay for parking facility acquisition or development. The impetus was a desire to preserve the historic character of the downtown. In 2002, the fee was $22,000 per stall. The city considers the program effective, and developers use the option frequently due to the scarcity of land available for parking (Ibid.).

- *Jackson*

Jackson, Wyoming, adopted an in-lieu fee policy in 1994, in conjunction with a new comprehensive plan and the adoption of minimum parking requirements. The policy was introduced in response to concerns that the parking requirements would hinder economic development. The per-stall fee ranges from $1,000 (up to four stalls) to $10,000 (more than 41 stalls). Revenues are dedicated to increasing parking supply, although the city does not specify when or where new public parking facilities will be constructed. When the in-lieu fee policy was adopted, existing properties that did not have parking were given transferable parking credits, so that even as the properties have been redeveloped, they have no parking requirement (Ibid.).

CHAPTER 5 (SHARE PARKING)
REFERENCES AND INFORMATION RESOURCES

The ACT Revenue Office (ACTRO) (2003), *Proposed ACT Parking Space Levy Discussion Paper for Consultation* (www.revenue.act.gov.au/docs/ACT%20Parking%20Space%20Levy%20Discussion%20Paper.pdf).

Barton-Aschman Associates (1982), *Shared Parking,* Urban Land Institute (Washington, DC) (www.uli.org).

Capitol Region Council of Governments (2002), *Shared Parking,* Capitol Region Council of Governments (www.crcog.org); available online (www.crcog.org/publications.htm).

Childs, Mark (1999), *Parking Spaces: A Design, Implementation and Use Manual for Architects, Planners, and Engineers,* The McGraw-Hill Companies (New York) (www.mcgraw-hill.com).

Gray, Judith (2004), "Policies for Rational Parking Development: Fee-In-Lieu Options," *The Parker,* Canadian Parking Association (www.canadianparking.ca), First Quarter 2004, pp. 10-14.

Institute of Transportation Engineers (ITE) (1995), *Shared Parking Planning Guidelines,* ITE (Washington, DC) (www.ite.org).

Institute of Transportation Engineers (ITE) (1999), *Transportation Planning Handbook,* ITE (Washington, DC) (www.ite.org).

Kodama, Michael (1999), *Parking Management Handbook; How to Use Parking Management to Better Utilize Parking Resources,* Oregon Department of Environmental Quality, State of Oregon (Salem) (www.deq.state.or.us).

Kuzmyak, J. Richard, Rachel Weinberger, Richard H. Pratt, and Herbert S. Levinson (2003), *Parking Management and Supply: Traveler Response to Transport System Changes,* Chapter 18, Report 95, Transit Cooperative Research Program; Transportation Research Board (www.trb.org); available online (http://gulliver.trb.org/publications/tcrp/tcrp_rpt_95c18.pdf).

Linssen, Barbara, John Fregonese, and Mary Weber (1997), *Shared Parking Handbook,* Metro Regional Planning (www.metro-region.org); available online (www.metro-region.org/article.cfm?articleid=435).

Oregon Downtown Development Association (2001), *Parking Management Made Easy: A guide to taming the downtown parking beast*, Transportation and Growth Management Program, Oregon Department of Transportation and the Oregon Department of Land Conservation and Development (www.lcd.state.or.us); available online (http://egov.oregon.gov/LCD/docs/publications/parkingguide.pdf).

Parsons Brinckerhoff (2002), "Parking and TOD: Challenges and Opportunities," *Transit-Oriented Development Study: Factors for Success in California*, California Department of Transportation (www.dot.ca.gov); available online (www.dot.ca.gov/hq/MassTrans/tod.htm).

Shoup, Donald C. (1999), "In Lieu of Required Parking," *Journal of Planning Education and Research*, Vol. 18, pp. 307-320; available online (www.sppsr.ucla.edu/dup/people/faculty/Shoup%20Pub%202.pdf).

Singer, Dick (2004), *City of Monrovia Downtown Parking Management*, City of Monrovia Public Information Office (Monrovia, CA), personal communication.

Stein Engineering (1997), *Shared Parking Handbook*, Portland Metro (www.metro-region.org); available online (www.metro-region.org/library_docs/land_use/sharedpark.pdf); including "Appendix A: Model Shared Parking Ordinance—Provisions," available online (www.metro-region.org/library_docs/land_use/appendixa.pdf).

Tri-Met (2001), *Park & Ride Policy*, Tri-County Metropolitan Transportation District of Oregon (www.tri-met.org).

Urban Land Institute (2000), *The Dimensions of Parking*, Urban Land Institute (Washington, DC) (www.uli.org) and National Parking Association (Washington, DC) (www.npapark.org).

U.S. Environmental Protection Agency (1999), *Parking Alternatives: Making Way for Urban Infill and Brownfield Redevelopment*, Urban and Economic Development Division, U.S. Environmental Protection Agency (www.epa.gov), EPA 231-K-99-001; available online (www.smartgrowth.org/pdf/PRKGDE04.pdf).

Victoria Transport Policy Institute (VTPI) (2005), *Online TDM Encyclopedia*, VTPI (www.vtpi.org); available online ("Shared Parking" (www.vtpi.org/tdm/tdm89.htm); includes a "Model Shared Parking Code").

REGULATE PARKING

Description

Parking regulations control who, when, and how long vehicles may park at a particular location in order to prioritize facility use. This ensures that the most convenient parking spaces are available to the most important users. Many of the concepts in this chapter also apply to parking pricing, which can also prioritize use of parking spaces.

There are three general steps in developing parking regulations. First, prioritize parking facility users. Here is a typical ranking:

1. Delivery and service vehicles.
2. Vehicles used by people with disabilities.
3. Rideshare and transit vehicles.
4. Customers, tourists, and visitors.
5. Employees and residents.
6. Long-term vehicle storage.

Second, choose appropriate regulations to favor the higher-priority activities. Table 5-2 describes common regulations and the type of parking activity they favor.

Third, determine how regulations will be indicated and enforced. Use signs, curb paint, maps, and brochures to denote which parking spaces are intended for which user type (see the section entitled "Improve User Information and Marketing" on page 171) and how violations will be punished (see the section entitled "Improve Enforcement and Control" on page 178).

In a typical commercial area, the most convenient parking spaces should be regulated for short-term use. Such spaces usually have 30- to 120-minute time limits, so each space can serve six to 12 vehicles per day. Shorter time limits increase turnover but constrain the types of activities that can be accommodated, which may frustrate customers who are unable to complete a transaction within the allowable parking period (see the sidebar entitled "How Much Time?").

Informal rules and encouragement can be used instead of formal regulations. For example, downtown business organizations can encourage commuters to leave more convenient parking spaces for customers. A reminder may be sent to employees who violate this policy.

Impacts on Parking Demand and Requirements

Parking regulations increase parking supply for higher-priority uses. They can also reduce parking demand in an area by encouraging location and mode shifts. For example, restrictions on long-term parking may cause some employees to park elsewhere, and others to commute by bicycle, rideshare, or transit. The magnitude of these impacts depends on the type of regulation and their specific circumstances. Efficient regulation is often

Table 5-2
Common Parking Regulations

Name	Description	Favored Users
User or vehicle type	Provide spaces dedicated to loading, service vehicles, taxis, customers, rideshare vehicles, disabled users, buses, and trucks.	As specified.
Duration	Limit parking duration (5-minute loading zones, 30 minutes adjacent to shop entrances, 1- or 2-hour limits).	Shorter-term users, such as deliveries, customers, and errands.
Time period restrictions	Prohibit occupancy at certain times, such as before 10 AM (to discourage use by employees) or between 10 PM and 5 AM (to discourage use by residents and campers). Prohibit chain parking (using a parking space multiple time periods).	Depends on restrictions.
Employee restrictions	Require or encourage employees to use less convenient parking spaces.	Deliveries, customers, and errands.
Special events	Have special parking regulations during special events.	Depends on restrictions.
Accommodation of multistop users	Provide special parking passes and bulk payment options for vehicles that make multiple short stops.	Delivery and service vehicles making multiple short stops.
Residential parking regulations and permits	Give area residents priority use of parking near their homes.	Area residents.
Special activities	Establish a system that allows specific parking spaces to be reserved for special activities, such as service and construction vehicles.	Vehicles used for special activities.
Street cleaning restrictions	Prohibit parking on a particular street one day of the week to allow street sweeping.	Street cleaning; ensures that motorists move their vehicles occasionally.
Large vehicle restrictions	Limit on-street parking of large vehicles, such as freight trucks and trailers.	Normal-size vehicles.
Arterial lanes	Prohibit on-street parking on arterials during peak periods to increase traffic lanes.	Vehicle traffic (as opposed to vehicle parking).
Removal of inoperable and abandoned vehicles	Have a system to identify and remove inoperable and abandoned vehicles from public parking facilities, and abandoned bikes from public areas (e.g., bike racks and sidewalks).	Operating vehicles.

Summary of various types of regulations that can prioritize the use of parking facilities.

Figure 5-4
Parking Regulations

Regulations control who can park, for what purpose, when, and where.

equivalent to a 10 to 30 percent increase in unregulated parking supply, reflecting the portion of higher-priority parking spaces occupied by lower-priority vehicles.

Benefits, Costs, and Consumer Impacts

Parking regulation increases parking system efficiency by favoring priority uses and by reducing demand. It increases convenience to some motorists (those given priority) and reduces convenience to others. It increases administrative and enforcement costs.

Suitable Applications

Regulations are appropriate virtually anywhere there are parking conflicts. The need for regulation tends to increase with density, growing parking demand, or declining parking supply. Regulation is particularly important for on-street parking spaces in busy commercial centers, off-street parking spaces in urban areas, and the most convenient spaces, such as those closest to a building entrance.

How Much Time?

One of the most common ways to manage parking is to limit parking duration. Shorter time periods increase turnover but constrain the activities that can be performed. Here are some general guidelines:

- Very short time periods (3 to 10 minutes) accommodate passenger drop-offs and deliveries. This is appropriate in busy loading areas, such as in front of transportation terminals, schools, theaters, hotels, and hospitals.
- Short time periods (15 to 30 minutes) accommodate quick errands. This is appropriate for the most convenient parking spaces at post offices, convenience stores, and other similar destinations.
- Medium time periods (1/2 to 4 hours) accommodate longer errands and activities, such as shopping and dining. Customers often find that 1 hour is inadequate for a shopping trip, meal, or errand, so 90-minute or 2-hour limits are common.
- 3- or 4-hour limits are commonly applied to prevent commuters from using parking spaces in business districts and nearby residential streets, although some commuters will simply move their vehicles once or twice each day.
- Long time periods (8+ hours) accommodate commute trips and residential parking.
- Special time restrictions can be used to discourage certain uses, such as parking prohibited before 10 AM (to discourage use by employees) or between 10 PM and 5 AM (to discourage use by residents and campers).

Implementation

Parking regulations are usually implemented by local governments (for on-street and municipal off-street parking) and by facility managers. Parking regulations should be flexible and adjusted as needed to reflect changing conditions. If possible, regulations should be set administratively rather than requiring legislative approval for every minor adjustment. For example, municipal traffic engineers can be given authority to establish and change parking regulations. It is important that regulations be clearly indicated to users (see the sidebar entitled "Curb Color"). User information on parking restrictions (e.g., "You can't park here") should generally include information on where parking is available (e.g., "You may park there").

Some cities establish parking regulation zones, sometimes designated by color. For example, on-street parking might be limited to 1 hour in a red zone (in major commercial areas), 2 hours in a blue zone (in minor commercial areas), and 4 hours in a yellow zone (in residential areas).

Residential Parking Permits

Residential parking permits are often used to ensure that neighborhood residents have priority use of on-street parking. In a typical program, residents may obtain permits that allow them to park on a particular block or in a particular area. To be effective, the total number of parking permits must be smaller than the number of available parking spaces. Permits may be free or sold for a fee. In some cases, a certain number of permits are sold to nonresidents, usually at a higher price. Each residence is usually limited to one or two permits. Some cities offer short-term guest permits. Permits are not generally provided to residents of multifamily buildings. Vehicles without permits may be prohibited altogether, have time restrictions (such as 1-hour limits), or may be required to pay a meter.

Residential parking permits are usually implemented in areas that frequently experience spillover parking problems from nearby businesses or schools, and so have chronic conflicts over on-street parking. Typically, an area must experience at least 75 percent on-street occupancy, have at least 25 percent of parked vehicles owned by nonresidents, and have a majority of residents who support the permit system to qualify.

When implementing residential parking permits, it is necessary to determine:
- The area to which each permit applies (a particular block or neighborhood).
- The total number of permits allocated in each area.
- How permits are allocated.
- What fee, if any, is charged for permits.
- Whether permits are assigned to a particular vehicle or are transferable.
- What parking restrictions or pricing apply to vehicles without a permit.
- Enforcement practices (regular patrols or enforcement only in response to complaints).

A typical urban parking space has an annualized value of $1,000 to $2,000 (what people would need to pay to rent an equivalent parking space), so residential parking permits are equivalent to handing out bundles of $100 bills. There is no single way to determine what arrangement is best because it depends on the needs and politics of the particular situation. However, to be effective, residential parking permits must ration the number of users to fit the number of available spaces, which means that somebody must lose access to desirable parking spaces. As a result, there are often conflicts over how permits are allocated.

Source: ITE, 2000.

Curb Color

Many communities use standard color codes to indicate curb parking regulations. These codes should be used consistently and publicized to motorists in a community. Typical color codes are listed below, although these may vary from one area to another.

Red indicates no stopping, standing, or parking at any time.

Yellow is used to designate a commercial loading zone to drop off or pick up freight. Commercial vehicle use is usually limited to 20 minutes; private vehicle use is usually limited to 3 minutes or is prohibited altogether.

White is designated for passenger loading zones to drop off or pick up passengers usually with a 3-minute limit. Drivers may not leave their vehicles. White curbs are enforced 24 hours a day, seven days a week, except as follows:

- When such zone is in front of an auditorium or theater, the restriction shall apply only when it is open for business.
- The length of time a vehicle is permitted to park in front of a mailbox shall be limited to the time a person is actually involved in the act of depositing mail in the adjacent mailbox.
- When such zone is posted or marked for valet parking, the restrictions shall apply only when businesses directly behind the posted zone are open.

Green indicates short-term, restricted, or limited time-zone parking. These zones are marked by signs that usually indicate 5 minutes to 2 hours of limited parking, and do not usually apply on Sundays or holidays.

Blue indicates disabled parking. Vehicles are required to display a valid permit when using these spaces.

It is important to anticipate possible spillover parking problems (the undesired use of off-site parking spaces) when implementing regulations. For example, new parking regulations in commercial areas may require additional regulations in nearby residential areas that would otherwise experience spillover problems.

Examples and Case Studies

Parking regulations are common. Below are some particularly interesting examples.

City of Highland Park

The Highland Park, Illinois, Intra-City Parking Committee is an organization of downtown merchants and public officials whose goal is to improve downtown parking options for customers and employees. In recent years, the Intra-City Parking Committee has worked to increase parking regulation and enforcement in the downtown core to favor customers. These measures include:

- Restricting on-street parking and certain surface parking lot spaces to 2 hours, and the first level of a municipal garage to 3 hours.
- Extending the 2-hour time limit for downtown, on-street parking to 7 PM.
- Requiring motorists to travel at least 500 feet to be considered a new space.
- Raising parking fines from $10 to $15, with increasing fines for multiple violations in a 30-day period (City of Highland Park, 2000).

Weekly Events

Some parking regulations and exemptions can be provided to accommodate special activities, such as religious services (Fridays for mosques, Friday nights and Saturday mornings for synagogues, and Sunday mornings for most churches), farmers' markets, or fairs. Regular, on-street parking regulations may be suspended and special arrangements made to use off-street parking facilities at these times.

City Parking Management

Portland, Oregon, requires at least 20 percent of parking spaces to be designated for short-term use. The city limits the amount of long-term parking that developers can supply downtown, but there is no limit to the amount of short-term parking that may be provided (City of Portland, 1994).

Santa Cruz Residential Parking Permits

Santa Cruz, California, restricts parking on residential streets. Residents may park unrestricted during the day but require a $20 annual permit to park on the street overnight. If residential streets are less than 75 percent occupied, nonresidents may purchase passes that allow daytime parking on a particular street for $1 per day or $60 per quarter. Additional regulations apply in particular areas, such as near high schools and commercial districts (Santa Cruz City, 2005).

Residential Parking Permits

- ### Miami Beach

Miami Beach, Florida, charges market rates for residential parking permits, which varies for different areas based on nearby on-street parking meter rates. In some areas, permits cost nearly $300 per year (City of Miami Beach, 2005).

- ### West Hollywood

West Hollywood, California, uses permits to limit use of on-street parking in many neighborhoods. Residents may purchase a three-month parking pass for $9, and any surplus, on-street capacity is sold to commuters for $90 for three months (ICLEI, 1998).

CHAPTER 5 (REGULATE PARKING)
REFERENCES AND INFORMATION RESOURCES

Barr, Mary (1998), *Downtown Parking Made Easy*, Downtown Research & Development Center (New York) (www.downtowndevelopment.com).

City of Highland Park (2000), *Parking Alert* (Highland Park, IL) (www.cityhpil.com/community/parkingalert.html).

City of Miami Beach (2005), *Residential Parking Permit Application* (Miami Beach, FL) (www.miamibeachfl.gov/newcity/depts/parking/resapp.pdf).

City of Portland (1994), *Central City Transportation Management Plan* (Portland, OR), Office of Transportation (www.trans.ci.portland.or.us).

Community Research & Development Information Service (2001), *COST 342: Parking Policy Measures and their Effects on Mobility and the Economy*, European Commission; available online (www.cordis.lu/cost-transport/src/cost-342.htm).

Heffron Transportation, Inc. (2002), *Seattle Parking Management Study*, City of Seattle (www.cityofseattle.net); available online (www.mrsc.org/govdocs/s42parkingstudyfinalreport.pdf).

Institute of Transportation Engineers (ITE) (2000), *Residential Permit Parking: Informational Report*, ITE (Washington, DC) (www.ite.org).

International Council for Local Environmental Initiatives (ICLEI) (1998), *Local Government's Guide to Parking Cash Out*, ICLEI (Toronto, ONT) (www.iclei.org).

International Parking Institute (2002), *Parking 101: A Parking Primer*, International Parking Institute (Fredericksburg, VA) (www.parking.org).

Kodama, Michael (1999), *Parking Management Handbook; How to Use Parking Management to Better Utilize Parking Resources*, Oregon Department of Environmental Quality, State of Oregon (Salem) (www.deq.state.or.us).

Kuzmyak, J. Richard, Rachel Weinberger, Richard H. Pratt, and Herbert S. Levinson (2003), *Parking Management and Supply: Traveler Response to Transport System Changes*, Chapter 18, Report 95, Transit Cooperative Research Program; Transportation Research Board (www.trb.org); available online (http://gulliver.trb.org/publications/tcrp/tcrp_rpt_95c18.pdf).

Santa Cruz City (2005), Traffic Engineering, Parking Section (Santa Cruz, CA) (www.ci.santa-cruz.ca.us/pw).

Seattle Department of Transportation (2001), *Parking Guide: Simple Ways to Improve Your Neighborhood's Parking*, City of Seattle (www.cityofseattle.net); available online (www.seattle.gov/transportation/parking/parkingguide.htm).

U.S. Environmental Protection Agency (1998), *Parking Management*, Transportation and Air Quality TCM Technical Overviews, U.S. Environmental Protection Agency (www.epa.gov); available online (www.epa.gov/oms/transp/publicat/pub_tech.htm).

ESTABLISH MORE ACCURATE AND FLEXIBLE STANDARDS

Description

"More accurate and flexible standards" (called "efficiency-based parking standards") means that parking requirements at a particular location are adjusted to account for the following:

- Geographic, demographic, and management factors that affect parking demand and parking requirements (see Table 5-3).
- Types of trips and users, including their priority and ability to rely on alternatives (higher requirements may be appropriate for delivery vehicles, at hospitals and for customers, with lower requirements for commuters, residents, and recreational uses).
- The cost and ease of adding parking capacity (requirements should be lower where increasing supply is relatively costly).
- The ability to implement parking management programs that reduce parking requirements.
- The availability of overflow parking supply nearby.
- The problems that result from spillover parking and the ability to address problems in other ways, such as improved user information, enforcement, or compensation.

Table 5-3
Factors Affecting Parking Requirements

Factor	Description
Geographic location	Variation in vehicle ownership and use in different areas
Land-use density	Number of residents, housing units, or employees per acre/hectare
Land-use mix	Different land uses located close together
Transit accessibility	Availability of transit service nearby
Carsharing	Whether a carsharing service is located nearby
Walkability	Quality of walking environment
Demographics	Age and physical ability of residents or commuters
Income	Average income of residents or commuters
Pricing	Degree to which parking is priced, unbundled, or cashed out
Parking and mobility management	Whether parking and mobility management programs are implemented at a site or within an area
Design hour	Number of allowable annual hours that a parking lot may be filled
Contingency-based planning	Identification of potential solutions to implement if needed

These factors can affect the amount of parking needed at a particular location and should be considered when establishing minimum parking requirements.

Source: From Chapter 3

As described in Chapter 2, conventional parking standards are often excessive and applied inflexibly, resulting in significantly more parking supply than is actually needed. Efficiency-based standards allow more accurate and reduced parking supply, and encourage use of other management strategies to address potential problems. Current planning practices often place a heavy burden of proof on reductions from conventional standards; efficiency-based planning shifts the burden of proof, so parking requirements can be reduced unless there is clear evidence that doing so will cause significant problems that cannot be addressed in other ways.

Many transportation professionals support the use of more accurate parking standards. Professional guides, such as the Institute of Transportation Engineers' *Parking Generation* (ITE, 2004), recommend conducting detailed analysis of parking requirements for each situation, but many jurisdictions ignore these recommendations and simply adopt generic standards applied with little flexibility.

Parking standards should be adjusted to reflect changing needs and conditions. Younger communities tend to have lower land values, densities, and traffic problems, so relatively high parking standards may be justified; however, as these communities grow and become more urbanized, the same standards become economically excessive. Parking demand at a particular location may vary over time as uses, occupants, and conditions change. Over its operating life, a building or district may experience various occupants, uses, and activities, with differing parking requirements. More flexible parking standards, coupled with parking management, allow a greater range of uses while reducing development costs.

Government-mandated parking standards may be unnecessary altogether. Eliminating minimum parking requirements does not eliminate parking supply; it simply allows developers and commercial parking operators to determine how much parking to supply based on market conditions, consumers' willingness to pay, the cost of providing parking, and the feasibility of applying management strategies. Many business districts have no parking requirements, relying on the market to supply parking. It makes sense to expand the areas with market-based parking supply as a community becomes more urbanized or wants to encourage more efficient transportation and land-use patterns.

One way to increase flexibility is to allow contingency-based standards, that is, minimum parking requirements that are flexible and adjusted over time based on performance indicators. Developers are allowed to provide less than the standard parking supply as long as they meet pre-established performance standards (e.g., if parking utilization rates do not exceed 90 percent more than 30 hours annually, or the city receives less than 25 legitimate spillover complaints annually). If these indicators are exceeded, the developer is required to either supply more parking or implement a parking management program. This can be enforced with a bond or fine.

"Context-sensitive design" refers to planning and design practices that are flexible and responsive to local conditions. This means, for example, that parking requirements should be adjusted to reflect a community's geographic, demographic, and historic conditions.

"Form-based codes" refers to building codes that define the type of development desired and provide maximum flexibility for achieving it (also called "design-based codes"). This encourages more innovative design, including more land-use mixing, and implementation of parking management to reduce parking requirements.

"Planning overlay districts" are areas where special zoning codes and development practices apply, such as a downtown or transit-oriented neighborhood. They often have reduced and more flexible parking requirements, and features (e.g., improved walkability, land-use mixing, and more clustered buildings) that support parking management.

Parking standards can sometimes be made more accurate simply by improving analysis methods. For example, some jurisdictions apply the same parking requirement to any sized housing unit, regardless of whether it is a small studio or a five-bedroom apartment. In that case, basing parking requirements on the number of bedrooms or floor area, and providing an alternative standard for housing with low parking demand (e.g., for students, elderly, and people with disabilities), can reduce excessive parking requirements.

Impacts on Parking Demand and Requirements

As described in Chapters 2 and 3, conventional parking standards tend to be excessive, resulting in parking facilities that are seldom or never fully occupied. Conventional standards can usually be reduced 10 to 30 percent with modest, cost-effective management activities, and greater reductions are often feasible with more comprehensive parking management, mobility management, and smart growth programs.

Benefits, Costs, and Consumer Impacts

More accurate and flexible standards can significantly reduce the economic, social, and environmental costs of excessive parking supply. They allow higher density and more infill development, leading to more efficient transport and land-use patterns. More flexible parking standards allow property owners to save money when they reduce parking demand, providing an incentive to implement parking and transportation management, which helps reduce traffic congestion, accidents, and pollution emissions. They increase equity by reducing parking costs imposed on nondrivers and increasing housing affordability. Costs can include additional planning analysis, additional administrative responsibilities, motorist inconvenience, spillover problems, and the costs of programs to address these problems.

Suitable Applications

Reduced and more flexible parking standards are appropriate in most situations. They are particularly justified in urban areas due to lower demand, high parking facility costs, and the effectiveness of parking and mobility management. On the other hand, suburban areas often have the most generous parking standards and the greatest degree of parking oversupply, and so also benefit from more accurate and flexible standards.

Implementation

More accurate and flexible parking standards can be implemented by eliminating minimum parking requirements altogether (allowing developers to determine how much parking to supply at each location) or by adjusting minimum parking requirements based on specific needs and conditions.

To help implement more flexible standards, governments can specify the analysis methods that may be used to determine parking supply at a particular location. The simplest approach is to establish adjustment factors or credits (specified reductions in parking requirements allowed for factors that increase efficiency or reduce parking demand) that can be applied to existing standards (see Chapter 3). However, such credits often account for just a few of the factors that can affect optimal parking supply. A better approach is to have traffic engineers perform a detailed study to determine optimal parking supply and management strategies at each site, taking into account a full range of geographic, demographic, and economic factors, and the severity of problems that result if parking lots fill. However, such studies can be costly and may be inappropriate for small projects. It is usually best to allow developers and property owners several options for determining parking supply, ranging from simple credits to comprehensive studies, depending on project scale and complexity.

The following activities can help implement more accurate and flexible standards:

- Educate decision-makers about the biases in conventional standards, the problems resulting from excessive supply, and potential parking management strategies.
- Adopt lower and more flexible minimum parking requirements in zoning codes and development standards.
- Identify acceptable methods for determining the amount of parking required at a particular location, ranging from simple to complex methodologies.
- Allow minimum parking requirements to be adjusted at an administrative level (e.g., by municipal traffic engineers) rather than requiring legislative action.

- Perform comprehensive, area-wide parking studies that provide data for determining optimal parking supply at a particular location, taking into account factors such as the availability of off-site parking facilities.
- Base parking requirements on the 50th (rather than 85th) percentile demand curve, a 30th annual design hour (rather than a 10th or 20th hour), and 100 percent occupancy for long-term parking (rather than the 85 to 90 percent often required, which is usually only needed for short-term parking).
- Use the most accurate measurement units when defining minimum parking requirements (e.g., base requirements on the number of employees or seats rather than building floor area).
- Reduce parking requirements where parking and mobility management programs are implemented. Provide support for such programs and develop procedures to ensure that such programs are implemented as promised.
- Establish procedures to allow conversion of unneeded parking facilities to other purposes (e.g., if shared parking eliminates the need for 40 parking spaces, municipal plans should allow those spaces to be leased, sold, or converted to other uses).
- Use contingency-based standards, which allow developers to reduce parking supply, provided they have a plan that identifies solutions to any parking problems that develop in the future, including management strategies and land banking (land set aside to be used for parking if needed in the future).
- Develop *form-based codes*, which specify the type of development desired in an area, and *overlay planning districts* (areas where special zoning codes and development practices apply, such as a downtown area or transit-oriented development), which allow reduced and more flexible parking standards and facilitate parking management in such areas.
- Allow a portion (e.g., 25 percent) of on-street parking within a reasonable distance (e.g., 500 feet) to be counted as part of the supply of parking available at a site.
- Include parking facilities when calculating development floor area ratio and revise floor area ratio upward accordingly, which provides an incentive to minimize parking supply since it can be traded off for leasable space.
- Wherever possible, eliminate mandatory parking requirements and let developers decide how much parking to provide. Expand areas where parking is not mandated such as around business districts and transit centers. Implement parking management programs in such areas to help address any problems that occur.

Examples and Case Studies

City of Concord

The zoning code in Concord, North Carolina, includes several provisions to support more flexible and accurate parking requirements:
- Minimum parking requirements are relatively low.
- Minimum parking requirements are not imposed in central business, traditional neighborhoods, and transit-oriented development zones.
- On-street parking can be counted as a portion of a building's parking requirements.
- Designated turf areas may be used for occasional overflow parking areas (maximum 10 uses per year).
- Further reduction is possible with shared parking arrangements (City of Concord, 2005).

Reduction of Minimum Parking Requirements

Many cities have implemented reduced and more flexible parking requirements, particularly in their major commercial centers, including Portland, Oregon; Seattle, Washington; San Francisco and Los Angeles, California; and Denver, Colorado (Kuzmyak et al., 2003). These revised requirements often allow developers to supply significantly less parking if they implement various parking management strategies (such as commute trip reduction programs for employees) and if located near transit stations or public parking facilities. These are often successful but, in some cases, few developers have taken advantage of these opportunities, due in part to pressure from lenders who fear that buildings with insufficient parking will have lower rents. This indicates that a more comprehensive parking management program may be needed to achieve desired changes, including education of developers and lenders about parking management opportunities and benefits, improved commuter transportation options, and additional incentives to encourage developers to try parking management strategies.

Minimum Parking Requirements Eliminated

Victoria, British Columbia, conducted a design charrette (a community planning exercise) to create a development plan for the Harris Green neighborhood at the edge of downtown. One result of this process was to eliminate minimum parking requirements for new buildings in that area and to redevelop the neighborhood to emphasize walkability and more efficient management of public parking. Since that plan was established the Harris Green area has experienced a boom in mixed residential and commercial development containing middle- and higher-priced condominiums. Although these developments all contain some parking, the amount is established by the developer and reflects market demand. Many area residents, including young professionals, retirees, and people with disabilities, do not own a vehicle, or one vehicle will be shared among two or three drivers in a household (City of Victoria, 2001).

CHAPTER 5
(ESTABLISH MORE ACCURATE AND FLEXIBLE STANDARDS)
REFERENCESAND INFORMATION RESOURCES

Childs, Mark (1999), *Parking Spaces: A Design, Implementation and Use Manual for Architects, Planners, and Engineers*, The McGraw-Hill Companies (New York) (www.mcgraw-hill.com).

City of Concord (2005), *Parking Management Program* (Concord, NC) (www.ci.concord.nc.us).

City of Victoria (2001), *Harris Green: A Neighborhood of Choice*, City of Victoria (www.city.victoria.bc.ca/business/profiles_neigh_harris.shtml).

Context Sensitive Design/Thinking Beyond the Pavement provides information on context-sensitive design (www.fhwa.dot.gov/csd).

Davidson, Michael and Fay Dolnick (2002), *Parking Standards*, Planning Advisory Service Report 510/511, American Planning Association (Chicago, IL) (www.planning.org).

Heffron Transportation, Inc. (2002), *Parking Management Study*, City of Seattle (www.cityofseattle.net).

Institute of Transportation Engineers (1999), *Transportation Planning Handbook*, Institute of Transportation Engineers (Washington, DC) (www.ite.org).

Institute of Transportation Engineers (ITE) (2004), *Parking Generation*, ITE (Washington, DC) (www.ite.org).

Kuzmyak, J. Richard, Rachel Weinberger, Richard H. Pratt, and Herbert S. Levinson (2003), *Parking Management and Supply: Traveler Response to Transport System Changes*, Chapter 18, Report 95, Transit Cooperative Research Program; Transportation Research Board (www.trb.org); available online (http://gulliver.trb.org/publications/tcrp/tcrp_rpt_95c18.pdf).

Local Government Commission (2003), *Smart Growth Zoning Codes: A Resource Guide*, Local Government Commission (Sacramento, California) (www.lgc.org); includes a CD that contains examples of progressive building codes.

Nelson/Nygaard Consulting (2002), *Housing Shortage/Parking Surplus*, Transportation and Land Use Coalition (www.transcoalition.org); available online (www.transcoalition.org/reports/housing_s/housing_shortage_home.html).

Pratt, Richard H. (2000), *Traveler Response to Transportation System Changes, Interim Handbook*, Transit Cooperative Research Program Web Document 12, Transportation Research Board (www.trb.org); available online (http://gulliver.trb.org/publications/tcrp/tcrp_webdoc_12.pdf).

Russo, Ryan (2001), *Planning for Residential Parking: A Guide For Housing Developers and Planners*, The Non-Profit Housing Association of Northern California (www.nonprofithousing.org) and the Berkeley Program on Housing and Urban Policy (http://urbanpolicy.berkeley.edu); available online (www.nonprofithousing.org/actioncenter/toolbox/parking/index.atomic).

Smith, Thomas P. (1983), *Flexible Parking Requirements*, Planning Advisory Service Report 377, American Planning Association (Chicago, IL) (www.planning.org).

U.S. Environmental Protection Agency (1998), *Parking Management*, Transportation and Air Quality TCM Technical Overviews, U.S. Environmental Protection Agency (www.epa.gov); available online (www.epa.gov/oms/transp/publicat/pub_tech.htm).

U.S. Environmental Protection Agency (1999), *Parking Alternatives: Making Way for Urban Infill and Brownfield Redevelopment*, Urban and Economic Development Division, U.S. Environmental Protection Agency (www.epa.gov) , EPA 231-K-99-001; available online (www.smartgrowth.org/pdf/PRKGDE04.pdf).

Voith, Richard (1998), "The Downtown Parking Syndrome: Does Curing the Illness Kill the Patient?" *Business Review* (www.phil.frb.org/econ/br/index.html), Vol. 1, 1998, pp. 3-14; available online (www.phil.frb.org/files/br/brjf98dv.pdf); also see Federal Reserve Bank of Philadelphia (www.phil.frb.org) Working Paper No. 95-11, 1995.

Washington State Department of Transportation (1999), *Local Government Parking Policy and Commute Trip Reduction: 1999 Review*, Commute Trip Reduction Office, Washington State Department of Transportation (www.wsdot.wa.gov); available online (www.wsdot.wa.gov/tdm/tripreduction/parking_policy.cfm).

ESTABLISH PARKING MAXIMUMS

Description

Parking maximums place an upper limit on supply of parking allowed, either at individual sites or over an area, such as a commercial district. Area-wide limits are called "parking caps." Maximums can apply only to certain types of parking (e.g., long-term, single-use, unpriced, or surface parking) depending on planning objectives. These can be in addition to or instead of minimum parking requirements. Excessive parking supply can also be reduced by reducing public parking supplies, imposing a special parking tax (see the section entitled "Reform Parking Taxes" on page 155), and by enforcing regulations that limit temporary or inferior design parking facilities.

These strategies are usually implemented in large urban centers as part of integrated programs to reduce excessive parking supply, encourage use of alternative modes, support more compact development, create more attractive streetscapes, preserve historic buildings, and support other transportation and land-use planning objectives.

It could be argued that parking maximums are as unnecessary and inefficient as minimum parking requirements. As discussed earlier, one approach is to simply allow property owners to determine how much parking to supply at their sites. However, parking minimums have been applied for decades, resulting in well-established transportation and land-use market distortions that increase parking supply beyond what is economically optimal, and lead motorists to expect free parking at each destination. As a result, individual developers and businesses often find it difficult to reduce supply. Parking maximums that apply equally to all businesses in an area may be more acceptable and effective than expecting each business to reduce their parking supply. Left to itself, the market may take decades to reach an optimal level of parking supply. Parking maximums may be necessary to achieve this more quickly.

Impacts on Parking Demand and Requirements

The impacts of parking maximums and supply reduction strategies depend on specific conditions, how much parking supply is reduced, and what other parking management strategies are implemented.

Benefits, Costs, and Consumer Impacts

Parking maximums can reduce excessive parking supply, providing economic, social, and environmental benefits. They encourage higher-density development and support other parking and mobility management strategies.

Reduced parking supply can reduce motorist convenience. Some businesses may consider parking maximums to give them a disadvantage compared with competitors who have unrestricted parking supply. It may shift some business activity from commercial districts that apply maximums to suburban locations where parking is abundant and free.

Suitable Applications

Parking maximums are appropriate in areas where, left to their own devices, developers and businesses are likely to supply excess parking, and other parking management strategies are being implemented to address potential problems. This strategy tends to be most appropriate in major commercial centers that want to encourage compact, infill development and shifts to alternative modes, and are implementing other parking management strategies.

Implementation

Parking maximums are usually developed as part of an overall transportation and land-use management plan. The following activities can help support parking maximums:

- Determine strategic planning objectives, such as encouraging more compact development and reducing automobile traffic, which will help determine how maximums will be applied (e.g., whether they apply to all types of parking, or just to free, long-term parking).
- Establish long-term, area-wide parking supply objectives (e.g., identify the number and type of parking desired in a downtown area 10 years into the future).
- Where appropriate, apply parking maximums in addition to or instead of minimum parking requirements.
- Use incentives, such as density bonuses, to encourage developers and businesses to reduce excessive parking supply and rely more on parking management strategies.
- Use tax incentives to discourage excessive supply (e.g., apply a higher tax rate on parking facilities that exceed a certain size).
- Make parking maximums and supply reductions predictable and gradual, so markets have time to adjust.
- Use maximum flexibility when reducing parking supply. Parking rights can be auctioned by governments or allocated to developers and treated as a transferable (sellable and tradable) resource. For example, if one development is allowed 50 parking spaces but only needs 40, and another is allowed 50 spaces but wants 60, the rights could be transferable.
- To reduce pavement and increase development densities, parking caps can limit the amount of land that may be devoted to parking, allowing developers to add parking supply if it is structured.
- Parking maximums and caps should be implemented in conjunction with other strategies to improve travel options and address spillover problems.

- Include parking facilities when calculating a building's development floor area ratio and revise floor area ratio upward accordingly, which provides an incentive to minimize parking supply since it can be traded off for leasable space.

Examples and Case Studies

Below are examples of parking maximum programs.

Portland

In 1975, Portland, Oregon, set a cap of approximately 40,000 parking spaces downtown, including existing and new facilities. This reduced the overall downtown parking ratio from approximately 3.4 long-term parking spaces per 1,000 square feet of office space in 1973 down to about 1.5 in 1990. The cap increased to 44,000 spaces by the 1980s and increased again in the 1990s to accommodate downtown business growth.

Maximum parking varies depending on the district within the city (see Table 5-4). City officials consider these policies successful, helping to make the downtown an attractive place for businesses, residents, and tourists, and increasing transit mode split from about 20 percent in the early 1970s to 48 percent in the mid-1990s (City of Portland, 2003).

Auckland

Auckland, New Zealand, limits parking supply in the central business district to reduce automobile traffic and encourage transit use. Within the central

Table 5-4
Portland Area Parking Maximums

	DD 2 & 3	DD 4	DD 1 & 5, UD	RD 5	RD 3 & 4, DD 6	Transit Zone	Rest of Region
Office	0.7	0.8	1.0	1.5	2.0	3.4	4.1
Retail	1.0	1.0	1.0	1.5	12.0	5.1	6.2
Medical centers	1.5	1.5	1.5	1.5	2.0	4.9	5.9
Schools/ colleges	1.0	1.0	1.0	1.5	2.0	0.3*	0.3*
Industrial	0.7	0.7	0.7	0.7	0.7	None	None
Community services	0.25	0.25	0.25	0.25	0.25	Varies	Varies

*DD = downtown district; UD = university district; RD = river district; * = per students and staff.*
Per 1,000 square feet net building area, unless noted otherwise.

Source: City of Portland, 2003.

parking district, the maximum parking allowed at each development is determined by the type of roadway it abuts. For most of the central business district, the maximum permitted parking ranges from one space per 105 square meters (1,130 square feet) to one space per 200 square meters (2,152 square feet) (Auckland City, 1999).

Washington, D.C.

The National Capital Planning Commission in Washington, D.C., limits the amount of parking allowed at federal office buildings, depending on location and transit accessibility. In suburban locations, this limit is currently one parking space per three employees and is projected to increase to one space per four employees in the future (although outside of the District, these rules are advisory, not required) (EDAW, Inc., 2002; NCPC, 2004).

San Francisco

The Transit First policy in San Francisco, California, allows a maximum of 7 percent of a building's gross floor area to be used for parking, and new buildings must have an approved parking plan prior to occupancy. In some cases, only short-term parking is approved; in others, a mix of long, short, and carpool parking is allowed. These reductions in private parking supply were implemented in conjunction with construction of additional municipal, priced parking. This policy has helped prevent increased peak vehicle traffic despite considerable growth in office space (Kuzmyak et al., 2003).

Boston

In 1977, Boston, Massachusetts, adopted a freeze on commercial parking but not parking reserved for individuals or company use within office buildings. While the number of commercial spaces has not increased, there was a 26 percent increase in exempt spaces between 1984 and 1987, and motor vehicle traffic increased along major corridors to the city (K.T. Analytics, Inc., 1995).

Seattle

Seattle, Washington, allows a maximum of one parking space per 1,000 square feet of downtown office space (Ibid.).

London

London, England, has maximum parking standards that vary with public transport accessibility. In the city center, one space is allowed per 1,500 square meters of commercial space, declining to one space per 300 square meters in outer areas.

CHAPTER 5 (ESTABLISH PARKING MAXIMUMS)
REFERENCES AND INFORMATION RESOURCES

Auckland City (1999), *Central Area Parking Policy* (Auckland, NZ) (www.aucklandcity.govt.nz); available online (www.aucklandcity.govt.nz/council/documents/parkingpolicy/default.asp).

City of Portland (2003), *Central City Plan District*, City of Portland, Oregon, Bureau of Planning (www.planning.ci.portland.or.us).

EDAW, Inc. (2002), *Federal Agency Transportation Management Program*, General Services Administration, National Capital Region (www.ncpc.gov/publications_press/transport/transportation.pdf).

K.T. Analytics, Inc. (1995), *Parking Management Strategies: A Handbook for Implementation*, Regional Transportation Authority (Chicago, IL); available online (www.fta.dot.gov/library/planning/tdmstatus/FTAPRKSP.HTM).

Kuzmyak, J. Richard, Rachel Weinberger, Richard H. Pratt, and Herbert S. Levinson (2003), *Parking Management and Supply: Traveler Response to Transport System Changes*, Chapter 18, Report 95, Transit Cooperative Research Program; Transportation Research Board (www.trb.org); available online (http://gulliver.trb.org/publications/tcrp/tcrp_rpt_95c18.pdf).

Mildner, Gerard, James Strathman, and Martha Bianco (1997), "Parking Policies and Commuting Behavior," *Transportation Quarterly*, Vol. 51, No. 1, Winter 1997, pp. 111-125.

Millard-Ball, Adam (2002), "Putting on Their Parking Caps," *Planning* (www.planning.org), April 2002, pp. 16-21.

Morrall, John and Dan Bolger (1996), "The Relationship Between Downtown Parking Supply and Transit Use," *ITE Journal*, February 1996, pp. 32-36.

National Capital Planning Commission (NCPC) (2004), *Comprehensive Plan for the National Capital: Transportation Element*, NCPC (www.ncpc.gov); available online (www.ncpc.gov/publications_press/CompPlan/Final/4-CP%20Transportation.pdf).

Voith, Richard (1998), "The Downtown Parking Syndrome: Does Curing the Illness Kill the Patient?" *Business Review* (www.phil.frb.org/econ/br/index.html), Vol. 1, 1998, pp 3-14; available online (www.phil.frb.org/files/br/brjf98dv.pdf); also see Federal Reserve Bank of Philadelphia (www.phil.frb.org) Working Paper No. 95-11, 1995.

PROVIDE REMOTE PARKING AND SHUTTLE SERVICES

Description

"Remote parking" (also called "overflow parking" or "satellite parking") involves the use of off-site parking facilities (see Figure 5-5). It often uses shared facilities, such as office workers parking at a restaurant parking lot during the day in exchange for restaurant employees using the office parking lot during the evening and on weekends (see the section entitled "Share Parking" on page 67).

Figure 5-5
Overflow Parking Sign

This sign indicates where to park when the lot is full.

Remote parking can also involve use of parking facilities at the periphery of a business district or other activity center, and use of overflow parking during special events that attract large crowds. Special shuttle buses or free transit service may be provided to allow use of more distant parking than would otherwise be acceptable. Another type of remote parking is Park & Ride facilities, located at the urban fringe, where commuters can leave their vehicles when they carpool or use public transit ("Park & Ride," VTPI, 2005).

Remote parking requires adequate user information and incentives to encourage use of more distant facilities. For example, signs and maps should indicate the location of peripheral parking facilities and their prices should be lower than in the core.

Impacts on Parking Demand and Requirements

On-site parking requirements can typically be reduced 10 to 30 percent if a destination has remote parking. The amount of reduction depends on the type of trip (longer duration trips, such as commuting, tend to be most suitable), the relative price of remote parking, the incentives used to encourage motorists to use more remote spaces, and the quality of walking conditions or shuttle services between a destination and remote parking facilities.

Benefits, Costs, and Consumer Impacts

Remote parking allows use of shared and less costly parking facilities. Park & Ride facilities encourage transit and ridesharing, reducing vehicle traffic. Costs can include inconvenience and insecurity to users, and the costs of any additional administration, security, and shuttle services.

Suitable Applications

Remote parking can be used where parking supply is inadequate and additional parking is available within an acceptable distance. Commute and special-event travel tend to be particularly suitable for remote parking. It is common in major commercial areas, campuses, airports, recreation and sports centers, and for events that attract large crowds. Park & Ride facilities tend to be most appropriate in large, urban areas where transit and ridesharing are promoted.

Implementation

Remote parking and shuttle services are generally implemented by facility managers, event managers, or local officials as part of an overflow parking plan (see the section entitled "Establish Overflow Parking Plans" on page 186). Park & Ride facilities are usually implemented by transit agencies or regional governments. The following activities can help implement remote parking:
- Create a comprehensive parking inventory, that is, a survey of the number and type of spaces throughout an area to help identify opportunities to use remote parking.

- Create a transportation management association or designate another organization (such as a chamber of commerce) to provide parking brokerage (see the section entitled "Establish Transportation Management Associations and Parking Brokerage" on page 182).
- Provide information and incentives for motorists to use remote sites, targeting those that are most suitable, such as commuters and long-term visitors.
- Integrate remote parking with other parking management strategies, such as shared parking, overflow parking plans, and smart growth.
- Use regulations and pricing to encourage use of remote and urban fringe parking facilities.
- Provide shuttle services, improve walking conditions, and create a free transit zone within commercial districts and other activity centers to facilitate use of more remote parking facilities.
- Provide security for vehicles in remote parking lots and for people walking between remote lots and destinations.

Examples and Case Studies

Northwestern University
Northwestern University in Evanston/Chicago, Illinois, provides scheduled shuttle bus service on weekdays and evenings between its Chicago campus to various remote parking lots and a rail station. The service is free to students (Evanston/Chicago Transportation Services of Northwestern University, 2005).

City of Chattanooga
Chattanooga, Tennessee, has redeveloped its once-depressed downtown to become a major commercial and tourist center that attracts millions of visitors a year. Since 1992, the Tennessee Aquarium, the world's largest freshwater aquarium, has become a trademark for a community that transformed itself from one of the dirtiest to one of cleanest and most sustainable cities in North America. To deal with growing parking demand, the local transportation authority constructed two parking garages (550 and 650 stalls) outside the downtown, and provides free shuttle service using electric buses that run every 5 minutes during peak periods. This service has encouraged downtown redevelopment while limiting traffic and parking problems there (Desman Associates, 2004).

City of Highland Park
The Highland Park, Illinois, Intra-City Parking Committee is an organization of downtown merchants and public officials working to improve downtown parking options for customers and employees. In recent years, the Intra-City Parking Committee has changed parking regulation and enforcement in the

downtown core to favor customers, while providing free employee parking lots outside but near downtown (City of Highland Park, 2000).

Peripheral Parking with Shuttles

Hospitals in San Francisco and San Jose, California; Portland, Oregon; and Syracuse, New York, provide shuttle buses to remote parking areas. The University of Maryland has operated 25 shuttle buses, serving parking areas, residential areas, their campus, and regional public transit stations. Hartford, Connecticut, has a policy allowing parking requirements for new development to be reduced up to 30 percent if shuttle service is provided from off-site parking. In Orlando, Florida, developers can reduce parking requirements up to 20 percent in exchange for contributing toward a mobility management fund. Orlando has constructed 8,000 spaces at the periphery of downtown (K.T. Analytics, Inc., 1995).

CHAPTER 5
(PROVIDE REMOTE PARKING AND SHUTTLE SERVICES)
REFERENCES AND INFORMATION RESOURCES

Al-Kazily, Joan (1991), "Analysis of Park-and-Ride Lot Use in the Sacramento Region," *Transportation Research Record 1321*, Transportation Research Board (Washington, DC) (www.trb.org), pp. 1-6.

City of Highland Park (2000), *Parking Alert* (Highland Park, IL) (www.cityhpil.com/community/parkingalert.html).

Desman Associates, A Division of Desman, Inc. (2004), *City of Chattanooga, TN, Downtown Parking Study*, submitted to Rivercity Company (www.rivercitycompany.com/pdfs/media/Parking_Study_2004.pdf).

Evanston/Chicago Transportation Services of Northwestern University (2005) (Evanston/Chicago, IL) (www.univsvcs.northwestern.edu/shuttles/index.htm).

K.T. Analytics, Inc. (1995), *Parking Management Strategies: A Handbook for Implementation*, Regional Transportation Authority (Chicago, IL); available online (www.fta.dot.gov/library/planning/tdmstatus/FTAPRKSP.HTM).

Kuzmyak, J. Richard, Rachel Weinberger, Richard H. Pratt, and Herbert S. Levinson (2003), *Parking Management and Supply: Traveler Response to Transport System Changes*, Chapter 18, Report 95, Transit Cooperative Research Program; Transportation Research Board (www.trb.org); available online (http://gulliver.trb.org/publications/tcrp/tcrp_rpt_95c18.pdf).

Victoria Transport Policy Institute (VTPI) (2005), *Online TDM Encyclopedia*, VTPI (www.vtpi.org); available online ("Park & Ride" (www.vtpi.org/tdm/tdm27.htm)).

IMPLEMENT SMART GROWTH POLICIES

Description

"Smart growth" is a general term for development practices that result in more compact and accessible land-use development. It is an alternative to sprawl. Table 5-5 compares these two development patterns.

Table 5-5
Sprawl and Smart Growth

	Sprawl	Smart Growth
Density	Lower density, dispersed activities.	Higher density, clustered activities.
Growth pattern	Urban periphery (greenfield) development.	Infill (brownfield) development.
Land-use mix	Single use, segregated.	Mixed.
Scale	Large scale; larger buildings, blocks, wide roads; less detail, since people experience the landscape at a distance, as motorists.	Human scale; smaller buildings, blocks and roads; attention to detail, since people experience the landscape up close, as pedestrians.
Public services (shops, schools, parks)	Regional, consolidated, larger; requires automobile access.	Local, distributed, smaller; accommodates walking access.
Transport	Automobile-oriented transportation and land-use patterns, poorly suited for walking, cycling, and transit.	Multimodal transportation and land-use patterns that support walking, cycling, and public transit.
Connectivity	Hierarchical road network with many unconnected roads and walkways, and barriers to nonmotorized travel.	Highly connected roads, sidewalks and paths, allowing more direct travel by motorized and nonmotorized modes.
Street design	Streets designed to maximize motor vehicle traffic volume and speed.	Streets designed to accommodate a variety of activities; traffic calming.
Planning process	Unplanned, with little coordination between jurisdictions and stakeholders.	Planned and coordinated between jurisdictions and stakeholders.
Public space	Emphasis on the private realm (e.g., yards, shopping malls, gated communities, and private clubs).	Emphasis on the public realm (e.g., streetscapes, pedestrian areas, public parks, and public facilities).

Comparison of various features of smart growth and sprawl.

Sources: "Smart Growth," VTPI, 2005; SGN, 2001.

Smart growth supports and is supported by parking management. Parking management reduces the amount of land required for parking facilities, allowing more compact development, and encourages use of alternative modes, such as walking, cycling, and public transit. These, in turn, tend to reduce vehicle ownership and use, which reduce parking demand. More compact development allows additional sharing and pricing of parking facilities. Smart growth usually incorporates specific parking management strategies (see Table 5-6).

Figure 5-6 compares sprawl and smart growth. The photo on the left (sprawl) shows destinations that are scattered along a busy roadway. It is difficult to walk from one to another, so it is infeasible to share parking and diffi-

Table 5-6
Conventional and Smart Growth Parking Policies

Conventional Parking Policies	Smart Growth Parking Policies
Managed for motorist convenience	Managed for transport system efficiency
Offers maximum parking supply	Offers optimal parking supply (not too little, not too much)
Prefers free parking	Prefers priced parking
Prefers single-use parking facilities	Offers shared parking facilities
Favors lower-density, dispersed development	Favors compact development

Parking management strategies that support smart growth.

Figure 5-6
Sprawl Versus Smart Growth

Sprawl   **Smart Growth**

Sprawled land-use patterns increase automobile travel and parking requirements. Smart growth allows more efficient management of transportation and parking.

cult to use public transit. People who live or work in such areas tend to make many vehicle trips, requiring generous parking supply.

The photo on the right (smart growth) shows an urban village where activities are clustered together in an area with good walking facilities and public transit services. People who live and work in this area tend to own fewer cars and drive less, and there are more opportunities to share parking facilities and apply other management strategies, thus reducing parking requirements.

Impacts on Parking Demand and Requirements

As discussed in Chapter 3, land-use factors affect parking and travel demand. Smart growth includes a variety of specific features that can help reduce parking requirements:

- Residents and employees of smart growth communities tend to own fewer cars and drive less than in more automobile-dependent communities.
- More compact development and mixed land use allow more shared parking.
- Building and streetscape design gives more emphasis to walking, cycling, and public transit.
- Smart growth often includes transit service improvements.
- Improved walkability reduces car trips and improves access between destinations and off-site parking facilities.

Smart growth typically reduces per capita motor vehicle ownership 10 to 30 percent and per capita vehicle mileage by 20 to 50 percent, compared with conventional sprawl development (USEPA, 2001; "Land Use Impacts on Transport," VTPI, 2005). Actual reductions depend on the specific smart growth strategies implemented, the scale of their implementation, as well as other geographic, demographic, and economic factors. Table 5-7 summarizes the projected vehicle miles traveled reduction impacts of several smart growth developments.

Benefits, Costs, and Consumer Impacts

Smart growth can provide a variety of benefits (see Table 5-8). Costs can include additional planning, construction, and operating expenses needed to develop higher-density facilities and increase travel choices. Higher-density infill development may increase local traffic congestion and exposure to noise and air pollution, but these are offset at the regional level by reduced per capita automobile travel. Consumer impacts are mixed: residents enjoy many benefits but tend to have smaller yards and less parking supply.

Suitable Applications

Smart growth can be applied in a variety of geographic conditions, including urban, suburban, and rural areas.

Table 5-7
Infill Vehicle Miles Traveled Reductions

Location	Description	VMT Reduction
Atlanta, Georgia	138-acre brownfield, mixed-use project	15% to 52%
Baltimore, Maryland	400 housing units and 800 jobs on waterfront infill project	55%
Dallas, Texas	400 housing units and 1,500 jobs located 0.1 miles from transit station	38%
Montgomery County, Maryland	Infill site near major transit center	42%
San Diego, California	Infill development project	52%
West Palm Beach, Florida	Auto-dependent infill project	39%

VMT = vehicle miles traveled.

Examples of vehicle travel reductions resulting from typical smart growth developments.

Source: CCAP, 2003.

Figure 5-7
Downtown Rutland

Many communities are working to revitalize their downtowns, such as Rutland, Vermont. Parking management supports and is supported by this type of urban redevelopment.

Source: Alex Maclean.

Table 5-8
Smart Growth Benefits

Economic	Social	Environmental
• Development cost savings • Public service cost savings • Consumer transport cost savings • Economies of agglomeration • More efficient transportation	• Improved transport options, particularly for nondrivers • Improved housing options • Increased community cohesion	• Greenspace preservation • Reduced air pollution • Reduced resource consumption • Reduced water pollution

Smart growth can provide a variety of benefits.

Sources: Burchell et al., 1998; Litman, 2004; "Smart Growth," VTPI, 2005.

Implementation

Smart growth is implemented by regional and local governments, usually through a strategic planning process. Many planning organizations provide resources to help implement smart growth (ITE, 2003; Dunphy et al., 2003). Below are specific smart growth implementation activities ("Smart Growth Policy Reforms," VTPI, 2005).

Comprehensive Plans

Regional and local governments should produce a comprehensive plan that identifies where activities will be located for maximum accessibility.

Capital Improvement Programs

Public infrastructure capital improvement programs (such as for roads, schools, and utilities) can be structured to encourage smart growth development by supporting compact development in existing urbanized areas.

Planning Policy Assessment

A planning policy assessment is a detailed analysis of policies, rules, and regulations to identify and correct policies that conflict with strategic goals.

Adequate Public Facility Standards

Adequate public facility standards limit development to areas adequately served by critical public infrastructure (e.g., water, sewer, and emergency services) or require developers to pay for upgrades.

Examples and Case Studies

Center Commons

A survey of residents of Center Commons—a mixed-income, transit-oriented development in Portland, Oregon—found that 30 percent of responding households own fewer cars than they did at their previous homes, almost 46 percent normally commute by public transit, and 56 percent do not drive on an average day. The number of households with no car increased 42 percent (Switzer, 2003) (see Table 5-9).

Portland Region

The Portland, Oregon, region is implementing numerous smart growth measures, including urban growth boundaries, multimodal transportation, and incentives for higher-density infill development. It has reduced parking requirements and encouraged parking management with complementary strategies, such as public transit improvements and carsharing. The region has shifted transportation investment funds away from highway capacity expansion into rail development, with supportive land-use policies to create transit-oriented development. It has significantly improved walking and cycling conditions, and implemented mobility management measures that encourage use of alternative modes (City of Portland, 2004).

Maryland Smart Growth

The State of Maryland's Priority Funding Areas legislation limits most state infrastructure funding and economic development programs to smart growth areas, which are designated by local governments. The Live-Near-Your-Work program supports this effort by providing cash contributions to workers buy-

Table 5-9
Center Commons Previous and Current Vehicle Ownership

Household Vehicle Ownership	Previous Home	Center Commons	Percent Change
No car	21	36	+42%
One car	60	54	−10%
Two cars	11	4	−64%
Three cars	3	2	−33%
Five cars	1	0	−100%
Totals	**96**	**68**	**−29%**

Households that moved to the Center Commons development tend to reduce their vehicle ownership and use.

Source: Switzer, 2003.

ing homes in certain older neighborhoods. To support preservation of undeveloped land, the new Rural Legacy Program provides financial resources for the protection of farm and forest land. This package is intended to save natural resources, redevelop existing communities, and save state expenses (Maryland Office of Smart Growth, 2004).

CHAPTER 5 (IMPLEMENT SMART GROWTH POLICIES) REFERENCES AND INFORMATION RESOURCES

Burchell, Robert W. et al. (1998), *The Costs of Sprawl—Revisited*, Transit Cooperative Research Program Report 39, Transportation Research Board (www.trb.org); available online (http://gulliver.trb.org/publications/tcrp/tcrp_rpt_39-a.pdf).

Campoli, Julie, Elizabeth Humstone, and Alex Maclean (2001), *Above and Beyond*, American Planning Association (Chicago, IL) (www.planning.org).

Center for Clean Air Policy (CCAP) (2003), *State and Local Leadership on Transportation and Climate Change*, CCAP (www.ccap.org); available online (www.ccap.org/pdf/statetransport_climat.pdf).

City of Portland (2004), Office of Transportation, plans, builds, manages, and maintains an effective and safe transportation system that provides people and businesses access and mobility (www.trans.ci.portland.or.us).

Dunphy, Robert, Deborah Myerson, and Michael Pawlukiewicz (2003), *Ten Principles for Successful Development Around Transit*, Urban Land Institute (Washington, DC) (www.uli.org).

Ewing, Reid (1996), *Best Development Practices; Doing the Right Thing and Making Money at the Same Time*, American Planning Association (Chicago, IL) (www.planning.org).

Institute for Location Efficiency works to encourage implementation of Location Efficient Development (www.locationefficiency.com).

Institute of Transportation Engineers (ITE) (2003), *Smart Growth Transportation Guidelines*, Smart Growth Task Force, ITE (Washington, DC) (www.ite.org).

Kuzmyak, J. Richard and Richard H. Pratt (2003), *Land Use and Site Design: Traveler Response to Transportation System Changes*, Chapter 15, Report 95, Transit Cooperative Research Program; Transportation Research Board (www.trb.org); available online (http://gulliver.trb.org/publications/tcrp/tcrp_rpt_95c15.pdf).

Litman, Todd (1995), *Land Use Impact Costs of Transportation*, World Transport Policy & Practice (www.eco-logica.co.uk/WTPPhome.html), Vol. 1, No. 4, pp. 9-16; updated version available online (www.vtpi.org/landuse.pdf).

Litman, Todd (2004), *Evaluating Criticism of Smart Growth*, Victoria Transport Policy Institute (www.vtpi.org); available online (www.vtpi.org/sgcritics.pdf).

Maryland Office of Smart Growth (2004) focuses on community revitalization, brownfields, transit-oriented development, priority funding areas, and local government involvement (www.smartgrowth.state.md.us).

Morris, Marya (1996), *Creating Transit-Supportive Land-Use Regulations*, Report Number 468, Planning Advisory Service, American Planning Association (Chicago, IL) (www.planning.org).

Nelson/Nygaard Consulting (2002), *Housing Shortage/Parking Surplus*, Transportation and Land Use Coalition (www.transcoalition.org); available online (www.transcoalition.org/reports/housing_s/housing_shortage_home.html).

Parsons Brinckerhoff (2002), "Parking and TOD: Challenges and Opportunities," *Transit-Oriented Development Study: Factors for Success in California*, California Department of Transportation (www.dot.ca.gov); available online (www.dot.ca.gov/hq/MassTrans/tod.htm).

Russo, Ryan (2001), *Planning for Residential Parking: A Guide For Housing Developers and Planners*, The Non-Profit Housing Association of Northern California (www.nonprofithousing.org) and the Berkeley Program on Housing and Urban Policy (http://urbanpolicy.berkeley.edu); available online (www.nonprofithousing.org/actioncenter/toolbox/parking/index.atomic).

Smart Growth Network (SGN) (2001), *What is Smart Growth*, SGN, U.S. Environmental Protection Agency (www.epa.gov/smartgrowth).

Switzer, Carl (2003), *The Center Commons*, Portland State University research, presented at the Rail~volution Conference (www.railvolution.com) (Atlanta, GA), September 11-14, 2003.

U.S. Environmental Protection Agency (USEPA) (2001), *Smart Growth Index (SGI) Model*, Smart Growth Program, USEPA (www.epa.gov/smartgrowth); available online (www.epa.gov/dced/topics/sg_index.htm).

U.S. Environmental Protection Agency (2004), *Smart Growth Policies Data Base*, U.S. Environmental Protection Agency (www.epa.gov); available online (http://cfpub.epa.gov/sgpdb/sgdb.cfm).

Victoria Transport Policy Institute (VTPI) (2005), *Online TDM Encyclopedia*, VTPI (www.vtpi.org); available online ("Land Use Impacts on Transport" (www.vtpi.org/tdm/tdm20.htm), "Smart Growth" (www.vtpi.org/tdm/tdm38.htm), and "Smart Growth Policy Reforms" (www.vtpi.org/tdm/tdm95.htm)).

IMPROVE WALKING AND CYCLING CONDITIONS

Description

Walking and cycling (together called "active transportation" or "nonmotorized transport") improvements support parking management strategies in several ways:

- Improving walkability (the quality of walking conditions) expands the range of parking facilities that serve a destination. This increases the feasibility of sharing parking facilities and use of remote parking facilities.
- Improving walkability increases park-once trips (parking in one location and walking rather than driving to other destinations), which reduces the amount of parking required at each destination.
- Walking and cycling improvements encourage transit use since most transit trips involve walking or cycling links.
- Walking and cycling improvements can help reduce total vehicle ownership and use in an area. People who live and work in more walkable and cyclable communities tend to own fewer vehicles and take fewer vehicle trips than those in more automobile-oriented locations.

Nonmotorized travel is affected by the quality of walking and cycling facilities (e.g., sidewalks, paths, and crosswalks), the distance between parking and destinations, and factors such as the speed of adjacent vehicle traffic and noise levels ("Evaluating Nonmotorized Transport," VTPI, 2005). Acceptable nonmotorized travel distances vary depending on the type of trip, the type of user, and conditions.

Table 5-10 indicates acceptable walking distances for various conditions (also see Table 6-1 in Childs, 1999). *Level of Service* is a qualitative measure describing the performance of a facility or service, rated A (best) through F (worst). For typical urban conditions, Level of Service A is less than one block, Level of Service B is one to four blocks, Level of Service C is four to eight blocks, and Level of Service D is more than eight blocks between a destination and its parking facilities.

Table 5-11 illustrates the acceptable walking Level of Service between parking facilities and destinations for various types of users and trips. Longer walking distances are acceptable for stops with longer duration (see Table 5-12).

Walkability within parking facilities is also important (see the section entitled "Improve Parking Facility Design and Operation" on page 192). Pedestrian safety, comfort, and convenience should be considered in parking facility design, including marked walkways that protect pedestrians from traffic, convenient sidewalk connections, and awnings for shelter from sun and rain. Urban parking lots can serve as midblock walkways, giving pedestrians a shortcut from one street to another, which improves nonmotorized accessibility and expands the number of destinations the parking facility can serve.

Table 5-10
Level of Service by Walking Distance (in Feet)

Walking Environment	LOS A	LOS B	LOS C	LOS D
Climate controlled	1,000	2,400	3,800	5,200
Outdoor/covered	500	1,000	1,500	2,000
Outdoor/uncovered	400	800	1,200	1,600
Through surface lot	350	700	1,050	1,400
Inside parking facility	300	600	900	1,200

LOS = Level of Service.

Walking LOS ratings under various conditions.

Source: PT, 2000.

Table 5-11
Recommended Walking Level of Service

Adjacent (LOS A)	Minimal (LOS A or B)	Medium (LOS B or C)	Long (LOS C or D)
• People with disabilities • Deliveries and loading • Emergency services • Convenience store	• Grocery stores • Professional services • Medical clinics • Residents	• General retail • Restaurant • Employees • Entertainment center • Religious institution	• Airport parking • Major sport or cultural event • Overflow parking

LOS = Level of Service.

Maximum acceptable walking distance from parking to destinations for different users and trips.

Source: "Evaluating Nonmotorized Transport," VTPI, 2005.

Table 5-12
Recommended Walking Distance by Duration

Stop Duration	Acceptable Walking Distance
½ hour	100 meters (300 feet)
1 hour	200 meters (600 feet)
2 hours	400 meters (1,200 feet)
4 hours	800 meters (2,500 feet)
8 hours	1,000 meters (3,000 feet)

Stops with shorter duration, such as quick errands, should generally have more convenient parking than longer duration stops, such as commuting.

Source: Carley, 2000.

Impacts on Parking Demand and Requirements

According to some estimates, 5 to 10 percent of motor vehicle trips can reasonably shift to nonmotorized transport; when parking fees or other disincentives reduce automobile travel, 10 to 35 percent of the reduced trips typically shift to walking and cycling (ADONIS, 1999). Parking requirements can usually be reduced 10 to 30 percent in pedestrian-friendly areas compared with conventional standards, due to shifts from automobile to nonmotorized modes and the increased feasibility of using shared and remote parking. Actual impacts depend on specific circumstances, the type of improvements provided, and the implementation of other parking management strategies (Litman, 2004b).

Benefits, Costs, and Consumer Impacts

Walking and cycling improvements provide a variety of economic, social, and environmental benefits, including road and parking facility cost savings, consumer cost savings, congestion reduction, energy and pollution emission reductions, improved public health, and improved mobility options (Litman, 2004a). Walking and cycling improvements directly benefit consumers by improving their convenience and safety, and expanding their parking and transportation options. Costs vary depending on the situation and can include facility construction and maintenance expenses, pedestrian security services, and sometimes vehicle traffic restrictions.

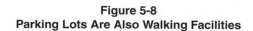

Figure 5-8
Parking Lots Are Also Walking Facilities

Parking facilities should be designed for pedestrian safety, comfort, and convenience.

Suitable Applications

Walking and cycling improvements can be appropriate in most geographic conditions. They tend to be particularly effective at reducing parking demand in dense, urban areas where destinations are clustered together, and in suburban areas by allowing more sharing of parking facilities and park-once trips. Cycling improvements are particularly appropriate for destinations that attract young people, such as schools, campuses, recreation centers, and some types of worksites.

Implementation

There are many specific ways to improve walking and cycling conditions:
- Implement a nonmotorized planning process, which identifies problems and implements improvements.
- Insure that parking facilities are safe and convenient for walking. Include marked paths that accommodate wheelchairs, and covered waiting areas for protection from rain and hot sun with benches and other pedestrian amenities.
- Give special attention to improving access between destinations and off-site parking facilities. This may involve improving paths, sidewalks, and crosswalks, and developing special shortcuts and entranceways that provide more direct access.
- If possible, provide multiple pedestrian access points to parking facilities so users can walk as directly as possible to various destinations.
- Improve walking facility design, maintenance, cleanliness, and aesthetics.
- Implement traffic calming, speed reductions, and vehicle restrictions.
- Implement universal design, which means that pedestrian facilities accommodate people with disabilities and other special needs.
- Address pedestrian security concerns by providing adequate lighting and visibility, security patrols, and alarm systems.
- Provide bicycle storage and changing facilities (see the section entitled "Provide Bicycle Facilities" on page 165).

Parking facility walkability improvements can be implemented by facility managers; comprehensive walking and cycling planning is usually implemented by local governments. Some improvements involve changing zoning codes and development regulations, for example, to require developers to provide and maintain sidewalks and paths. Cities can encourage the development of pedestrian connections, such as midblock walkways in commercial districts. Developers can provide sidewalks and other pedestrian improvements, and individual businesses or a local business organization can improve sidewalk cleanliness and security.

Examples and Case Studies

Downtown Toledo Revitalization

Toledo, Ohio, has a Citiwalk system—a network of a skywalk, subterranean tunnels, and internal connections—to accommodate pedestrians in inclement weather; however, it was not well maintained or well used. A local trail system provided recreational walking and biking opportunities, but it was not well integrated into the transportation system. There were directional signs for motorists but none were oriented to pedestrians.

The *2002 Downtown Toledo Master Plan* incorporates the following features to improve walkability and reduce vehicle trips:

- Within the existing sidewalk width, new landscaping and street furniture treatments will soften and enhance the main corridors.
- New directional signs will be added, including real-time informational signs about parking conditions at three key gateways into the downtown.
- Pedestrian kiosks and directional signs will be located at strategic locations throughout downtown.
- A walking and cycling greenway system will be developed.
- Park-once trips will be promoted and downtown parking supply will be limited to what currently exists (TMACOG, 2003).

City of Portland

Portland, Oregon, has adopted a two-part pedestrian improvement plan:

- Part One outlines the policies and plans for improving conditions for walking.
- Part Two is a detailed design manual for pedestrian facilities.

The *Portland Pedestrian Design Guide* and *Portland Pedestrian Master Plan* are outstanding pedestrian planning resources that create a process for prioritizing pedestrian improvements, taking into account demand and current conditions. The downtown Portland business association works to maintain high standards of sidewalk cleanliness and pedestrian security (City of Portland, 2004).

City Center Walkability

Research on downtown commercial districts indicates that pedestrian environmental quality is an important factor in their economic vitality and in the willingness of downtown customers to use remote parking facilities and transit. Where walking conditions are good, downtown shoppers are willing to walk longer distances and accept more limited and costly parking facilities (Carley, 2000).

CHAPTER 5 (IMPROVE WALKING AND CYCLING CONDITIONS) REFERENCES AND INFORMATION RESOURCES

Analysis and Development of New Insight into Substitution (ADONIS) (1999), *Best practice to promote cycling and walking* and *How to substitute short car trips by cycling and walking*, ADONIS, Transport RTD Programme, European Union; available online (www.cordis.lu/transport/src/adonisrep.htm).

Bicycle and Pedestrian Program Office is responsible for promoting bicycle and pedestrian transportation accessibility, use, and safety (supported by the U.S. Department of Transportation, Federal Highway Administration) (www.fhwa.dot.gov/environment/bikeped).

Carley, Michael (2000), *Sustainable Transport and Regional Vitality: State of the Art for Towns & Cities*, Donaldsons, National Trust for Scotland; summary available online (www.cockburnassociation.org.uk/helen/pages/sustainabletransport.htm).

Childs, Mark (1999), *Parking Spaces: A Design, Implementation and Use Manual for Architects, Planners, and Engineers*, The McGraw-Hill Companies (New York) (www.mcgraw-hill.com).

City of Portland (2004), Office of Transportation (www.trans.ci.portland.or.us), *Portland Pedestrian Design Guide* (1998); *Portland Pedestrian Master Plan* (1998). This Web site provides planning information and resources, including extensive information on pedestrian and bicycle planning techniques.

Litman, Todd et al. (2002), *Pedestrian and Bicycle Planning: A Guide to Best Practices*, Victoria Transport Policy Institute (www.vtpi.org); available online (www.vtpi.org/nmtguide.doc).

Litman, Todd (2004a), "Economic Value of Walkability," *Transportation Research Record 1828*, Transportation Research Board (www.trb.org), pp. 3-11; available online (www.vtpi.org/walkability.pdf).

Litman, Todd (2004b), *Quantifying the Benefits of Nonmotorized Transportation For Achieving Mobility Management Objectives*, Victoria Transport Policy Institute (www.vtpi.org); available online (www.vtpi.org/nmt-tdm.pdf).

Parking Today (PT) (2000), "How Far Should Patrons Have to Walk After They Park?" *Parking Today* (www.parkingtoday.com), May 2000, pp. 34-36; originally published in Mary S. Smith and T.A. Butcher, "How Far Should Parkers Have to Walk?" *Parking*, Vol. 33, No. 8, September 1994.

Pedestrian and Bicycle Information Center is a pedestrian planning and safety information clearinghouse (supported by the U.S. Department of Transportation, Federal Highway Administration) (www.walkinginfo.org).

Toledo Metropolitan Area Council of Governments (TMACOG) (2003), *2002 Downtown Toledo Master Plan—Fundamentals* (www.tmacog.org/Transportation/Regional%20core/Fundamentals.pdf).

Victoria Transport Policy Institute (VTPI) (2005), *Online TDM Encyclopedia*, VTPI (www.vtpi.org); available online ("Evaluating Nonmotorized Transport" (www.vtpi.org/tdm/tdm63.htm) and "Nonmotorized Transportation Planning" (www.vtpi.org/tdm/tdm25.htm)).

INCREASE CAPACITY OF EXISTING PARKING FACILITIES

Description

The capacity of existing parking facilities can often be increased without requiring more land or major facility construction. Here are some strategies to do this:

- Use currently wasted areas (e.g., corners, edges, or undeveloped land), which can be particularly appropriate for small car spaces and motorcycle and bicycle parking.
- Where there is adequate street width, change on-street parking orientation from parallel to angled spaces (see Figure 5-9).
- Allow tandem parking (one vehicle parked behind another on a driveway) and count this toward minimum parking requirements.
- Maximize the number of on-street parking spaces (e.g., using a curb lane for parking rather than traffic during off-peak periods, minimizing unnecessary restrictions to on-street parking, eliminating unused driveways, and designating undersized spaces for small cars or motorcycles).
- Reduce parking space size. A portion of spaces can be sized for compact vehicles, which require about 20 percent less space than full-sized stalls. Employee and residential parking spaces can be somewhat smaller than shorter-term parking, which must accommodate more movement and loading activity.

Figure 5-9
Angled Parking

Compared with parallel parking, angled parking approximately doubles the number of parking spaces.

Figure 5-10
Motorcycle Parking

Special areas can be dedicated for motorcycle parking.

Figure 5-11
Car Stackers

Car stackers allow more vehicles to be stored in a given space.

Source: Car Parking Solutions.

- Provide special, small parking spaces for motorcycles. Allow and encourage motorcycles to share parking spaces when possible (see Figure 5-10).
- Use car stackers and mechanical garages, which can significantly increase parking capability, although they are only suitable for certain applications. They generally require an attendant to move lower-level vehicles when needed to access upper-level vehicles, and stackers may be unable to accommodate larger vehicles, such as sport utility vehicles, vans, and trucks (see Figure 5-11).
- Use valet parking (attendants park each vehicle), particularly during busy periods, which can increase parking capacity by 20 to 40 percent, compared with self-park (drivers park their own vehicles).
- Remove or consolidate nonoperating vehicles, equipment, material, and junk stored in parking facilities, particularly in prime locations.

Impacts on Parking Demand and Requirements

The potential for increasing parking capacity varies depending on circumstances. Capacity increases of 5 to 10 percent are often possible if a facility was poorly designed, and greater increases are possible in some situations, such as shifting from self-park to valet parking or if parallel parking is converted to angled parking.

Benefits, Costs, and Consumer Impacts

Increasing existing parking facility capacity can provide economic savings and increased user convenience. Costs may include repainting, new equipment (such as stackers), labor for valet parking, and reduced motorist convenience from smaller spaces.

Suitable Applications

Increased capacity of existing parking facilities tends to be most appropriate in areas with high land values, such as major commercial centers. Smaller spaces and mechanical parking systems tend to be most suitable for longer-term parking, such as for commuters and residents. Valet parking is most suitable for special events and other predictable periods of high demand. Conversion from parallel to angled parking tends to be suitable along relatively wide streets.

Implementation

These strategies usually require consultation with a parking planning expert to assess their appropriateness in a particular situation and develop an implementation plan.

Examples and Case Studies

Valet Parking Services

Valet parking is popular as a prestige service at elite clubs and restaurants, and as a way to address parking problems during special events. Most major cities have private companies that offer uniformed, bonded, valet parking services.

Tandem Parking

Some cities (e.g., San Diego, California, and Edmonds, Washington) allow tandem parking to count toward minimum residential parking requirements.

Automated Parking

Automated parking systems are widely used in Japan, Korea, and Europe. Japan is estimated to have 1.6 million parking stalls in mechanical and automated parking facilities, more than the number of spaces in concrete ramp garages there. Automated parking is accepted in these areas because it is space efficient and motorists have become familiar with such systems (Automated & Mechanical Parking Association, 2004).

Hamburg Mechanical Parking Garage

A parking system in Hamburg, Germany, is the first automatic parking system to receive the Car Park Seal of Quality conferred by the German Automotive Club. The system has over 132 parking spaces and fulfills all the criteria of the extensive award checklist. "Automatic parking systems provide great advantages because they make maximum use of the available space," says Dr. Erhard Oehm of the German Automobile Association ADAC. "They also provide effective protection against theft and damage." (Wöhr, 2003)

CHAPTER 5 (INCREASE CAPACITY OF EXISTING PARKING FACILITIES) REFERENCES AND INFORMATION RESOURCES

Automated & Mechanical Parking Association (2004) is an organization of companies that provide car stackers and mechanical parking equipment (www.ampapark.org).

Car Parking Solutions provides automated parking solutions including car stackers that maximize vehicle parking supply at minimal cost (www.carstackers.co.nz).

Edwards, John D. (2002), "Changing On-Street Parallel Parking to Angle Parking," *ITE Journal*, Vol. 72, No. 2, February 2002, pp. 28-33.

EXPO1000 *Parking Industry Guide* is a comprehensive catalogue of products and services related to parking (www.expo1000.com/parking).

International Parking Institute provides information and other resources for parking management professionals (www.parking.org).

National Parking Association and the Automated & Mechanical Parking Association (2003), *Guide to the Design & Operation of Automated Parking Facilities*, National Parking Association (Washington, DC) (www.npapark.org) and the Automated & Mechanical Parking Association (Chicago, IL) (www.ampapark.org).

Stover, Vergil G. and Frank J. Koepke (2002), "Parking Design," *Transportation and Land Development, Second Edition,* Institute of Transportation Engineers (Washington, DC) (www.ite.org).

Wöhr (2003), ADAC Award for WÖHR Parksafe 580, Wöhr Auto Park Systems (www.woehr.de/engl/home/detail.php3?Kennung=19).

II. STRATEGIES THAT REDUCE PARKING DEMAND

IMPLEMENT MOBILITY MANAGEMENT

Description

"Mobility management" (also called "transportation demand management") is a general term for strategies that increase transportation system efficiency by changing travel behavior (VTPI, 2005). It can affect travel frequency, mode, destination, or timing (for example, by shifting to a closer destination, from driving to public transit travel, or from peak to off peak). There are many different mobility management strategies (see Table 5-13 and Figure 5-12).

Mobility management both supports and is supported by parking management. Mobility management usually reduces parking demand and many parking management strategies encourage travel changes. Some strategies, such as parking pricing and walkability improvements, are considered both parking and mobility management measures.

Impacts on Parking Demand and Requirements

An integrated mobility management program that includes various strategies often reduces automobile trips and parking demand by 10 to 30 percent among participants, and even more if implemented as part of a comprehensive regional effort that includes transit improvements and smart growth land-use development. Information on mobility management travel impacts is available at VTPI (2005), OUM (2001), and in other references listed on page 127.

Benefits, Costs, and Consumer Impacts

Mobility management can provide a variety of benefits, including:
- Road and parking facility cost savings
- Congestion reduction
- Consumer cost savings
- Improved travel options
- Increased road safety
- Support for strategic land-use objectives (reduced sprawl)
- Pollution reductions
- Improved community livability

Consumers directly benefit from mobility management strategies that improve travel options or reduce travel costs (see the sidebar entitled "Carsharing"). Motorists may consider themselves worse off from negative incentives, such as increased parking fees, but they may benefit overall from reduced congestion and financial savings if revenues substitute for other fees or taxes. Costs may include expenses for additional administration and services, and sometimes reduced consumer convenience.

Table 5-13
Mobility Management Strategies

Improved Transport Options	Incentives to Shift Mode	Land-Use Management	Policies and Programs
• Flextime • Bicycle improvements • Bike/transit integration • Carsharing • Guaranteed ride home • Security improvements • Park & Ride • Pedestrian improvements • Ridesharing • Shuttle services • Improved taxi service • Telework • Traffic calming • Transit improvements	• Bicycle and pedestrian encouragement • Congestion pricing • Distance-based pricing • Commuter financial incentives • Fuel tax increases • High-occupant-vehicle priority • Pay-As-You-Drive vehicle insurance • Parking pricing • Road pricing • Vehicle use restrictions	• Car-free districts • Compact land use • Location-efficient development • New urbanism • Smart growth • Transit-oriented development • Street reclaiming	• Access management • Campus transport management • Data collection and surveys • Commute trip reduction • Freight transport management • Marketing programs • School trip management • Special event management • Tourist transport management • Transport market reforms

Mobility management includes numerous strategies that affect vehicle travel behavior, many of which affect parking demand.

Source: VTPI, 2005.

Figure 5-12
Public Transit

Shifting travel from automobile to public transit reduces parking demand.

Carsharing

"Carsharing" refers to automobile rental services that substitute for private vehicle ownership. To be effective, such services must be located in residential areas and priced for hourly use. Carsharing can help reduce per capita vehicle ownership and therefore parking requirements. A carshare service that is located in or near a residential development typically reduces parking requirements by 5 to 10 percent.

Figure 5-13
Carsharing

Example of a carshare vehicle, available for rent by the hour or day.

Suitable Applications

Mobility management is appropriate in many situations to help address a variety of problems. Mobility management is most common in large cities and activity centers; it can also be implemented at suburban worksites, college campuses, schools, residential neighborhoods, transportation terminals (e.g., airports), during major events, and at resorts.

Implementation

Mobility management programs can be established and supported by local, regional, or state/provincial governments. These programs can be implemented by transportation management associations (see the section entitled "Establish Transportation Management Associations and Parking Brokerage" on page 182), campus and mall managers, and individual businesses. Government policies can encourage or require developers and employers to implement travel-reduction programs. Some mobility management strategies, such as road-pricing reforms and investments in alternative modes, require government action. Mobility management programs can be required in exchange for reduced parking requirements.

Examples and Case Studies

There are many examples of successful mobility management programs that reduce parking problems and costs ("Success Stories," VTPI, 2005).

Trip Reduction Ordinances

Some jurisdictions have ordinances that encourage or require commute trip reduction programs. Below are some examples.

- *Maricopa County*

Maricopa County, Arizona, requires major worksites with 50 or more employees to implement trip reduction programs (Valley Metro Employer Services & Trip Reduction Program, 2004).

- *City of Cambridge*

Cambridge, Massachusetts, has an ordinance requiring businesses to implement transportation demand management programs at new developments (City of Cambridge, 2004).

- *South Natomas*

South Natomas, California, allows developers to use transportation demand management programs to help gain municipal acceptance of new developments (South Natomas Transportation Management Association, 2005).

- *San Francisco Bay Area*

California's San Francisco Bay Area requires all public and private employers with 100 or more employees at a worksite to establish employee trip reduction targets and identify strategies they will implement to help achieve these targets (Bay Area Air Quality Management District, 2004).

- *Washington State's Commute Trip Reduction Law*

The Commute Trip Reduction law is designed to reduce traffic congestion, pollution, and fuel consumption. Employers in major urban areas with more than 100 employees at a worksite are required to develop Commute Trip Reduction Programs that encourage employees who drive alone to work to consider using alternative commute modes (e.g., buses, vanpools, carpools, biking, walking, and teleworking) and flexible work schedules (Washington State General Administration, 2004).

Car Sharing in Vancouver

Carsharing is growing in Vancouver, British Columbia. More than 1,300 residents were members of a carsharing organization in 2003. The city is considering new planning rules that reward developers who encourage carsharing. The idea is inspired by the success of Electric Avenue, a downtown condominium development whose developers were given permission by the city to build fewer parking spots in return for agreeing to provide spaces for seven carshare vehicles on the site. The developers only expected about 10 percent of the building's 426 residents to join the carshare organization but 26 percent actually became members (Carplus, 2003).

Kamloops TravelSmart Plan

The TravelSmart Plan in Kamloops, British Columbia, promotes changes in travel behavior and encourages more efficient development in order to reduce demands on the municipal transportation system and improve the community's quality of life. Launched in 1997, TravelSmart includes these ongoing initiatives:

- *More Efficient Roadway Utilization*

  To avoid expensive improvements to road networks, the city has limited development in some areas and encouraged more development in more accessible locations.

- *Improved Public Transit*

  A comprehensive travel plan was developed to improve the level of transit service, including increased service to outlying communities.

- *Promotion of Bicycle Use*

  The Kamloops Bicycle Plan identifies $6 million worth of additional cycle routes and initiatives for businesses to provide end-of-trip facilities to cyclists, such as showers and bike racks.

- *Promotional Programs*

  Transportation alternatives (e.g., carpooling, biking, and walking) are promoted through workshops and campaigns in workplaces, schools, and neighborhoods. The plan recognizes the need for ongoing community involvement.

Total project planning costs $300,000, of which $245,000 was funded by the city and $55,000 by the province. TravelSmart will be updated every five years as one component of *Kamplan*, the city's growth management strategy. After three years of operation, the program has improved air quality and reduced planned road expenditures by 75 percent (City of Kamloops, 1999).

CHAPTER 5 (IMPLEMENT MOBILITY MANAGEMENT)
REFERENCES AND INFORMATION RESOURCES

Bay Area Air Quality Management District (2004) (www.arb.ca.gov/DRDB/BA/CURHTML/R13-1.HTM).

Carplus (2003), *Key Lessons From a World Wide Car Club Tour,* Carplus (www.carclubs.org.uk/carplus/whatcarplus.htm).

Centre for Sustainable Community Development: Case Studies, Federation of Canadian Municipalities (www.fcm.ca); available online (http://kn.fcm.ca); includes various examples of successful mobility management strategies.

City of Cambridge (2004), "Parking and Transportation Demand Management" (www.ci.cambridge.ma.us).

City of Kamloops (1999), TravelSmart Plan (www.city.kamloops.bc.ca/transportation/plans/travelsmart.shtml).

European Local Transport Information Service is an online guide to over 400 transportation measures, policies, and practices in Europe (www.eltis.org.htm).

International Council for Local Environmental Initiatives (2005), *Case Studies* (www3.iclei.org/iclei/casestud.htm), *Case Reference & Cities Database* (www.iclei.org), and European Good Practice Information Service, "Local Sustainability" (http://cities21.com/coldfus/citylist.dbm).

Kuzmyak, J. Richard, Rachel Weinberger, Richard H. Pratt, and Herbert S. Levinson (2003), *Parking Management and Supply: Traveler Response to Transport System Changes,* Chapter 18, Report 95, Transit Cooperative Research Program; Transportation Research Board (www.trb.org); available online (http://gulliver.trb.org/publications/tcrp/tcrp_rpt_95c18.pdf).

Moving the Economy, *Moving the Economy On-line Best Practices Database* (http://w4.metrotor.on.ca/inter/mte/mte.nsf/$defaultview?OpenView&Count=5) is an ever-expanding searchable inventory of economic success stories in sustainable transportation.

National Center for Transit Research (www.nctr.usf.edu/clearinghouse/tro), National Transportation Demand Management and Telework Clearinghouse, University of South Florida, has compiled a list of nearly 40 trip reduction ordinances to provide examples of various ordinances that local and state governments have applied to address traffic congestion, air quality and quality of life needs.

Office of Urban Mobility (OUM) (2001), *TDM Success Stories*, Washington State Department of Transportation (www.wsdot.wa.gov); available online (www.wsdot.wa.gov/mobility/TDM/TDMsuccess.html).

South Natomas Transportation Management Association (2005) works cooperatively with the greater South Natomas community on transportation management and air quality issues (www.southnatomastma.org).

TELLUS—Bringing CIVITAS onto the road, European Union, describes projects that integrate urban transport policies to help reduce urban traffic problems (www.tellus-cities.net).

U.S. Environmental Protection Agency (2002), *Transportation Control Measures Program Information Directory,* U.S. Environmental Protection Agency (www.epa.gov); available online (http://yosemite.epa.gov/aa/tcmsitei.nsf).

U.S. Environmental Protection Agency, Commuter Choice describes federal
Commute Choice program, which encourages more efficient commute modes
(www.commuterchoice.com).

U.S. Environmental Protection Agency (2004), *Smart Growth Policies Data Base*,
U.S. Environmental Protection Agency (www.epa.gov); available online
(http://cfpub.epa.gov/sgpdb/sgdb.cfm).

Valley Metro Employer Services & Trip Reduction Program (2004)
(www.valleymetro.org/Rideshare3/1Employer/Index.html) provides services
and resources to help motivate employees to commute to work by ways other than
driving alone.

Victoria Transport Policy Institute (VTPI) (2005), *Online TDM Encyclopedia*, VTPI
(www.vtpi.org); available online ("Success Stories" (www.vtpi.org/tdm/
tdm71.htm)).

Washington State General Administration (2004), Commute Trip Reduction Program,
Washington State (www.ga.wa.gov/ctr).

PRICE PARKING

Description

Pricing parking is the practice of requiring motorists to pay directly for using parking facilities. It may be implemented as a parking management strategy (to reduce parking problems), as a mobility management strategy (to reduce transport problems), to recover parking facility costs, or to raise revenue for any purpose (such as funding local transport programs or downtown improvements). It is often intended to achieve a combination of objectives.

Currently, most parking is inefficiently priced, that is, the prices consumers pay do not accurately reflect the costs imposed by their parking decisions. Most parking is provided free, significantly subsidized, or bundled (automatically included with building purchases and rents), which forces consumers to pay for parking regardless of whether or not they want it. Prices seldom vary by time or location to accurately reflect marginal costs. When parking is priced, motorists often pay a flat annual or monthly fee, providing little incentive to use alternative modes occasionally.

Of course, motorists generally prefer unpriced parking; however, the choice is not really between free and paid parking. It is between paying directly or indirectly, since consumers ultimately bear parking facility costs through rents, taxes, or wages (Shoup, 2005). Paying directly is more efficient and fair. It gives consumers an opportunity to save money by consuming less, or less costly, parking.

For example, by paying for parking directly, a commuter saves money each time they shift to an alternative mode or park at a cheaper location. The less you drive, the more you save, which reflects the parking cost savings that result from that decision. When parking is paid indirectly, consumers do not have this option. Efficient pricing allows higher-value trips to outbid lower-value trips for the most convenient spaces, so motorists can find a space when they really need it. The choice, therefore, is actually between paying indirectly for inefficiently allocated parking or paying directly for efficiently allocated parking.

Pricing previously free parking is politically difficult, but there are ways to overcome this resistance. For example, rather than simply pricing parking, cash out free parking, allowing commuters to choose between a subsidized parking space or the cash equivalent (see the section entitled "Provide Financial Incentives" on page 144). Similarly, rather than charging extra for residential parking, offer a discount to renters who do not use a parking space. It is also possible to overcome political resistance by using revenue in ways that address objections. For example, revenues can be used to fund transportation improvements, new community services, or tax reductions.

Much of the objection to priced parking reflects users' frustration with the methods used to collect fees. Current pricing methods often require motorists to pay with a particular denomination, predict the maximum amount of time they will be parked, and purchase relatively large time blocks, such as 2 hours or a day. There is often no provision for parking for just a few minutes or for an uncertain amount of time. New pricing methods (as described in the section entitled "Improve Pricing Methods" on page 138) can address these problems, making pricing more convenient and fair.

Below are guidelines for more efficient parking pricing:

- Wherever possible, charge consumers directly rather than indirectly for parking.
- Use improved pricing methods that are more convenient. For example, use pricing systems that charge for just the amount of time a vehicle is parked rather than for fixed time blocks.
- Use small time units, so motorists can avoid paying for more time than they need. For short-term parking, charge by the minute rather than by the hour; for long-term parking, charge by the hour rather than by the day or month.
- Charge higher rates and use shorter pricing periods at the most convenient parking spaces to increase turnover and favor higher-priority uses. Prime spaces should generally be at least twice as expensive per unit of time as less convenient spaces. For example, in a central business district, charge $.25 for each 15-minute period with a 2-hour limit; at the fringe, charge $4 per day. Adjust the ratio between short- and long-term spaces as needed to optimize use.
- Use a progressive price structure in more convenient spaces to favor short-term users (e.g., charge $1 for the first hour, $1.50 for the second hour, and $2 for each subsequent hour).
- Minimize discounts for long-term parking passes (e.g., set daily rates to at least six times the hourly rates and monthly rates to at least 20 times the daily rates).
- Eliminate unlimited-use weekly, monthly, and annual passes altogether. Instead, sell books of daily tickets so commuters save money every day they avoid driving.
- Eliminate early-bird discounts, which encourage automobile commuting.
- To increase revenues, expand when and where parking is priced rather than raising rates at existing priced facilities. For example, rather than increasing rates from $1 to $1.25 per hour where parking is already priced, maintain the current rate but price more spaces and begin charging $.50 per hour during evening and weekends.
- Use parking payment revenues to fund transportation management associations, business improvement districts, and other services that directly benefit area visitors, residents, and businesses.
- Set parking prices based on transit fares (e.g., set daily rates to exceed the cost of two single fares and monthly rates to exceed the cost of a monthly pass).

- Encourage or require businesses to price parking. For example, allow developers to reduce their minimum parking requirements and increase density if parking is priced.
- Tax parking spaces and encourage or require that this cost be passed on to users. Reform existing tax policies that favor free parking (see the section entitled "Reform Parking Taxes" on page 155).
- If parking must be subsidized, use targeted discounts and exemptions. For example, allow businesses to validate customer parking and provide direct discounts to people with disabilities rather than provide free parking to everybody.
- If parking must be subsidized, offer comparable benefits for use of other travel modes, such as cash-out payments and transit subsidies.
- Unbundle parking so people who rent or purchase building space can choose how much parking is included (see the section entitled "Unbundle Parking" on page 151).
- Lease on-street parking spaces. For example, let residents and businesses lease the parking spaces in front of their homes or shops, which they could use themselves, reserve for their visitors and customers, or rent to other motorists (Solomon, 1995).
- Provide free or discounted parking to rideshare vehicles.

Impacts on Parking Demand and Requirements

Pricing parking is one of the most effective ways of affecting parking and travel demand. Pricing parking can change parking location, destination, mode, travel time, parking duration, and vehicle ownership rates. These impacts vary depending on the price structure that is implemented, the type of location and user, and the relative convenience and price of alternative parking facilities and modes.

Cost-based pricing (prices set to recover the full costs of providing a good or service) typically reduces parking demand 10 to 30 percent compared with free parking. Overall, the elasticity of vehicle trips with respect to parking price is typically –0.1 to –0.3, which means that a 10 percent parking fee increase reduces vehicle use by 1 to 3 percent (Kuzmyak et al., 2003; Vaca and Kuzmyak, 2005; "Transportation Elasticities," VTPI, 2005).

Hess (2001) finds that shifting from free parking to a $6 daily parking fee in downtown Portland, Oregon, reduces automobile commutes by 21 percent. Time-variable rates (prices that vary over time, with higher rates during peak periods), combined with improved travel options (e.g., walking, cycling, ridesharing, public transit, and telework), are particularly effective at reducing peak parking demand. (See Chapter 3 and the references on page 136 for more information on how pricing impacts parking and travel demand.)

Figure 5-14
Paying Directly for Parking

Parking is never really free—consumers either pay directly or indirectly. Paying directly is more economically efficient and equitable, and supports parking management objectives. Newer payment systems are more convenient and flexible and reduce many objections to parking pricing.

Benefits, Costs, and Consumer Impacts

Pricing parking can provide a wide range of benefits, including reductions in parking and roadway facility costs, reduced traffic congestion, reduced urban sprawl, reduced traffic accidents, energy consumption and pollution emissions, and revenues. It allows taxes, rents, and retail prices that currently subsidize parking to be reduced or provides new funds for community services. Pricing parking tends to increase equity by charging users for their parking costs and by reducing the parking costs imposed on nondrivers. Paying directly rather than indirectly for parking tends to benefit consumers overall because it reduces traffic and parking problems, and allows individuals to decide how much parking to purchase, giving consumers a new opportunity to save money.

Parking fees themselves are an economic transfer, a cost to consumers, and a source of revenue to governments. Pricing increases administration and enforcement costs and motorist inconvenience compared with abundant, free parking, although it is often cheaper and more convenient than using regulations to manage parking because enforcement officers only need to pass each vehicle once (to check for violations) rather than twice (first to mark each vehicle and then to check for violations), and motorists can use a space as long as they want, provided they are willing to pay for it. New pricing methods reduce these costs and inconveniences (see the section entitled "Improve Pricing Methods" on page 138).

Suitable Applications

Pricing parking is appropriate for implementation in a wide range of situations, particularly in areas with high land values, traffic and parking congestion problems, or other problems associated with excessive vehicle traffic, and whenever a community needs a new revenue source.

Implementation

Parking pricing is usually implemented by local governments and property owners. Pricing is often administrated by private operators that serve many property owners. When implementing parking pricing, it is usually best to consult an expert familiar with local conditions to identify appropriate pricing methods and rates, and anticipate potential problems.

Current planning practices that result in parking oversupply tend to drive down prices, often to the point that it does not seem cost effective to collect fees. Policy changes to reduce parking oversupply help implement parking pricing. To facilitate implementation, it is helpful to develop an area-wide parking plan that coordinates parking supply, pricing, management, and enforcement activities.

Governments often control a major portion of parking supply and can therefore influence prices directly. Regional planning organizations can help coordinate policies between different jurisdictions so parking pricing practices are consistent in different areas. Parking pricing should generally be implemented with improved user information, enforcement, and other management strategies that address potential problems.

It is important to define the objectives for pricing parking in order to determine how prices will be structured:

- For *traffic* management, peak period prices should be high enough to shift travel modes or times.
- For *parking* management, prices during peak periods and at the most convenient locations should be high enough to shift modes, times, and destinations, resulting in a maximum 85 to 90 percent occupancy rate. If charges are too low, parking supply becomes saturated, causing motor-

Table 5-14
Cost Recovery Parking Fees (Cost Per Space)

Type of Facility	Capital Costs	Annual O & M	Total Annual Cost	Monthly Cost	Daily Cost
Suburban, on-street	$1,700	$200	$360	$30	$1.20
Suburban, surface, free land	$1,500	$200	$342	$28	$1.42
Suburban, surface	$1,955	$200	$384	$32	$1.60
Suburban, 2-level structure	$6,227	$300	$888	$74	$3.70
Urban, on-street	$3,000	$200	$483	$40	$1.61
Urban, surface	$4,083	$300	$685	$57	$2.86
Urban, 3-level structure	$8,694	$400	$1,221	$102	$5.09
Urban, underground	$20,000	$400	$2,288	$191	$9.53
CBD, on-street	$10,500	$300	$1,291	$108	$4.30
CBD, surface	$17,885	$300	$1,988	$166	$6.63
CBD, 4-level structure	$13,846	$400	$1,707	$142	$5.69
CBD, underground	$22,000	$500	$2,388	$199	$7.96

O & M = operation and maintenance; CBD = central business district.

Typical fees needed to recover parking costs in various conditions. These are base values, which must be increased to account for utilization factors (the portion of parking spaces that are rented at any time) and to provide profits.

Source:"Parking Evaluation," VTPI, 2005.

ists to cruise around in search of a space. If prices are too high, parking supply will be underutilized.

- For *revenue generation*, prices should be as high as the market will bear and should at least exceed cost recovery (see Table 5-14).

Prices should vary by location and time (e.g., $2 per hour may be optimal for central parking spaces during business hours, but only $1 per hour during evenings and only $.50 per hour at less convenient locations).

When first introduced, there is often opposition to pricing parking, so it is important to build support and address concerns. Pricing tends to be more accepted if:

- Pricing methods are convenient and structured so motorists only pay for the amount of time they are parked.
- Pricing is implemented in conjunction with improvements in alternative modes.
- Information is provided to users on parking availability, price, pricing methods, and travel options.

- Enforcement is courteous and fair (see the section entitled "Improve Enforcement and Control" on page 178).
- Revenues are used in ways that clearly benefit communities.
- Special groups (e.g., low-income motorists, people with disabilities, and tourists) may be offered discounts or exemptions. These should be targeted and limited so that only a small portion of total parking fees is discounted.

Examples and Case Studies

Below are a few examples of communities that successfully implement priced parking as a way to encourage more efficient use of parking facilities.

City of Aspen

Aspen, Colorado, experienced growing parking problems due to its success as an international resort. In 1991, the city built a 340-space, underground parking structure in the city center but, despite its convenient location and low price, it remained half empty most days while motorists fought over on-street parking spaces nearby. Many on-street spaces were occupied by locals and downtown commuters who would perform the "90-minute shuffle," moving their cars every 90 minutes to avoid a parking ticket.

In 1995, the city began charging for on-street parking using multispace meters. Parking fees are highest in the center and decline with distance from the core. Parking is priced on nearby residential streets but residents are allowed a limited number of passes. The city had a marketing campaign to let motorists know about the meters, including distribution of one free $20 pre-paid parking meter card to each resident to help familiarize them with the system. Each motorist was allowed one free parking violation and parking control officers provided an hour of free parking to drivers who were confused by the meters.

Although some downtown workers initially protested (opponents organized a "Honk if you hate paid parking" campaign the day pricing began), pricing proved effective at reducing parking problems. Six months later, the program was supported 3 to 1 in the municipal election. Most downtown business people now support pricing as a way to ensure that convenient parking is available for customers and to raise funds for city programs (Shoup, 2002).

Employee Parking Pricing

CH2M Hill, a leading engineering firm, began charging employees who drive alone $49 per month to park, while carpoolers parked for free and each employee received a $40 monthly travel allowance. Solo driving declined from 89 percent to 64 percent. Pacific Northwest Bell charged employees who drive alone $60 per month to park, with discounts for carpools. This resulted in only 25 percent of employees driving alone to work, compared with 80 percent for other employers in the area (K.T. Analytics, Inc., 1995).

City Parking Pricing

- *Portland*

Portland, Oregon, has a SmartPark program that favors shorter-term users at municipal parking facilities downtown. Motorists pay only $.95 per hour for up to 4 hours, but $3 per hour for longer periods (City of Portland, 2004).

- *Madison*

When Madison, Wisconsin, imposed a surcharge of $1 per day at four parking facilities, and introduced new shuttle services, 5 to 8 percent of commuters switched to transit (K.T. Analytics, Inc., 1995).

- *Chicago*

Chicago, Illinois, raised fees at municipal lots 30 to 120 percent, bringing them to levels at nearby commercial lots. The number of cars parked declined 35 percent, with no significant increase in parking at nearby lots (Ibid.).

- *Eugene*

Eugene, Oregon, approximately doubled monthly rates at municipal parking lots from $6 to $16 for surface lots and from $16 to $30 for garages. Parking demand declined 35 percent, about half of previous users changing parking locations and the other half switching to public transit or other alternative modes (Ibid.).

- *San Francisco*

San Francisco, California, sets parking prices to favor short-term users and encourage turnover. The city requires that parking rates for 4 hours must be no more than four times the rate for the first hour, and the charge for 8 hours be no less than 10 times the first hour fee. This policy applies to both municipally owned facilities and, through the zoning code, new private parking facilities (Ibid.).

CHAPTER 5 (PRICE PARKING)
REFERENCES AND INFORMATION RESOURCES

City of Aspen & Pitkin County (www.aspenpitkin.com).

City of Portland (2004), *Central City Transportation Management Plan*, City of Portland Transportation Planning Department (www.portlandonline.com/smartpark).

Community Research & Development Information Service (2001), *COST 342: Parking Policy Measures and their Effects on Mobility and the Economy*, European Commission; available online (www.cordis.lu/cost-transport/src/cost-342.htm).

Hess, Daniel B. (2001), *The Effects of Free Parking on Commuter Mode Choice: Evidence from Travel Diary Data*, The Ralph and Goldy Lewis Center for Regional Policy Studies, University of California, Los Angeles; available online (http://lewis.sppsr.ucla.edu/publications/workingpapers/35Hess.pdf).

Kodama, Michael (1999), *Parking Management Handbook; How to Use Parking Management to Better Utilize Parking Resources*, Oregon Department of Environmental Quality, State of Oregon (Salem) (www.deq.state.or.us).

K.T. Analytics, Inc. (1995), *Parking Management Strategies: A Handbook for Implementation*, Regional Transportation Authority (Chicago, IL); available as FTA, *TDM Status Report: Parking Supply Management* and *TDM Status Report: Parking Pricing*, Federal Transit Administration (www.fta.dot.gov/library/planning/tdmstatus/tdm.htm).

Kuzmyak, J. Richard, Rachel Weinberger, Richard H. Pratt, and Herbert S. Levinson (2003), *Parking Management and Supply: Traveler Response to Transport System Changes*, Chapter 18, Report 95, Transit Cooperative Research Program; Transportation Research Board (www.trb.org); available online (http://gulliver.trb.org/publications/tcrp/tcrp_rpt_95c18.pdf).

Shaw, John (1997), *Planning for Parking*, Public Policy Center, The University of Iowa (Iowa City, IA) (www.uiowa.edu).

Shoup, Donald (1995), "An Opportunity to Reduce Minimum Parking Requirements," *Journal of the American Planning Association*, Vol. 61, No. 1, Winter 1995, pp. 14-28.

Shoup, Donald (2002), *Buying Time at the Curb*, Paper 615, The University of California Transportation Center (www.uctc.net); available online (www.uctc.net/scripts/countdown.pl?615.pdf).

Shoup, Donald (2004), *Cruising for Parking*, presented at the World Parking Symposium (www.worldparkingsymposium.ca), Toronto, Ontario, May 2004.

Shoup, Donald (2005), *The High Cost of Free Parking*, American Planning Association (Chicago, IL) (www.planning.org).

Solomon, Lawrence (1995), "On the Street Where You Park: Privatizing Residential Street Parking Will Keep the Lilacs Blooming, the Larks Singing and the Pavement to a Minimum," *The Next City*, Vol. 1, No. 2 (www.nextcity.com), Winter 1995, pp. 58-61; available online (www.urban-renaissance.org/urbanren/index.cfm?DSP=content&ContentID=565).

Vaca, Erin and J. Richard Kuzmyak (2005), *Parking Pricing and Fees*, Chapter 13, TCRP Report 95, Transit Cooperative Research Program, Transportation Research Board, Federal Transit Administration (www.trb.org/publications/tcrp/tcrp_rpt_95c13.pdf).

Victoria Transport Policy Institute (VTPI) (2005), *Online TDM Encyclopedia*, VTPI (www.vtpi.org); available online ("Parking Evaluation" (www.vtpi.org/tdm/tdm73.htm) and "Transportation Elasticities" (www.vtpi.org/tdm/tdm11.htm)).

IMPROVE PRICING METHODS

Description

Much of the resistance to parking pricing results from inconvenient pricing methods:

- Many systems require payment in specific denominations (coins or bills).
- Many systems require motorists to predict how long they will be parked, with no refund available if they leave earlier than predicted.
- Some payment systems cannot easily handle discounts or variable rates.
- Some systems are confusing or time consuming to use.
- Some systems have high equipment or enforcement costs.
- Enforcement often seems arbitrary or excessive.

Better payment methods are available (see Table 5-15). Newer electronic systems are more convenient, accurate, flexible, and cost effective. They can

Table 5-15
Summary of Parking Pricing Options

Type	Description	Capital Costs	Operating Costs	User Convenience	Price Adjustability	Enforceability
Pass	Parkers purchase and display a pass.	Low	Low	Medium	Poor to medium	Good
Time-coded tickets	Parkers purchase a ticket for a certain amount of time (such as 2 hours or a day) with punch out tabs indicating the start time.	Low	Medium	Medium	Poor to medium	Good
Single-space meters	Parkers prepay a mechanical or electronic meter located at each space.	High	High	Mechanical meters: low; electronic meters: medium	Mechanical meters: poor; electronic meters: good	Mechanical meters: poor; electronic meters: good
Smart meters	Parkers prepay an electronic meter located at each space. A detector determines when a vehicle leaves and resets the meter.	High	High	Medium	Good	Good
Pay box	Parkers prepay into a box with a slot for each space.	Low	Medium	Low	Poor to medium	Poor

Table 5-15 (cont.)
Summary of Parking Pricing Options

Type	Description	Capital Costs	Operating Costs	User Convenience	Price Adjustability	Enforceability
Pay-and-Display meters (Figure 5-15)	Parkers prepay a meter, which prints a ticket that is displayed in their vehicle.	Medium	Medium	Medium	Mechanical meters: poor; electronic meters: good	Good
Electronic pay-per-space (Figure 5-16)	Parkers prepay an electronic meter.	Medium	Medium	Medium	Very good	Good
Debit card	Parkers prepay a meter using a debit card. Some rebate unused time.	Medium	Medium	Medium	Very good	Good
In-vehicle meter	Parkers display a small electronic meter with prepaid credits inside their vehicle when it is parked.	Medium	Low	High	Moderate	Good
Attendant	Parkers pay an attendant when entering or leaving the parking lot.	High	High	High	Good	Good
Valet	Parkers pay an attendant who parks their car.	Low	High	High	Good	Good
Automated controlled access system	Parkers pay a machine when entering or leaving the parking lot.	High	Moderate	Medium	Good	Poor
Automatic vehicle identification	System automatically records vehicles entering and leaving a parking area, and bills for use.	High	Medium	High	Good	Good
Global location technology	Satellite-based system tracks vehicle location, which automatically calculates parking fees.	High initially, declining over time	High initially, declining over time	High	Very high	Good

Various systems can be used to price parking. Newer systems tend to provide various advantages.

Source:"Pricing Methods," VTPI, 2005.

accommodate various payment methods (e.g., by using coins, bills, and credit and debit cards, and by cellular telephone or the Internet), charge only for the amount of time parked, incorporate variable rates and discounts, automatically calculate rates for specific times, and are convenient to use. Some can be integrated with payment systems for other public services, such as transit, road tools, and telephone use. Some employ contactless technology, which automatically deducts payment. Newer systems produce printed receipts and record data for auditing, which prevents fraud and increases convenience for customers, operators, and local governments. They can also automatically record data on utilization and turnover, which improves planning and administration.

Alternatively, pricing can be more convenient and secure with parking facility attendants. Some parking facilities use attendants during peak periods and rely on mechanical or electronic payment during off-peak periods. Better equipment maintenance and more courteous enforcement (see the section entitled "Improve Enforcement and Control" on page 178) can also improve pricing (see Figure 5-16).

Figure 5-15
Pay-and-Display Parking

A modern Pay-and-Display ticket terminal accepts various payment options, including credit cards, debit cards, and coins and bills, and accommodates various time periods. This is more convenient than older, mechanical meters.

Impacts on Parking Demand and Requirements

Improved pricing methods make parking pricing more acceptable to consumers and cost effective to implement, which increases the amount of parking that can be priced, and allows more efficient rate structures. Impacts on parking and travel demand vary depending on circumstances.

Benefits, Costs, and Consumer Impacts

Improved parking pricing provides various benefits, including increased convenience, flexibility, integration, security, and cost effectiveness. Most new systems are more attractive and use less sidewalk space than older, single-space meters. Costs include new equipment, training, and user information. Newer electronic systems tend to have higher initial costs but are generally cheaper to operate.

Figure 5-16
Parking Payment Systems

New pricing systems allow users to pay for just the amount of time they are parked, and some allow payment by telephone and Internet.

Suitable Applications

Improved payment methods are appropriate just about anywhere parking is priced, and are particularly important as part of a comprehensive parking management program, for example, to allow more flexible and accurate rates.

Implementation

Implementation requires evaluating, selecting, and installing the most appropriate pricing technique for a particular situation. It is usually best to consult a parking expert when choosing parking payment methods to help identify the best option. If possible, parking pricing methods should be standardized within an area, so one system with a single payment card is used throughout a community for parking, transit fares, and other public services.

When new pricing methods are first introduced, there are often complaints by motorists unfamiliar with the system. It is important to help motorists learn to use new pricing methods (see the section entitled "Improve User Information and Marketing" on page 171). Once users become familiar with the new system, they will generally accept it and help visitors learn to use it as well.

Examples and Case Studies

Many cities and facilities are now converting from older parking payment technologies to various types of electronic systems. Below are some examples.

Italian Parking Payment Smart Cards

A cooperative effort involving parking facility operators and technology companies will promote use of smart cards for paid parking and transit services in Italy. It involves the development of a national smart card standard that secures multiple transactions between driver, e-purse (an Internet payment system), and parking management companies. The public will be able to pay for parking with electronic money at on-street parking terminals or directly from their cars using Europark, an electronic in-car unit. This device accesses the appropriate parking facilities (parking terminal and management system), calculates the duration of parking, and authorizes payment. The card can also be used with Pay-and-Display, parking meters, car park access controls, and other systems. The smart card can be recharged through a fast and simple operation either by using a cash dispenser card via the bank branch terminal, by paying in cash, and via the Internet (Europolis, 2000).

Pay-By-Phone Parking Systems

Many commercial parking operators now use systems that allow motorists to pay by cellular telephone. This is particularly helpful when users want to add time without having to return to the parking facility (e.g., when a business meeting or shopping expedition takes longer than expected).

San Francisco's Commercial Parking Control Systems

Like many cities, San Francisco, California, imposes a tax on commercial parking transactions. To help improve administration, the city mandates that operators use specific revenue control systems that provide a receipt to users and securely record transactions for auditing purposes. This has reduced fraud and increased total revenue collection (City of San Francisco, 2001).

CHAPTER 5 (IMPROVE PRICING METHODS) REFERENCES AND INFORMATION RESOURCES

City of San Francisco (2001), *Revenue Control Equipment Ordinance* (www.sfgov.org/site/dpt_index.asp?id=22619).

Co-ordinating Urban Pricing Integrated Demonstrations is a European Commission program to support urban transport pricing (www.transport-pricing.net/cupid.html).

E-Parking is a project involving the European Union, research institutes, and technology companies to develop Internet-based tools that allow drivers to easily identify parking availability and price in a particular area, make reservations, and pay for parking use (www.parkres.com).

Europolis (2000), *Partnership Will Simplify Parking Payment With Smart Cards*, The Europolis Project (www.obs-ost.fr/en/europolis_project.php).

EXPO1000, *Parking Industry Guide* is a comprehensive catalogue of products and services related to parking (www.expo1000.com/parking).

International Parking Institute provides information for parking management professionals; *Electronic Buyers Guide* provides information on parking pricing systems and consultants (www.parking.org).

ITS International provides information on Intelligent Transportation System technologies, some of which apply to parking pricing (www.itsinternational.com).

Parking Today (2001), "Pay by Space and Pay & Display" *Parking Today* (www.parkingtoday.com), April 2001, pp. 42-44.

U.S. Department of Transportation, Intelligent Transportation System Joint Program Office provides information on programs to develop Intelligent Transportation Systems, some of which apply to parking pricing (www.its.dot.gov).

Victoria Transport Policy Institute (VTPI) (2005), *Online TDM Encyclopedia*, VTPI (www.vtpi.org); available online ("Pricing Methods" (www.vtpi.org/tdm/tdm83.htm)).

PROVIDE FINANCIAL INCENTIVES

Description

Financial incentives provide travelers, particularly commuters, with financial rewards for reducing their vehicle trips or shifting to cheaper parking facilities ("Commuter Financial Incentives," VTPI, 2005). These rewards reflect the resulting cost savings. There are various types of incentives:

- Parking cash-out (commuters can choose cash instead of a parking subsidy) (Shoup, 2005).
- Transit benefits (commuters can choose a subsidized transit pass instead of a parking subsidy).
- Universal transit passes (a group purchases discounted transit passes for all members, such as all students at a college or all employees at a worksite).
- Discounted or preferential parking for rideshare (carpool and vanpool) vehicles.

Impacts on Parking Demand and Requirements

Financial incentives, such as transit benefits and parking cash-out, typically reduce automobile travel 10 to 30 percent, depending on the value of the incentive, the quality of travel alternatives, and other factors. Figure 5-17 illustrates the effects of parking cash-out in one study, indicating a 17 percent average reduction in car trips. The larger and more flexible the incentives, the greater the impact. For example, parking cash-out tends to cause larger auto-

Figure 5-17
Cashing Out Impacts on Commute Mode

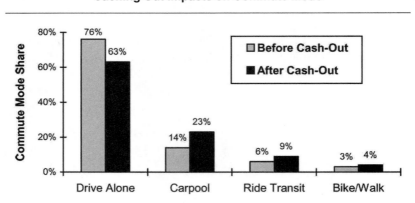

A study of eight California worksites found that parking cash-out reduced automobile commute trips an average of 17 percent.

Source: Shoup, 1997.

mobile trip reductions than do transit benefits because it encourages shifts to a variety of alternative modes including walking, cycling, ridesharing, and telecommuting, not just public transit.

Table 5-16 shows the percentage reduction in vehicle trips that typically results from a transit or rideshare subsidy. For example, a $1 (1993 U.S. dollars) per-day transit subsidy at a transit-oriented activity center is likely to reduce automobile commute trips by about 11 percent; in a rideshare-oriented central business district, the same subsidy would only induce about 5 percent trip reduction.

These vehicle trip reductions tend to increase over time as travelers become more familiar with alternative modes and take these incentives into account when making long-term vehicle purchase and home location decisions. By itself, discounted and preferred rideshare parking is a relatively modest incentive, but it can be more effective if implemented in conjunction with other rideshare encouragement and commute transport management strategies.

Benefits, Costs, and Consumer Impacts

Financial incentives are an effective way to reduce parking and vehicle travel demand, congestion, traffic accidents, and pollution emissions. They tend to increase equity by offering nondrivers benefits comparable to parking subsidies provided to motorists. These benefits are economically neutral if they are funded through parking cost savings. Costs primarily consist of any additional administrative requirements to distribute benefits (generally minimal for businesses with automated payroll systems) and any additional enforcement.

Table 5-16
Percent Vehicle Trips Reduced by Daily Subsidy (1993 U.S. Dollars)

Worksite Setting	$1	$2	$3	$4
Low-density suburb, rideshare oriented	6.5	12.6	20.2	27.6
Low-density suburb, mode neutral	2.5	6.1	11.0	17.0
Low-density suburb, transit oriented	1.4	3.6	6.8	11.1
Activity center, rideshare oriented	8.4	17.0	24.9	31.4
Activity center, mode neutral	4.1	9.4	15.3	21.3
Activity center, transit oriented	0.5	1.2	2.4	4.3
Regional CBD/corridor, rideshare oriented	8.1	14.7	19.6	23.0
Regional CBD/corridor, mode neutral	3.9	8.1	2.3	15.9
Regional CBD/corridor, transit oriented	0.5	1.2	2.3	3.8

CBD = central business district.

Reduction in automobile commute trips that can be expected from various incentives.

Sources: Comsis Corporation, 1993; for the complete set, see "Trip Reduction Tables," VTPI, 2005.

Suitable Applications

Financial incentives can be implemented in any geographic condition, including urban and suburban areas. They are particularly appropriate if an employer has inadequate parking supply, leases parking spaces, or in other ways can save money by reducing parking demand.

Implementation

These incentives are usually implemented by employers as part of a commute trip reduction program. Employers establish rules that employees must observe to receive these benefits. For example, employers should specify the maximum number of days per month that employees may drive to work and still qualify, and how participation will be monitored. Many programs allow commuters to drive occasionally (typically two to four days a month) and still receive full benefits.

Ideally, parking cash-out and transit benefits should equal the value of a parking space, which is typically $50 to $100 per month (see Chapter 4); however, this is sometimes difficult to determine. An alternative is to set these benefits equal to the price of a monthly transit pass. Incentives can be prorated to accommodate part-time participation (e.g., commuters who reduce their car trips 30 percent of workdays receive 30 percent of the full benefit).

Local governments and business organizations can help implement this strategy by supporting other parking management strategies that allow employers to capture savings from reduced parking demand, including reduced and more flexible parking requirements, and transportation management associations to provide parking brokerage.

Examples and Case Studies

Ernst & Young

The accounting firm of Ernst & Young offers pretax commuter transportation and parking benefits to its employees. This is estimated to save employees 40 percent of their commuting and work-related parking costs and reduce the firm's payroll expenses. "Adding commuter benefits to our innovative benefits offerings is just one more reflection of Ernst & Young's commitment to make the firm a great place to work," says Vice Chairman of Human Resources James L. Freer. "When we surveyed a group of employees regarding what benefits they value, a pretax commuter program was the most frequent enhancement by far, with 62 percent of the respondents asking for it. We are pleased to offer such a program that will make our people's commute to work a bit easier." (WageWorks, 2001)

CH2M Hill

Upon moving into new offices in the Seattle suburb of Bellevue, Washington, the 430 employees of the engineering firm of CH2M Hill were offered $40 per month if they walked, bicycled, carpooled, or took transit to work—or free parking if they drove alone. The firm's drive-alone rate declined from 89 percent to 54 percent, while the percentage of biking or walking increased from 1 percent to 17 percent (see Table 5-17).

With parking demand down by 39 percent, the firm's problem of "too many parkers for too few spaces" disappeared. This approach reduced costs to the company, reduced traffic and pollution, and increased tax revenue. The company won the 1999 Commuter Challenge Diamond Award for this program (Commuter Challenge, 1999).

Transit Voucher Programs

- *New York City*

The New York City region's TransitChek program sells vouchers to 6,000 employers, providing more than $25 million worth of transit benefits (Commuter Check, 2004).

- *San Francisco Bay Area*

The Commuter Check program in California's San Francisco Bay Area sells $6 million worth of vouchers to about 700 employers. This has increased transit use an average of 31 percent among those who receive vouchers, resulting in an estimated 17 million miles of reduced automobile travel and $1.6 million in increased transit revenue in 1994 (Ibid.).

Table 5-17
Commute Mode Shift

CH2M Hill Employee Commute Mode	Before Program	After Program
Drive alone	89%	54%
Carpool	9%	12%
Bus	1%	17%
Bike, walk	1%	17%

A $40 per month financial benefit for alternative modes reduced automobile commuting by 39 percent.

Source: Commuter Challenge, 1999.

Parking Cash-Out Programs Sponsored by Local Governments

- *Oakland*

Oakland, California, successfully implemented parking cash-out as a short-term solution to the loss of 88 employee parking spaces due to construction. Employees were offered $40 a month in Commuter Checks to not drive to work at least three days a week. Employees who agreed not to drive to work just one day a week were offered $20 per month. In one year, the program reduced 14,650 automobile commute trips (ICLEI, 1998).

- *Pleasanton*

Since 1994, Pleasanton, California, has offered $1.50 per day to employees who use a commute alternative instead of driving to work alone. The program has resulted in an annual reduction of 20,625 vehicle trips. Before the program was implemented, only 28 employees commuted using alternative modes. Average participation in 1994 was 55 employees per month, which grew to 66 participants in 1995 (Ibid.).

- *Bellevue*

Bellevue, Washington, requires building owners to include parking costs as a separate line item in leases and to charge a minimum rate for monthly long-term parking that is equal or greater than the cost of a bus pass. This makes it easier for employers to determine the value of their current parking subsidies (Washington State Department of Transportation, 1999).

Universal Transit Passes

More than two dozen college and university campuses in North America now offer universal transit passes in order to help reduce traffic and parking problems and improve transportation options for students and staff (Brown et al., 1998).

- *Boulder*

In Boulder, Colorado, a residential transit pass program resulted in a 50 percent increase in transit ridership (GO Boulder, 2004).

- *Santa Clara County*

The Valley Transportation Authority in Santa Clara County, California, offers an EcoPass program to residents (Santa Clara Valley Transportation Authority, 2005).

- *Portland*

Some developers in Portland, Oregon, provide transit passes to all residents, which significantly increases transit use (Office of Operations, 2005).

CHAPTER 5 (PROVIDE FINANCIAL INCENTIVES) REFERENCES AND INFORMATION RESOURCES

Association for Commuter Transportation supports mobility management programs (www.actweb.org).

Association for Commuter Transportation (http://tmi.cob.fsu.edu/act) is a professional organization for employee transportation managers that provides a variety of useful resources.

Brown, Jeffrey, Daniel Hess, and Donald Shoup (1998), *Unlimited Access*, Institute of Transportation Studies, University of California at Los Angeles; available online (www.sppsr.ucla.edu/its/research/UA).

Center for Urban Transportation Research (1998), *AVR Employer Trip Reduction Software*, Center for Urban Transportation Research (Tampa, FL) (www.cutr.usf.edu).

Commuter Challenge (1999), *Diamond Award: CH2M Hill*, Washington State Commuter Challenge Program (www.commuterchallenge.org/cc/daw99ch2m.html).

Commuter Check (2004) works with transit agencies to provide transit vouchers as a tax-exempt employee benefit (www.commutercheck.com).

Commuter Choice—America's Way to Work Program (www.commuterchoice.com) is a nationwide partnership to help employers develop commuter trip management programs.

Commuter Choice provides information on Commute Trip Reduction programs and benefits, particularly U.S. income tax policies related to commuter benefits (www.commuterchoice.com).

Comsis Corporation (1993), *Implementing Effective Travel Demand Management Measures: Inventory of Measures and Synthesis of Experience*, U.S. Department of Transportation and Institute of Transportation Engineers (www.ite.org); available online (www.bts.gov/ntl/DOCS/474.html).

GO Boulder (2004), Neighborhood Eco Pass Program, GO Boulder, City of Boulder, CO (ww.ci.boulder.co.us/goboulder/html/transit/eco_pass/neco/index.htm).

ICF Consulting (2003), *Strategies for Increasing the Effectiveness of Commuter Benefits Programs*, Transit Cooperative Research Program Report 87, Transportation Research Board (www.trb.org); available online (http://gulliver.trb.org/publications/tcrp/tcrp_rpt_87.pdf).

International Council for Local Environmental Initiatives (ICLEI) (1998), *Local Government Guide to Parking Ca$h Out*, ICLEI (www.iclei.org); available online (www.iclei.org/us/cashout).

Office of Operations (2005), *Orenco Station Mixed-Use Development— Hillsboro, OR*, Office of Operations, Federal Highway Administration (http://ops.fhwa.dot.gov/publications/mitig_traf_cong/orenco_case.htm).

Santa Clara Valley Transportation Authority (2005), "EcoPass," VTA (Santa Clara, CA) (www.vta.org/ecopass/ecopass_corp).

Shoup, Donald (1997), "Evaluating the Effects of California's Parking Cash-out Law: Eight Case Studies," *Transport Policy*, Vol. 4, No. 4, pp. 201-216.

Shoup, Donald (2005), "Parking Cash Out," Planning Advisory Service Report 532 (Chicago: American Planning Association) (www.planning.org/pas).

Shoup, Donald and Richard Willson (1992), *Commuting, Congestion, And Pollution: The Employer-Paid Parking Connection*, Policy Study 147, Reason Public Policy Institute (www.rppi.org); available online (www.rppi.org/es147.html).

Shoup, Donald C. (1998), *Congress Okays Cash Out*, ACCESS No. 13, The University of California Transportation Center (www.uctc.net), Fall 1998, pp. 2-8; available online (www.uctc.net/access/access13.pdf).

U.S. Environmental Protection Agency (1998), *Commute Alternative Incentives*, Transportation and Air Quality TCM Technical Overviews, U.S. Environmental Protection Agency (www.epa.gov); available online (www.epa.gov/oms/transp/publicat/pub_tech.htm).

Victoria Transport Policy Institute (VTPI) (2005), *Online TDM Encyclopedia*, VTPI (www.vtpi.org); available online ("Commuter Financial Incentives" (www.vtpi.org/tdm/tdm8.htm) and "Trip Reduction Tables" (www.vtpi.org/tdm/tdm41.htm)).

WageWorks (2001), *Ernst & Young To Offer Its Employees A Transportation and Parking Program Through WageWorks*, WageWorks (www.wageworks.com).

Washington State Department of Transportation (1999), *Local Government Parking Policy and Commute Trip Reduction, 1999 Review* (www.wsdot.wa.gov).

UNBUNDLE PARKING

Description

"Unbundle parking" means that parking spaces are rented and sold separately from building space so occupants only pay for the parking they actually want to use. For example, rather than renting an apartment with two "free" parking spaces for $1,000 per month, the apartment could rent for $800 per month plus $100 per month for each parking space the renter chooses. This is more equitable and efficient since it allows consumers to choose how much parking to purchase based on their individual requirements.

Parking can be unbundled in several ways:
- Facility managers can unbundle parking when renting building space.
- Developers can make some or all parking optional when selling buildings. For example, a condominium could sell with just one space, with additional spaces available for rent.
- In some cases, it may be easier to offer a discount or rebate to renters who use fewer than average parking spaces. For example, an office or apartment might rent for $1,000 per month with two "free" parking spaces, but renters who only use one space receive a $75 monthly discount.
- Minimum parking requirements can be reduced for developments with unbundled parking in recognition that it tends to reduce parking demand.
- Informal unbundling can be encouraged by helping to create a secondary market for available spaces. For example, office, apartment, and condominium managers can maintain a list of residents who have excess parking spaces that are available for rent, and parking brokerage can help lease, rent, and trade parking supply between buildings.

Impacts on Parking Demand and Requirements

Unbundling impacts parking demand similar to pricing parking, as discussed in Chapter 3. Figure 5-18 indicates the reduction in vehicle ownership likely to result from various residential parking fees. For example, a $50 per month parking fee is likely to reduce automobile ownership by 8 to 15 percent, and a $100 per month parking fee can cause a 15 to 30 percent reduction, assuming average consumers and no free off-site parking available nearby. These impacts may vary depending on geographic and demographic factors.

Benefits, Costs, and Consumer Impacts

Unbundled parking increases efficiency and equity, and supports other parking and mobility management programs. The impacts are comparable to parking pricing but usually face less opposition. Unbundled residential parking typically reduces vehicle ownership by 5 to 15 percent, and more where park-

Figure 5-18
Reduction in Vehicle Ownership from Residential Parking Prices

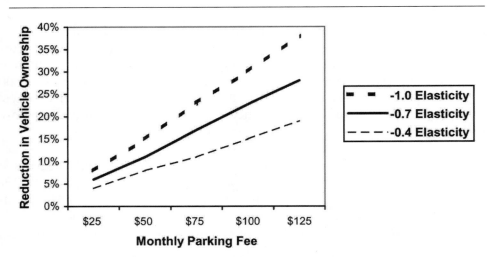

Typical vehicle ownership reductions due to residential parking pricing or unbundling, assuming that the fee is unavoidable (free parking is unavailable nearby).

Source: Based on Table 3-4 on page 40.

ing facility costs are higher than average. Unbundled commercial parking allows businesses that rent building space to save money by reducing parking demand, giving them an incentive to support parking and mobility management programs. For example, employers can use the savings to offer parking cash-out benefits (see the section entitled "Provide Financial Incentives" on page 144).

Unbundled parking may increase administrative and enforcement costs to property managers. It may lead to spillover problems if some renters avoid the fee by parking off site, so additional regulation and enforcement may be needed. Unbundled parking benefits consumers by offering them a new opportunity to save money, and is particularly beneficial to lower-income households since they tend to own fewer than average vehicles and place a relatively high value on financial savings. It is an important strategy for increasing housing affordability.

Suitable Applications

Parking can be unbunbled in virtually any situation where building space is rented, leased, or sold. It can be applied to most types of building space, including residential, office, retail, and industrial. It is particularly appropriate in buildings with parking shortages and where increased housing affordability is a planning objective.

Implementation

Parking is unbundled by individual developers and building owners, but public policies can encourage or require it. Several specific reforms can support unbundling:

- Reduce or eliminate minimum parking requirements for buildings with unbundled parking.
- Require that parking be a separate line item in building leases in order to make the cost of parking explicit to renters.
- Create transportation management associations and parking brokerage services to facilitate unbundling.
- Increase enforcement of parking regulations to avoid spillover problems from vehicle owners parking off site.

Examples and Case Studies

Soma Studios and Apartments

The new five-story building at 8th and Howard Streets in San Francisco, California, combines 74 affordable family apartments and 88 small studios, a childcare center, and a market, providing 246 bedrooms and 24,000 square feet of commercial space on 1 acre. The building contains a 66-space parking garage, 0.38 spaces per unit, with parking rented separately from housing units. Unbundled parking freed up space for the childcare center and neighborhood retail, and significantly reduced apartment rents (Baker, 2002).

Harris Green Redevelopment

In 1997, Victoria, British Columbia, sponsored a community planning project to encourage redevelopment in the Harris Green neighborhood adjacent to downtown. As a result, minimum parking requirements were eliminated there. In subsequent years, numerous condominiums and apartments were constructed; to minimize costs and accommodate the large portion of residents who do not own an automobile, most units are sold or rented without parking. Residents rent parking spaces if they need them. Developers find that they need only about 0.5 parking spaces per unit, as opposed to 1.0 to 2.0 in conventional multifamily buildings (City of Victoria, 2001).

CHAPTER 5 (UNBUNDLE PARKING) REFERENCES AND INFORMATION RESOURCES

Baker, David (2002), *Why it's a good idea to unbundle new urban housing and parking*, David Baker + Partners Architects, (www.dbarchitect.com); available online (www.dbarchitect.com/firm/writing/writing_pdfs/parking_and_housing.pdf).

City of Victoria (2001), *Harris Green: A Neighborhood of Choice*, City of Victoria (www.city.victoria.bc.ca/business/profiles_neigh_harris.shtml).

Nelson/Nygaard Consulting (2002), *Housing Shortage/Parking Surplus*, Transportation and Land Use Coalition (www.transcoalition.org); available online (www.transcoalition.org/reports/housing_s/housing_shortage_home.html).

Russo, Ryan (2001), *Planning for Residential Parking: A Guide For Housing Developers and Planners*, The Non-Profit Housing Association of Northern California (www.nonprofithousing.org) and the Berkeley Program on Housing and Urban Policy (http://urbanpolicy.berkeley.edu); available online (www.nonprofithousing.org/actioncenter/toolbox/parking/index.atomic).

San Francisco Planning and Urban Research Association (1998), *Reducing Housing Costs by Rethinking Parking Requirements*, San Francisco Planning and Urban Research Association (www.spur.org); available online (www.spur.org/documents/spurhsgpkg.pdf).

Shoup, Donald (2005), *The High Cost of Free Parking*, American Planning Association (Chicago, IL) (www.planning.org).

U.S. Environmental Protection Agency (1999), *Parking Alternatives: Making Way for Urban Infill and Brownfield Redevelopment*, Urban and Economic Development Division, U.S. Environmental Protection Agency (www.epa.gov) , EPA 231-K-99-001; available online (www.smartgrowth.org/pdf/PRKGDE04.pdf).

REFORM PARKING TAXES

Description

Parking tax reform includes various changes to current tax policy to support parking management. Major categories of parking tax reforms are described below:

- *Commercial Parking Taxes*

"Commercial parking taxes," which are special taxes on user-paid parking transactions, are fairly common and relatively easy to implement, but they tend to discourage parking pricing since they make free parking relatively more valuable to motorists and are considered unfair since they are borne primarily in urban centers where parking is priced.

- *Per-Space Levies*

"Per-space levies" are special taxes imposed on parking facilities, such as a $30 annual tax on each nonresidential parking space. If applied specifically to employee parking, it is called a "workplace parking levy." This is more difficult to implement than a commercial parking tax since it requires an inventory of all qualifying parking spaces, but it tends to be more efficient and fair since it applies to more types of parking, not just commercial parking.

- *Free Parking Levies*

"Free parking levies" are special taxes imposed on unpriced parking, such as a $50 annual tax per space provided free to employees. They are a variation on per-space levies designed to discourage unpriced parking.

- *Stormwater Management Fees*

"Stormwater management fees" are utility fees based on a property's impervious surface area to fund stormwater management services, such as a $15 annual fee per 1,000 square feet of pavement or a $5 annual fee per parking space.

- *Car-Free Tax Discounts*

"Car-free tax discounts" are property tax discounts provided to households that do not own an automobile, reflecting the lower roadway and traffic service costs that they impose. For example, if municipal roadway maintenance and traffic service costs average $200 annually per vehicle owned in the community, a tax discount up to this amount could be provided to households that do not own a car.

- *Parking Facility Assessment Reforms*

"Parking facility assessment reforms" means that property tax assessments value land devoted to parking facilities at the same rate as adjacent land used for other purposes. With current practices, land used for unpriced parking is often given a low assessment value since it does not directly earn a profit. Charging a higher rate encourages property owners to devote less land to parking.

- *Income Tax Policy Reforms*

"Income tax policy reforms" means that employee parking subsidies are treated as a taxable benefit, employee parking tax exemptions are limited (for example, only $100 per month is income tax exempt), or tax exemptions are provided to subsidies of other modes, such as employer-provided transit passes. Current tax policies make parking subsidies an attractive employee benefit. A typical employee must earn $1,500 or more in pretax income to pay for a parking space that costs their employer only $1,000 to provide. U.S. tax policy makes transit benefits income tax exempt, but other countries have yet to implement such reforms, and many employers are unaware of these options or have yet to offer them to employees.

- *Smart Growth Tax and Pricing Reforms*

Several tax and pricing reforms can encourage compact development and discourage sprawl ("Smart Growth Policy Reforms," VTPI, 2005). For example, development fees, utility rates, and tax rates can reflect the higher costs of providing public services to more dispersed locations, creating additional financial incentives for more compact, infill development. Tax discounts can reward businesses that choose more accessible locations.

These tax reforms may be justified on several grounds. If governments must tax something, parking facilities and activities can be particularly appropriate because doing so helps achieve parking and transportation management objectives in addition to raising revenue, providing what economists call a "double dividend" (additional benefits that result from a policy or management strategy). Parking taxes encourage property owners to reduce parking supply and implement more parking management strategies. Special parking taxes and car-free discounts can be considered a road-user fee: They provide incentives to reduce vehicle ownership and use and therefore traffic problems. Parking tax revenues can be used to fund parking facilities, transportation programs, stormwater management programs, or other beneficial services.

Impacts on Parking Demand and Requirements

Tax reforms can have various impacts on parking demand, depending on the type of reform and the circumstances in which they are applied. To the degree that taxes are passed on to consumers, they increase parking prices, so their impacts can be predicted based on price response information in Chapter 3.

For example, if half of a 20 percent commercial parking tax is passed on to consumers (that is, rates increase 10 percent) and the elasticity of parking demand with respect to price is –0.7, demand will decline 7 percent. This decline in demand may involve a combination of shifts to alternative destinations, modes, and shorter parking duration.

Commercial parking taxes make priced parking less profitable, which can reduce the total amount of parking that is priced. By increasing costs in urban centers (where parking is priced) but not at the urban fringe (where parking is usually free), such taxes may encourage sprawl and increase total automobile travel in the long run. A per-space levy or fee based on impervious surface area gives businesses an incentive to reduce parking supply. In Sydney, Australia, a per-space parking tax reduced downtown parking supply about 10 percent (Enoch, 2001). Taxes that specifically target unpriced parking or parking subsidies can encourage parking pricing. If parking taxes only apply in certain areas (such as a central business district), it may shift business activity and parking demand to other areas.

Benefits, Costs, and Consumer Impacts

Parking tax reforms can provide several benefits. To the degree that it corrects existing distortions that undertax parking and automobile travel, it increases economic efficiency and equity. To the degree that it reduces parking supply and increases parking prices, it supports parking and mobility management objectives, reducing total parking facility costs and traffic problems. A commercial parking tax tends to reduce the amount of parking that is priced and encourage sprawl; a per-space levy tends to increase pricing and reduce parking supply, which supports smart growth.

Tax payments themselves are an economic transfer, a cost to consumers, and a source of revenue to governments. True resource costs include any additional costs to collect taxes, such as additional equipment and time for property owners, operators, and consumers. Taxes on commercial parking may reduce their profits and shift some business activity from urban centers to outlying areas where parking is free. Tax reforms that increase parking prices or reduce supply in a particular area may lead to spillover problems.

Suitable Applications

Parking taxes can be applied in just about any situation where governments want to raise parking prices, reduce parking supply, generate revenue, or reduce vehicle traffic.

Implementation

Parking tax reforms can be implemented by various levels of government. They require careful analysis to identify the best policy to implement in order to achieve planning objectives. Below are recommendations for effective implementation of parking taxes based on interviews with various parking officials (Berk & Associates, 2002):

- The tax base should be broad and well defined. A broad tax base spreads the financial burden and does not give certain groups a competitive advantage. For example, it is considered most equitable to tax publicly owned as well as private parking facilities.
- Exemptions for certain types of facilities (e.g., hospitals and churches) must be well defined and understood by all affected parties.
- Enforcement must be effective and practical and given sufficient priority (see the section entitled "Improve Enforcement and Control" on page 178).
- Taxes should be structured for efficient compliance and auditing. For example, revenue data are easier to collect than data on individual transactions, although new electronic pricing systems facilitate data collection.
- When implementing a commercial parking tax, operators should be required to use a ticketing system that provides receipts and creates secure transaction records suitable for auditing.
- Stakeholders, such as commercial parking operators, should be consulted to insure that regulations, administrative procedures, and enforcement policies are efficient and fair.
- Travel and economic impacts of a tax should be carefully assessed. Establish an evaluation program, with before-and-after analysis, to determine the impacts a tax has on parking supply and pricing, local business activity, vehicle traffic, and parking spillover problems.
- Before imposing special parking taxes, local governments should increase their own parking prices. Commercial operators tend to be more accepting of a parking tax if governments are already maximizing income from other parking-related revenue sources, such as meters and enforcement of parking regulations.
- As much as possible, parking tax reforms should be part of overall parking and mobility management programs and coordinated between jurisdictions in a region.

As mentioned earlier, a commercial parking tax is easier to implement than a per-space levy, but it tends to be inefficient and unfair and must be much higher to raise a given amount of revenue. For example, to raise $1 million annually for transportation improvements, a community could either impose a tax that collects $200 annually from 5,000 commercial parking spaces or a $20 levy on each of 50,000 nonresidential parking spaces. In addition, commercial parking taxes tend to distort parking and land-use markets in undesirable ways, encouraging more unpriced parking and sprawl.

Table 5-18
Parking Taxes in Various Cities

City	Parking Tax
Bainbridge Island, Washington	12% of revenues on both public and private parking facilities
Bremerton, Washington	6% of commercial operator revenues
Burien and SeaTac, Washington	$1 per parking transaction; exemptions for people with disabilities, government vehicles, and carpools
Baltimore, Maryland	$14 flat fee on monthly parking transactions; 11% on daily and weekly parking
Detroit, Michigan	30% tax on airport commercial parking
Los Angeles, California	10% of parking revenues
Miami, Florida	27.8% of revenues
New York, New York	18.5%, or 10.5% for Manhattan residents
Oakland, California	10% of revenues
New Orleans, Louisiana	12% of revenues
Pittsburgh, Pennsylvania	31% of revenues
Santa Monica, California	10% of revenues

Many jurisdictions impose commercial parking taxes for local revenue generation.

Examples and Case Studies

Commercial Parking Taxes

Many cities impose special sales taxes on commercial parking transactions (see Table 5-18).

* *San Francisco*

San Francisco, California, imposes a 25 percent tax on all commercial parking transaction ("any rent or charge required to be paid by the user or occupant of a parking space") (City of San Francisco, 2001). To allow auditing of parking transactions, the city requires commercial parking operators to use certified pricing systems. The city collects nearly $50 million annually and revenue is expected to increase as improved revenue control systems are implemented. Revenues are divided between the city's general revenue, public transportation, and senior citizen funds (Ibid.).

* *Cleveland*

Cleveland, Ohio, implemented an 8 percent parking tax in 1995 to fund a new football stadium. This tax was relatively easy to implement because the city planning department maintains a comprehensive inventory of both public and private parking spaces and their respective turnover rates (City of Cleveland, 2004).

Parking Space Levies

Two Australian cities have special levies on nonresidential urban parking spaces intended to encourage use of alternative modes and fund transport facilities and services:

- *Sydney*

In Sydney, Australia, the levy is AU$800 annually per space in the central business district and AU$400 annually per space in other business districts. This raises more than AU$40 million annually (OSR, 2000).

- *Perth*

In Perth, Australia, a parking levy is applied within the central business district and the immediate surrounding area. When first introduced in 1999, the levy was $AU70 per space and raised in 2002 to AU$155 for short-stay parking, AU$180 for commuter-oriented parking, and AU$77.50 for motorcycles. This raises about AU$8.2 million annually (DPI, 2002).

Perth and Sydney have similar levy collection procedures. The state government's revenue agency sends a parking license application to all nonresidential property owners within the designated area. Owners are required to return the completed application indicating all parking spaces on their property. It does not matter whether or not a parking space is marked. In Sydney, where an unmarked area is used for parking, the number of spaces is determined by dividing the total area, in square meters, by 25.2 square meters. (This formula takes into account access lanes required for off-street parking.) Based on the application, owners are sent an annual assessment. In Perth, the parking license holder is responsible for ensuring that the number of vehicles parked anywhere within the boundary of their property is within the number licensed. Also in Perth, the levy applies to on-street parking. Local governments pay using the revenue generated from their on-street parking operations. Table 5-19 compares these two parking levies.

The Sydney parking levy applies to privately owned, nonresidential, off-street parking and is imposed whether or not a parking space is currently in use. The levy is applied proportionately to infrequently used parking spaces, such as church parking lots, in which case property owners must maintain daily records indicating how often such spaces are used.

In Perth, owners only pay the levy on spaces that are actually in use rather than on the number of potential parking spaces. Owners may change a parking space from one category to another (from "in use" to "out of use" or vice versa) and pay a prorated amount if appropriate for part of a year. The city

Table 5-19
Parking Levy Comparison

Feature	Perth, Australia	Sydney, Australia
Annual levy	Short-term: AU $155 Long-term (commuter): AU $180 Motorcycle: AU $77.50	Central area: AU $800 Other business districts: AU $400
First implemented	1992	1999
Use of revenues	Downtown transit service	Transportation infrastructure
On-street	Not exempt	Exempt
Residential use	Exempt	Exempt
Part-time use	No reduction	Prorated by use
Publicly owned parking facilities	Not exempt	Exempt
Potential parking spaces, not currently used	Exempt	Not exempt
Small businesses (less than six parking spaces)	Exempt	Not exempt
Parking for disabled persons	Exempt	Exempt
Loading zones, including taxi and bus bays	Exempt	Exempt
Community service and emergency service spaces	Exempt	Exempt
Spaces for service vehicles (such as trades and repairs)	Exempt	Exempt
Car sales and service spaces (excludes staff parking)	Exempt	Exempt

Comparison of Perth and Sydney, Australia, parking levy features.

Sources: Enoch, 2001; Parliament of New South Wales, 2000; DPI, 2002.

allows additional parking to be provided for special events that require additional downtown parking.

When first applied in Perth, of 58,500 licensed spaces, about 4,000 were exempt on usage grounds and 2,000 were exempt because they are owned by small businesses. The small-business exemption reduced the number of fee payers and associated administrative costs by a third with little revenue loss. Governments must pay the levy, including 6,000 on-street parking spaces owned by the city.

During the first year of implementation, the revenue agency emphasized education and outreach to property owners and only later applied enforcement. As a result, the noncompliance rate was less than 2 percent after the first year and local business organizations, although opposed to the levy, worked with officials to improve administration and address concerns. Parking supply in the area fell by about 6,000 spaces—a 10 percent reduction. Some small businesses decommissioned parking to meet the five-space limit. As a result of this levy and the reduced supply, parking is generally better managed with less wasted parking and better enforcement, and more pricing and regulation to favor short-stay uses (e.g., shoppers and clients) over long-term commuter use.

Toronto Parking Property Tax

During the early 1990s, a Commercial Concentration Tax of $1 per square foot per year was imposed on commercial properties larger than 200,000 square feet in the Toronto, Ontario, region, including large commercial parking facilities, to fund transit and road improvements (IBI, 2000). Because it only applied to priced parking, and revenues were used to fund projects in other parts of the province, it was perceived as anti-Toronto.

However, some of the largest impacts were on suburban parking facilities, where the tax was relatively large compared with existing parking prices, so some suburban municipal lots and transit Park & Ride lots abolished their parking fees to avoid the tax. The tax had no apparent impact on regional vehicle travel since it caused a relatively small price increase in downtown areas where automobile mode split is low, and caused little or no increase in suburban areas where most parking was unpriced. This tax was highly criticized as unfair because it only applied to commercial parking, its impacts were concentrated in certain markets, and it was repealed after three years (Ibid.).

Workplace Parking Levies

Some European jurisdictions allow parking space levies to raise revenues, increase parking turnover, and encourage the use of alternative modes. For example, local councils in the United Kingdom can charge a workplace parking levy. Employers will be charged a license reflecting the number of susceptible spaces. Employers can decide whether or not to pass the fee on to employees. Exemptions are provided for disabled people, small businesses, emergency vehicles, and parking for motorbikes, scooters, and bicycles. Discounts will be provided to companies that implement workplace travel management plans (Department for Transport, 2002).

Stormwater Management Fees

Some jurisdictions impose stormwater management fees, a utility fee based on a property's impervious surface area to find stormwater management ser-

Table 5-20
Impervious Surface Stormwater Charges

Location	Fee	Approximate Annual Fee Per Parking Space
Columbia County stormwater utility, Georgia	$1.75 monthly per 2,000 square feet	$4.00
Spokane County stormwater utility, Washington	$10 annual fee per ERU	$1.00
Oviedo stormwater utility, Florida	$4 per month per ERU	$5.00
Bellingham, Washington	$5 per month per 3,000 square feet	$7.00

ERU = equivalent runoff unit, 3,200 square foot impervious surface.

Source: Project Clean Water, 2004.

vices (see Table 5-20). These fees range from about $1 to $7 annually per off-street parking space.

Employee Parking Tax Exemptions

In the U.S., up to $180 per month worth of employee parking and up to $100 per month in transit benefits is income tax exempt (Commuter Choice, 2005). This is considered more balanced than the previous policy of all parking being tax exempt and all transit benefits being taxable. Making transit benefits tax exempt has motivated many employers to offer subsidized transit passes in addition to free parking (Ibid.).

In Canada, transit benefits are taxable as income, so few employers offer them (employees would just as well receive cash), while free or subsidized employee parking is common (employee parking is officially a taxable benefit, but this is not generally applied or parking benefits are taxed with a low assessment value). There are current efforts to make transit benefits federal income tax exempt in Canada (CUTA, 2002). One study concluded that it is one of the most cost-effective emission reduction strategies available to the federal government (IBI, 2000). Various European countries are considering tax reforms to discourage employee parking subsidies and encourage use of other commute modes (Wang and Sharples, 1999; TNO Inro, 2001).

CHAPTER 5 (REFORM PARKING TAXES)
REFERENCES AND INFORMATION RESOURCES

Berk & Associates (2002), *Parking Tax Analysis: An Assessment of the Potential Implications of Implementing a Commercial Parking Tax in the City of Seattle*, City of Seattle (www.cityofseattle.net); available online (www.cityofseattle.net/transportation/pdf/SeattleParkingTaxFinalReport.pdf).

Canadian Urban Transportation Association (CUTA) (2002), *Tax-exempt transit benefits: The case for action—now!*, CUTA (www.cutaactu.ca); available online (www.cutaactu.ca/pdf/IssuePaperSpec2ENG.pdf).

City of Cleveland (2004), *Administrative Code—Taxation, Chapter 196—Parking Facility Tax*, City of Cleveland (http://caselaw.lp.findlaw.com/clevelandcodes/cco_part1_196.html).

City of San Francisco (2001), *San Francisco Commercial Parking Tax* (San Francisco, CA) (www.ci.sf.ca.us).

Commuter Choice (2005) provides information on Commute Trip Reduction programs and benefits, particularly U.S. income tax policies related to commuter benefits (www.commuterchoice.com).

Department for Planning and Infrastructure (DPI) (2002), *Licensed Parking in Perth: A guide for commercial property owners about licensing their parking bays*, DPI, Government of Western Australia (www.dpi.wa.gov.au); available online (www.dpi.wa.gov.au/planning/parking/guide.pdf).

Department for Transport (2002), *Road User Changes and Workplace Parking Levy Regulations* (www.dft.gov.uk).

Enoch, Marcus (2001), "Workplace parking charges Down Under," *Traffic Engineering & Control*, Vol. 42, No. 10, November 2001, pp. 357-360; available online (http://eeru.open.ac.uk/staff/marcus/Workplace%20parking.PDF).

Feitelson, Eran and Orit Rotem (2004), "The Case for Taxing Surface Parking," *Transportation Research Part D*, Vol. 9, Issue 4, Elsevier (www.elsevier.com/locate/trd), July 2004, pp. 319-333.

IBI (2000), *Transit-Supportive Parking Policies: North American Experience and Model Policies for Municipalities*, Canadian Urban Transit Association (Toronto, Ontario) (www.cutaactu.on.ca).

Office of State Revenue (OSR) (2000), *Parking Space Levy*, Office of State Revenue, New South Wales Treasury (Sydney, Australia) (www.osr.nsw.gov.au).

Parliament of New South Wales (2000), *Parking Space Levy Amendment Bill 2000*, Parliament of New South Wales (Sydney, Australia) (www.parliament.nsw.gov.au).

Project Clean Water (2004) provides information on surface water management strategies (www.projectcleanwater.org).

TNO Inro (2001), *The Fiscal Taxation of the Company Parking Space: A Study of the Opportunities, Feasibility and Possible Effects*, Department of Traffic & Transport, TNO Inro (Delft, The Netherlands) (www.inro.tno.nl).

Victoria Transport Policy Institute (VTPI) (2005), *Online TDM Encyclopedia*, VTPI (www.vtpi.org); available online ("Parking Pricing" (www.vtpi.org/tdm/tdm26.htm) and "Smart Growth Policy Reforms" (www.vtpi.org/tdm/tdm95.htm)).

Wang, T. and J. Sharples (1999), *Workplace Parking Levy*, TRL 399, Transport Research Laboratory (Wokingham, Berkshire, United Kingdom) (www.trl.co.uk) for the Chartered Institute of Transport and the Royal Town Planning Institute.

PROVIDE BICYCLE FACILITIES

Description

Bicycle parking, storage, and shower/changing rooms (collectively called "end-of-trip facilities") increase the convenience and security of cycling. Bicycle parking can sometimes substitute for a portion of automobile parking.

Optimal bicycle parking supply depends on the level of cycling activity in an area and the type of destination. Some destinations, such as schools, campuses, and recreation centers, have 10 to 20 percent of visitors who arrive by bicycle (at least during fair weather). Table 5-21 shows examples of bicycle parking requirements, but these should be adjusted to meet specific conditions. To determine whether additional bicycle parking may be needed, observe entrance areas to see if bicycles are frequently locked to posts and trees—an indication that bicycle parking facilities are inadequate, either because there are too few bicycle racks or because existing bike racks are not well designed or located. Survey cyclists and potential cyclists to determine what type of facilities they prefer.

It is important that bicycle facilities have appropriate design, construction, and maintenance, or cyclists will refuse to use them. There are two general categories of bicycle parking requirements:

- *Short-term* (Class II) parking is needed where bicycles will be left for short stops. It should be located as close to destinations as possible. At least some short-term bicycle parking should be protected from the weather (a portion can be unprotected, since demand tends to increase during dry weather).
- *Long-term* (Class I) parking is designed to accommodate bicycles that will be left for extended periods. It requires a high degree of security and weather protection with well-designed racks in covered areas, lockers, storage rooms, or fenced areas with restricted access (see Figure 5-19).

Most destinations require some long-term (Class I) bike storage for employees and residents and some short-term (Class II) racks for customers and visitors. Locate bicycle parking where it is convenient to use, secure, visible, protected from weather, and has adequate clearance. Do not locate bicycle racks where they block pedestrian or vehicle traffic or fire hydrants. Adequate lighting and surveillance are essential for security. Bicycle racks and lockers must be well anchored to the ground to avoid vandalism and theft.

Sometimes a single bicycle storage or changing facility can serve several destinations. For example, a downtown gym can open early so bicycle commuters can shower before arriving at work; a building with a large central bicycle storage area may be managed to accommodate cyclists who work at various nearby locations.

Table 5-21
Typical Minimum Bicycle Parking Requirements

Type of Establishment	Minimum Number of Bicycle Parking Spaces
Primary or secondary school	10% of the number of students plus 3% of the number of employees
College or university classrooms	6% of the number of students plus 3% of the number of employees
Dorms, fraternities, and sororities	One space per three residents
Commercial (retail or office)	One space per 3,000 square feet of commercial space or 5% to 10% of the number of automobile spaces
Sport and recreation centers	10% to 20% of the number of automobile spaces
Movie theaters or restaurants	5% to 10% of the number of automobile spaces
Industrial	2% to 5% of the number of automobile spaces
Multiunit housing	One space per one to two apartments
Public transit stations	Varies, depending on usage

Typical minimum bicycle parking requirements, which should be adjusted to reflect the needs of specific locations.

Sources: "Bicycle Parking," VTPI, 2005; Davidson and Dolnick, 2002.

Figure 5-19
Bicycle Parking

It is important to provide suitable bicycle parking at destinations, such as schools, recreational centers, and worksites. Long-term (Class I) bicycle parking should be secure and covered from the weather.

Source: Peter van der Waerden.

Impacts on Parking Demand and Requirements

If bicycle use is constrained by inadequate storage or opportunity to change clothes, end-of-trip facility improvements can increase cycling and reduce automobile trips. Cycling tends to be most common during mild weather. Where this coincides with a destination's peak parking demand, bicycle parking improvements may reduce parking requirements. In some situations, 5 to 15 percent of peak-period trips will shift to cycling if adequate facilities are provided—particularly if implemented as part of a comprehensive bicycle program that improves cycling conditions and encourages bicycle use.

Benefits, Costs, and Consumer Impacts

Quality bicycle parking and other end-of-trip facilities make cycling more convenient and secure. This can reduce automobile travel and parking demand and provide various benefits associated with shifts from motorized to nonmotorized travel, including reduced traffic congestion and pollution emissions, and improved public health. Costs include space requirements, and construction and maintenance expenses, which can be offset by reduced automobile parking costs. Consumers benefit from improved travel options, increased convenience and security, and various user benefits from shifts from driving to cycling, such as improved physical fitness and enjoyment.

Suitable Applications

Many destinations can benefit from improved bicycle parking and changing facilities, particularly in areas with high potential levels of bicycling. Transportation terminals (e.g., train and bus stations), schools, campuses, employment centers, recreation centers, multifamily housing, and commercial districts are all suitable candidates.

Implementation

Bicycle parking can be provided as part of parking facilities or through a special bicycle planning program. The following activities can support bicycle facility implementation:

- Establish minimum bicycle parking standards in zoning codes and allow bicycle parking to substitute for a portion of required automobile parking.
- Provide well-protected, long-term bicycle parking for commuters, residents, or anywhere else cyclists will leave a bicycle for several hours.
- Provide long-term bicycle storage in transportation terminals, such as in train and bus stations and at Park & Ride lots.
- Provide changing facilities for bicycle commuters.
- Provide information to developers, designers, and facility managers concerning best practices for bicycle parking facility planning and design.

Examples and Case Studies

Required Bicycle Parking

The following requirements are incorporated in the Grand Rapids, Michigan, zoning code: "Bicycle parking shall be provided in conjunction with new automobile parking facilities. Any new facility providing parking for more than fifty (50) automobiles shall provide bicycle parking at a rate of one bicycle parking space for each forty (40) automobile spaces, with a minimum of six (6) spaces. In lieu of providing bicycle parking within the parking facility, the owner may provide bicycle parking at an alternative location well suited to meet the needs of potential users. Public parking facilities designed to provide remote employee parking on the fringe of the district shall be exempt from this requirement." (City of Grand Rapids, 1998)

Vancouver Bicycle Parking Requirements

"Requirement for Shower/Change Rooms" (By-law 7481) in Vancouver, British Columbia, specifies the number of water closets (toilets), wash basins, and showers required at a new building, based on the number of bicycle racks required (City of Vancouver, 2003) (see Table 5-22).

Parkade Bicycle Parking

Victoria, British Columbia, owns seven downtown parkades (multistory parking facilities). Each has an area set aside for bicycle parking with secure bicycle racks and some have individual bicycle storage lockers available for rent by the month. These bicycle parking areas are located near entranceways where they are visible to parking attendants (most parkades are staffed during the day and evenings), police patrols, and by-passers. They occupy otherwise unused space, providing secure, covered bicycle storage suitable for downtown commuters, shoppers, and tourists at minimal cost.

Rail Station Bicycle Parking

The United Kingdom Department for Transport has established guidelines and programs for improving bicycle parking at transportation terminals and commercial centers. Improving bicycle storage has significantly increased the amount of cycling to such destinations. In Hampshire and Glasgow, cycle trips increased 600 to 800 percent after secure bicycle parking was installed at train stations (Department for Transport, 2003).

Table 5-22
Vancouver Shower/Change Rooms

Required Class A Bike Spaces	Minimum Number for Each Sex		
	Water Closets	Wash Basins	Showers
0-3	0	0	0
4-29	1	1	1
30-64	2	1	2
65-94	3	2	3
95-129	4	2	4
130-159	5	3	5
160-194	6	3	6
Over 194	6 plus 1 for each additional 30 bike spaces or part thereof	3 plus 1 for each additional 30 bike spaces or part thereof	6 plus 1 for each additional 30 bike spaces or part thereof

Minimum number of water closets, wash basins, and showers that must be provided for use by cyclists at new developments in the City of Vancouver, British Columbia.

Source: City of Vancouver, 2003.

CHAPTER 5 (PROVIDE BICYCLE FACILITIES)
REFERENCES AND INFORMATION RESOURCES

Analysis and Development Of New Insight into Substitution (1999), *Best Practice to Promote Cycling and Walking* and *How to Substitute Short Car Trips by Cycling and Walking*, Analysis and Development Of New Insight into Substitution of short car trips by cycling and walking, Transport RTD Program, European Union; available online (www.cordis.lu/transport/src/adonisrep.htm).

Association of Pedestrian and Bicycle Professionals (2002), *Bicycle Parking Guidelines*, Association of Pedestrian and Bicycle Professionals (www.apbp.org), Pedestrian and Bicycle Information Center (www.bicyclinginfo.org); available online (www.bicyclinginfo.org/pdf/bikepark.pdf).

Browning, Rick (1999), *End-of-The-Trip Facility Design Program*, Oregon Department of Environmental Quality (www.deq.state.or.us). This set of excellent information sheets on bicycle parking facilities is available online at the Victoria Transport Policy Institute Web site: "Installing Secure & Convenient Bike Racks" (www.vtpi.org/bp1.pdf); "Providing Covered Bike Parking" (www.vtpi.org/bp2.pdf); "Bike Parking in Public Areas" (www.vtpi.org/bp3.pdf); "Indoor Bicycle Parking" (www.vtpi.org/bp4.pdf); and "Lockers, Showers & Changing Rooms" (www.vtpi.org/bp5.pdf).

City of Grand Rapids (1998), *City Code, Article 16. C-3 Central Business District, Sec. 5.167. Transportation and Parking* (Grand Rapids, MI) (http://library4.municode.com).

City of Portland Office of Transportation (2004), *Bicycle Parking Facilities Guidelines,* City of Portland Office of Transportation (www.trans.ci.portland.or.us); available online (www.trans.ci.portland.or.us/bicycles/parkguide.htm).

City of Vancouver (2003), *Bicycle Parking Design Supplement* and *Requirement for Shower/Change Rooms* (By-law 7481), Community Services (Vancouver, BC) (www.city.vancouver.bc.ca); available online (www.city.vancouver.bc.ca/engsvcs/parking/admin/developers.htm).

Davidson, Michael and Fay Dolnick (2002), *Parking Standards,* Planning Advisory Service Report 510/511, American Planning Association (Chicago, IL) (www.planning.org).

Department for Transport (2003), "Parking and Security," *National Cycling Strategy* (www.nationalcyclingstrategy.org.uk); available online (www.nationalcyclingstrategy.org.uk/parking_and_security.html).

Litman, Todd et al. (2002), *Pedestrian and Bicycle Planning: A Guide to Best Practices,* Victoria Transport Policy Institute (www.vtpi.org); available online (www.vtpi.org/nmtguide.doc).

National Center for Bicycling & Walking provides extensive resources for bicycle and pedestrian planning (www.bikewalk.org).

Pedestrian and Bicycle Information Center provides information on nonmotorized transport planning and programs (www.bicyclinginfo.org).

U.S. Department of Transportation, Federal Highway Administration (1998), *Implementing Bicycle Improvements at the Local Level,* U.S. Department of Transportation, Federal Highway Administration (www.fhwa.dot.gov); available online (http://safety.fhwa.dot.gov/fourthlevel/pdf/LocalBike.pdf).

Victoria Transport Policy Institute (VTPI) (2005), *Online TDM Encyclopedia,* VTPI (www.vtpi.org); available online ("Bicycle Parking" (www.vtpi.org/tdm/tdm85.htm)).

III. SUPPORT STRATEGIES

IMPROVE USER INFORMATION AND MARKETING

Description

"User information" refers to information provided to travelers about parking availability, regulations, price, and alternative travel options. Many parking problems result in part from inadequate user information. User information can be provided by signs (see Figure 5-20), maps, brochures, Web sites, and electronic guidance systems. Some systems provide real-time information (systems that indicate exactly where parking spaces are available at the current time).

Figure 5-20
Parking Facility Directional Sign

This sign lets motorists know where parking is available.

Figure 5-21 illustrates one creative way of making parking information available: by covering traffic signal switch boxes and other appropriate street furniture with maps showing the location of parking facilities and local attractions.

Parking information can be incorporated into visitor materials, such as event announcements, yellow pages, and newspaper advertisements. Local governments can produce brochures and Web sites that identify the location of parking facilities, indicate parking prices, describe parking planning and management activities, explain parking regulations, describe opportunities for citizen involvement, and answer other common questions about parking issues. Destinations, such as commercial centers, hospitals, and campuses, can produce an "access guide" (a document that provides concise, customized information on how to reach a particular destination, such as a hospital, campus, or business district, including information on parking options) ("Multi-Modal Access Guides," VTPI, 2005). All materials should have parking program contact information, such as a telephone number or Web site.

"Intelligent Transportation Systems" (various communication technologies used to improve transportation services) can provide useful parking informa-

Figure 5-21
Parking Information Posted on Switch Box

Maps showing the location of downtown attractions, including parking facilities, are pasted on traffic signal switch boxes in downtown Victoria, British Columbia.

tion, including changeable signs and in-vehicle guidance systems that indicate parking location, availability, and price in a particular area. Some use sensors that determine which spaces are occupied, allowing signs and guidance systems to indicate where parking is currently available (see Figure 5-22). The 511 area code number is reserved for transportation information, including parking services, traffic reports, and transit information.

User information is one component of marketing. "Marketing" is a general term for activities to determine consumer needs and preferences, and provide suitable services, information, and encouragement to help achieve an objective. Parking management marketing activities involve studies to help understand motorists' needs, preferences, and attitudes regarding parking options, and to identify opportunities for changing parking and travel behavior ("TDM Marketing," VTPI, 2005). Market studies can help planners anticipate and address possible objections to parking management strategies. It is important to educate the public about the full costs of expanding parking supply, and the full benefits of parking management programs in order to build community support for parking innovations.

Figure 5-22
Parking Sign with "Full" Indicator

This Victoria, British Columbia, sign shows the location of a parking facility and indicates when it is full.

Impacts on Parking Demand and Requirements

Improved user information can increase the effective parking supply serving a destination, often by 5 to 15 percent, reflecting parking facilities that are inefficiently used because motorists lack information about their parking and travel options. Improved user information and marketing are critical to the success of most parking management programs. Impacts on parking and travel demand depend on the type of information provided, which other parking management strategies are implemented, and the specific circumstances in which it is applied.

Benefits, Costs, and Consumer Impacts

Improved information can increase motorist convenience, shift where people park, make more efficient use of available parking supply, and help shift modes. It can help expand the range of parking facilities that serve a destination, reduce vehicle mileage and driving costs caused by motorists searching for parking (in some congested areas, a significant portion of vehicle traffic is cruising for a parking space), and increase the effectiveness of other parking management strategies. Consumers benefit significantly from improved parking information. It reduces their frustration and costs and lets consumers decide which option best suits their needs. Costs include planning, production, and maintenance of information resources.

Suitable Applications

Information and marketing are critical to the success of most parking management programs. They are particularly important where some parking spaces are underused because they are not visible to potential users, when new regulations or pricing technologies are introduced, to promote alternative travel modes, or when any other new management strategy is implemented. Directional information is also important within parking facilities, including information on the location of available spaces in large parking facilities, and wayfinding information for people when they leave their vehicles.

Implementation

Parking user information can be provided by governments, business organizations, and individual businesses. Establish a transportation and parking information plan that identifies what information users need, what types of information should be provided, and how the materials will be produced and distributed. Survey users to determine their parking and travel problems and to learn about what types of information resources they prefer. Since marketing is a specialized field, it is often appropriate to hire a consultant or expert staff to help plan and implement the marketing component of a parking management program.

Transportation and parking information can be incorporated into maps, visitor brochures, and invitations. All staff members who work with clients and visitors should be familiar with these travel information resources. Below are recommendations for effective information materials:

- Design user information materials to support parking management strategies. For example, brochures and maps can indicate parking regulations, pricing, where and when parking facilities are shared, off-site and overflow parking options, walking directions, travel alternatives, and enforcement practices.
- Materials indicating parking restrictions ("You can't park here") should also include information on parking availability ("You may park there").
- Produce special notices to discourage unwanted use of specific parking spaces. For example, downtown associations can produce reminders to put on the windshields of employees' vehicles using customer parking, and neighborhood associations can produce warnings for nonresident vehicles parked in resident-only spaces.
- All materials should be updated as needed to reflect changing conditions, and have a publication date clearly indicated.
- Include parking program contact information, such as telephone numbers and Web sites, in all information materials.

Examples and Case Studies

Parking Maps and Brochures

Many downtowns or other commercial centers produce maps, brochures, and Web site information on parking facility location, regulations, and prices. For example, the Eugene, Oregon, Diamond Parking Lot Map, produced by the downtown association and a private parking operator, is an online map showing the location and price of public and private parking lots. Users can also purchase parking permits on the Web site.

Parking Program Web Sites

Many cities, campuses, and business associations have parking information Web sites. A good example is the Seattle, Washington, parking program Web site, which begins with the question, "How May We Serve You?" and provides information on parking regulations and enforcement, payment options, how to use new payment machines, neighborhood parking planning and management activities, parking studies and plans, parking permits, and program staff contact information (City of Seattle Parking Resources, 2005).

Parking Search

Parking Search is a private company that offers parking space brokerage throughout the U.S. The company maintains a national database of parking

Figure 5-23
Electronic Sign with Real-Time
Information on Parking Availability

New, variable electronic signs can provide real-time information on parking availability and price.

Source: Signal-Technologies Inc.

spaces that enable buyers or renters to quickly locate those that meet their needs. The site's search engine allows users to quickly locate available parking spots for sale or rent in a particular geographic area. Users specify the city and state (or zip code), the transaction type (sale, lease, or sublease), and the price range, and receive a report listing available properties (Parking Search, 2005).

Variable Signs

Electronic signs along roadways and at parking facility entranceways can provide real-time information on current parking availability and prices. Some rely on sensors that automatically track which parking spaces are occupied, indicating to motorists where parking is available (see Figure 5-23).

CHAPTER 5 (IMPROVE USER INFORMATION AND MARKETING)
REFERENCES AND INFORMATION RESOURCES

Barr, Mary (1998), *Downtown Parking Made Easy*, Downtown Research & Development Center (New York) (www.downtowndevelopment.com).

Chartered Institute of Logistics and Transport (1999), *Netting More Passengers: The fundamentals of travel information on the web*, Chartered Institute of Logistics and Transport (www.iolt.org.uk); available online (www.trg.soton.ac.uk/news-features/ilt-web/report.pdf).

City of Seattle Parking Resources (2005) (www.ci.seattle.wa.us/html/citizen/parking.htm) is a Web site that provides comprehensive information on parking options, services, and programs in the City of Seattle.

Department for Transport (2002), *A Review of the Effectiveness of Personlised Journey Planning Techniques*, Local Transport, UK Department for Transport (London) (www.local-transport.dft.gov.uk).

Diamond Parking Lot Map is a government and private enterprise partnership for better community parking (www.adeptcomputers.com/diamond/map.html).

Edwards, John D. (1994), *Parking: The Parking Handbook for Small Communities*, Institute of Transportation Engineers (Washington, DC) (www.ite.org) and National Main Street Center (Washington, DC) (www.mainstreet.org).

E-Parking is a project involving the European Union, research institutes, and technology companies to develop Internet-based tools that allow drivers to easily identify parking availability and price in a particular area, make reservations, and pay for parking use (www.parkres.com).

Information and Publicity Helping the Objective of Reducing Motorized Mobility is an organization that supports mobility management marketing efforts (www.wmin.ac.uk/transport/inphormm/inphormm.htm).

International Parking Institute provides information and other resources for parking management professionals (www.parking.org).

Parking Search (2005) maintains a national database of parking spots that enable buyers or renters to quickly locate spots with an easy-to-use web interface (www.parkingsearch.com).

Schade, Jens (2003), *The Acceptability of Travel Demand Management Measures*, research project by Traffic and Transportation Psychology (www.verkehrspsychologie-dresden.de), Dresden University of Technology.

Seattle Department of Transportation (2001), *Parking Guide: Simple Ways to Improve Your Neighborhood's Parking*, City of Seattle (www.cityofseattle.net); available online (www.seattle.gov/transportation/parking/parkingguide.htm).

Signal-Technologies Inc. is one of many companies that provide variable message signs suitable for parking facilities (www.signal-tech.com).

TAPESTRY is a research project to develop better communication programs and campaigns that encourage sustainable travel behavior (www.eu-tapestry.org).

U.S. Department of Transportation, Intelligent Transportation Systems Joint Program Office, provides access to federal Intelligent Transportation Systems programs and information (www.its.dot.gov).

Victoria Transport Policy Institute (VTPI) (2005), *Online TDM Encyclopedia*, VTPI (www.vtpi.org); available online ("Multi-Modal Access Guides" (www.vtpi.org/tdm/tdm113.htm) and "TDM Marketing" (www.vtpi.org/tdm/tdm23.htm)).

IMPROVE ENFORCEMENT AND CONTROL

Description

"Improve enforcement and control" means that parking regulations and pricing are enforced more effectively and more considerately. Adequate enforcement is important for many management strategies and to avoid spillover problems. As parking management activities expand, so too should enforcement activities.

To be effective and politically acceptable, the entire enforcement process must be perceived as efficient, considerate, and fair. The need for fines and punishments should be minimized by providing adequate user information and options. For example, motorists sometimes violate parking regulations simply out of ignorance, because they lack the particular coins required by a parking meter, or because they are unexpectedly delayed. Better user information and newer pricing methods can help address these problems, thus reducing violations. It may be appropriate to have exemptions to parking regulations and fines, such as "First Time Free," so the first time a motorist violates parking rules they are given information about parking regulations instead of a citation. It is useful to survey motorists who receive parking citations to determine how their parking needs can be better met and future violations avoided.

New, hand-held data systems allow enforcement officers to track individual vehicles, identifying those that overstay (e.g., commuters who feed meters) and habitual violators (motorists who ignore numerous parking regulations). It is important to have a system to collect outstanding parking fines. This may include use of a wheel clamp that immobilizes a vehicle (often called a "boot"), towing of vehicles with numerous unpaid fines, restrictions on renewing vehicle registrations or drivers' licenses if parking fines are outstanding, or use of collection agencies.

Parking enforcement officers and private parking operators must be given adequate training and clear guidelines on how to enforce parking rules. They should be friendly, considerate, and helpful. Parking enforcement officials and operators should strive to be perceived as helpful community ambassadors. They should provide maps and brochures about local parking options as well as general directions and tourist information.

Parking passes sold or allocated to employees, officials, or visitors should have clear limitations regarding where, when, and by whom they may be used. They should be audited regularly to insure they are used as intended.

It is also important to have effective procedures for enforcing parking management agreements with developers and facility managers. For example, cities may require bonds or impose penalties if a developer fails to implement a trip reduction program or a facility manager fails to support a parking sharing agreement as promised.

Impacts on Parking Demand and Requirements

Improving enforcement increases the effectiveness of parking regulations, pricing, and tax collection. It can reduce abuse of parking regulations and increase turnover, improving the availability of prime parking spaces. Impacts vary depending on specific conditions.

Benefits, Costs, and Consumer Impacts

Improved parking enforcement increases parking management effectiveness, providing various benefits. It reduces parking spillover problems and can increase the political acceptability of parking management programs. Effective enforcement requires adequate financial investment, but these costs may be offset by increased payment and fine revenues, more efficient use of parking facilities, and reduced vehicle and facility vandalism. Improved enforcement benefits consumers overall, although motorists may consider themselves worse off when faced with a citation.

Suitable Applications

Good enforcement is important anywhere parking is regulated or priced, particularly where there are frequent complaints about spillover impacts.

Implementation

An enforcement plan should be part of any parking management program, and parking enforcement practices should be regularly reviewed and updated to reflect changing needs and best practices. Parking enforcement is usually implemented by parking facility operators and municipal governments. Below are recommendations for effective enforcement programs:

- Develop a professional parking enforcement program with clearly established procedures and adequate training and tools.
- Ensure that parking enforcement is perceived as efficient, considerate, and fair. Have parking enforcement officers provide directions, maps, and tourist information, and serve other community functions that create a positive image.
- Educate motorists, residents, and businesses concerning the laws that apply to parking, how these laws are enforced, and how they benefit from effective enforcement.
- Develop a progressive enforcement policy that starts with education and warnings, and then applies fines and towing, if necessary.
- Make fines high enough and enforcement frequent enough to motivate motorists to follow regulations, but not so high to be considered excessive or unfair. Fines should generally be two to five times the daily parking rate. Fines should increase the longer they are unpaid (e.g., double after a week and quadruple after a month).

- Offer "First Time Free" exemptions, so that the first time a vehicle violates parking rules, the motorist is given a brochure explaining local parking regulations and indicating the location of parking facilities instead of a citation.
- Distribute information (e.g., signs, brochures, fact sheets, and Web sites) on parking facility locations, parking regulations, and the consequences of violations (see the section entitled "Improve User Information and Marketing" on page 171). Whenever you indicate where parking is prohibited, also indicate where it is allowed.
- Establish suitable exemptions for parking regulations and fines. For example, determine under what circumstances service and delivery vehicles can ignore parking regulations.
- Establish an effective system to collect outstanding parking fines. Use hand-held data devices to track parking violations and identify vehicles with outstanding violations.
- Develop suitable controls on the distribution, use, and enforcement of parking passes.
- Have a system to quickly identify and remove abandoned vehicles.
- Establish appropriate parking enforcement policies and activities for special events.

Common Parking Mistakes That Result in Tickets

- Overstaying the allowed time.
- Parking at expired meters (purchase a Cash Key to use instead of cash or tokens).
- Parking within 5 feet of a driveway, alley, or fire hydrant.
- Parking within 20 feet of or blocking a crosswalk/corner (marked or unmarked crossings apply).
- Parking in an alley and not leaving at least 10 feet of clearance for other vehicles to pass.
- Blocking a sidewalk (even a bumper is illegal).
- Not displaying current registration tags on license plate.
- Occupying more than one parking space (you must park within the markings).
- Parking on the street for more than 72 consecutive hours.
- Parking in a loading zone and not visibly loading or unloading (simply having blinkers on or opening your trunk doesn't work).
- Giving your permit to another person (if you don't need it, return it).

Source: City of Boulder, 2004.

Examples and Case Studies

Parking Regulation Reminder

Boulder, Colorado, uses notices to remind motorists of common mistakes that result in parking tickets, summarized in the sidebar entitled "Common Parking Mistakes That Result in Tickets."

Inadequate Enforcement in Berkeley

A parking study in Berkeley, California, found a high rate of parking violations. Between the hours of 9 and 5 on weekdays, spaces with 1-hour limits had a turnover rate (number of cars observed over the 8-hour period) of about 4.2; 2-hour spaces had a turnover rate of about 3.5. This indicates that many cars are overstaying legal time limits. Had vehicles observed legal time limits, nearly twice the number of cars could have been accommodated.

Numerous violations were observed (e.g., in the 1-hour metered spaces, 32 percent of the vehicles observed exceeded the time limit and in 2-hour metered spaces, 27 percent exceeded the limit). This high rate of violations is partly explained by poor enforcement and broken equipment. During the survey period, 27 to 37 percent of parking meters were found to be inoperable. Many cars were observed to park for long periods or even all day at these meters. Commuters used spaces with broken meters or, by being aware of enforcement officers' routines, would feed operating meters just before they arrived or wiped away tire chalk marks just after they left. In response to this study, the city is improving parking enforcement (Deakin et al., 2003).

CHAPTER 5 (IMPROVE ENFORCEMENT AND CONTROL) REFERENCES AND INFORMATION RESOURCES

Barr, Mary (1998), *Downtown Parking Made Easy*, Downtown Research & Development Center (New York) (www.downtowndevelopment.com).

City of Boulder (2004), *Common Parking Mistakes That Result in Tickets*, Planning and Public Works, City of Boulder (www.ci.boulder.co.us/publicworks/about/welcome/parking_mistakes.htm).

Deakin, Elizabeth et al. (2003), *Parking Management and Downtown Land Development: The Case of Downtown Berkeley, CA*, University of California Berkeley, College of Environmental Design, City & Regional Planning (www-dcrp.ced.berkeley.edu).

Edwards, John D. (1994), *Parking: The Parking Handbook for Small Communities*, Institute of Transportation Engineers (Washington, DC) (www.ite.org) and National Main Street Center (Washington, DC) (www.mainstreet.org).

Heffron Transportation, Inc. (2002), *Parking Management Study*, City of Seattle (www.cityofseattle.net), September 2002; available online (www.cityofseattle.net/td/plan_parkingtax_study.asp).

Scrutiny Committee (2002), *Parking Enforcement Scrutiny Review: Report of Findings and Recommendations*, Tonbridge & Malling Borough Council (www.tmbc.gov.uk); available online (www.tmbc.gov.uk/assets/businesslinks/Parking.pdf).

ESTABLISH TRANSPORTATION MANAGEMENT ASSOCIATIONS AND PARKING BROKERAGE

Description

Transportation management associations are private, nonprofit, member-controlled organizations that provide transportation and parking management services in a particular area, such as a commercial district, mall, or medical center ("Transportation Management Associations and Coordinators," VTPI, 2005). Transportation management associations can be an effective way to implement parking management programs and reduce total parking demand. Transportation management associations are typically funded through dues paid by member businesses and local government grants.

Transportation management associations can:
- Coordinate parking planning in the area.
- Maintain an inventory of parking facilities to help with parking planning and management activities.
- Perform regular parking utilization surveys.
- Provide parking brokerage services.
- Coordinate shared parking (e.g., help establish and enforce sharing agreements).
- Produce and distribute user information.
- Administrate commuter financial incentives, such as parking cash-out.
- Coordinate shuttle services and other special public transit programs.
- Manage overflow parking programs.
- Provide bicycle parking.
- Deal with spillover problems.
- Provide other mobility management services.
- Advise on parking facility design and management.
- Advise on regulations and enforcement policies.
- Coordinate enforcement services.
- Monitor parking problems.

Transportation management associations can provide parking brokerage (also called "parking banks" or "parking exchanges"), that is, they can help businesses share, trade, lease, rent, and sell parking facilities. For example, they can match businesses that have extra parking supply with nearby businesses that need parking at a particular time, and help develop and enforce sharing agreements. This helps businesses deal with changing parking demands and allows businesses to benefit when their parking management programs free up existing parking spaces. Transportation management associations can also be responsible for monitoring activities to identify potential problems and evaluate parking management program effectiveness. A parking authority or parking management association can provide many of the same services as a transportation management association but with a narrower scope that often excludes activities such as commute trip reduction programs.

Impacts on Parking Demand and Requirements

Transportation management associations provide an institutional structure for parking and mobility management programs. They can significantly improve program effectiveness and cost efficiency compared with transportation and parking management programs implemented by individual businesses. A transportation management association can significantly reduce traffic parking requirements in an area compared with what would otherwise occur.

Benefits, Costs, and Consumer Impacts

Transportation management associations can help implement most of the parking management strategies described in this book and so help achieve the diverse benefits they provide. In addition to supporting parking management, they also support transportation management strategies that help address various traffic problems, including traffic congestion and inadequate mobility for nondrivers. Costs are primarily direct program expenses, which typically average $5 to $20 annually per covered employee, although this varies significantly depending on the services provided. Consumers benefit from improved services and options.

Suitable Applications

Transportation management associations are appropriate for any geographic area where multiple businesses are clustered together. They are particularly beneficial in major activity centers with significant parking and traffic problems, such as downtowns and other commercial centers, large medical and educational centers, suburban malls, industrial parks, and resort areas.

Implementation

Transportation management associations can be created by regional or local governments, chambers of commerce, or managers of large facilities, such as a mall or hospital. A transportation management association may exist within another organization, such as a downtown association or a chamber of commerce. Developers or facility managers may be required to establish and support a transportation management association as part of a congestion or parking problem mitigation program.

Examples and Case Studies

Transportation Management Association of San Francisco

The Transportation Management Association of San Francisco is a privately funded association of building owners and managers that encourages the use of alternatives to single-occupant commuting in order to reduce traffic and parking problems. The association was established in 1989 as a cooperative effort between San Francisco city/county governments and office building developers in the downtown area. It has more than 45 business members and 50,000 individual members who use the organization's services. These services include online ridematching, transit trip planning and referral, a business resource library, comprehensive marketing, surveys, public and community relations programs, interagency relations, and event planning. The organization is run by an executive director who reports to a board of directors made up of member representatives (Transportation Management Association of San Francisco, 2004).

The BWI Business Partnership, Inc.

The BWI Business Partnership, Inc., is a nonprofit, member-run organization established in 1985 to support economic development in and around the Baltimore/Washington International Airport. It promotes ridesharing, flextime, preferential parking, telecommuting, guaranteed ride home services, and other traffic management techniques (The BWI Business Partnership, Inc., 2004).

Parking Brokerage

Several types of businesses provide parking brokerage services (although they do not always call it that), including specialized national organizations, such as Parking Search, local parking operators, and the classified sections of local newspapers and organization newsletters, particularly in large cities where parking is a valuable commodity.

CHAPTER 5 (ESTABLISH TRANSPORTATION MANAGEMENT ASSOCIATIONS AND PARKING BROKERAGE) REFERENCES AND INFORMATION RESOURCES

Association for Commuter Transportation is a nonprofit organization supporting Transportation Demand Management programs (www.actweb.org).

Association for Commuter Transportation (2001), *TMA Handbook*, Association for Commuter Transportation (Atlanta, GA) (www.actweb.org).

The BWI Business Partnership, Inc. (2004) provides transportation management services in the Baltimore and Washington, DC, areas (www.bwipartner.org).

Loveless, Shirley Morrison and Jill Sebest Welch (1999), "Growing to Meet the Challenges; Emerging Roles for Transportation Management Associations," *Transportation Research Record 1659*, Transportation Research Board (Washington, DC) (www.trb.org), pp. 121-128.

Mobility Management Strategies for the next Decades (2001), "Mobility Centres and Mobility Consulting," *MOST News*, No. 3 (http://mo.st), December 2001.

Parking Search is a private company that offers a variety of services, including parking space brokerage (e.g., for a fee, it helps match parking space buyers, sellers, and renters) (www.parkingsearch.com).

TDM Resource Center (1997), *Transportation Management Association (TMA) Profiles*, TDM Resource Center, Washington State Department of Transportation (Olympia, WA) (www.wsdot.wa.gov).

Transportation Management Association of San Francisco (2004), Commuter Resource Site (www.tmasf.org).

Victoria Transport Policy Institute (2005), *Online TDM Encyclopedia*, Victoria Transport Policy Institute (www.vtpi.org); available online ("Transportation Management Associations and Coordinators" (www.vtpi.org/tdm/tdm44.htm)).

ESTABLISH OVERFLOW PARKING PLANS

Description

Overflow parking plans identify the responses that will be applied when parking demand exceeds the available supply at a destination, for example, during special events, peak shopping periods, or temporary reductions in parking supply ("Special Event Transport Management," VTPI, 2005). Below are some possible components of an overflow parking plan:

- Use signs and maps to direct motorists to alternative parking facilities nearby.
- Establish shared and remote parking arrangements, with walkability improvements and shuttle services to connect them if necessary.
- Provide information on parking and travel options for special event participants. For example, when people purchase tickets to a major sport or cultural event, give them a brochure or map showing the location of parking facilities and describing how to arrive by transit.
- Encourage travelers to shift their mode or use remote parking during peak periods. For example, retail employees can be required to use remote parking facilities or alternative commute modes during busy shopping periods.
- Apply special parking regulations to favor priority vehicles (e.g., emergency, service, high occupancy, and disabled) during busy periods.
- Provide special parking and transport services during peak periods, such as shuttle buses to remote parking, and valet parking to increase parking facility capacity.
- Design plazas, courtyards, and lawns so they can be used occasionally for vehicle parking.
- Provide adequate traffic and parking management staff during peak periods. Additional staff may be hired for special events.

Impacts on Parking Demand and Requirements

An overflow parking plan allows parking requirements to be reduced, since many parking facilities are sized to accommodate infrequent peaks (see Chapter 2). The amount of the reduction depends on the degree to which parking supply is oversized to accommodate occasional peak demands, the nature of these peak demands, and overflow plan effectiveness.

Benefits, Costs, and Consumer Impacts

Overflow parking plans can provide a variety of benefits. They can reduce parking requirements, reduce traffic congestion, and improve service quality (convenience, comfort, and safety as perceived by users). Costs include any additional staff time, equipment, and special services required to develop and implement the plan. Consumers tend to benefit from an effective parking overflow plan that reduces confusion, makes efficient use of available facilities, and prevents spillover problems.

Suitable Applications

This strategy is appropriate at any location where peak parking demands create problems. It is particularly useful during special events that attract large crowds, for retail centers during peak shopping periods, for resort communities during holiday seasons, and when parking supply is temporarily reduced.

Implementation

Overflow parking plans are usually implemented by facility managers and special event organizers, sometimes with the assistance of local planning and law enforcement officials. Overflow parking and traffic plans may be required for approval of special events. Facility managers, government agencies, mobility management associations, or private companies may arrange overflow parking areas (e.g., by renting available parking spaces from nearby businesses) and provide shuttle buses and special traffic management services.

Examples and Case Studies

City of Concord

Concord, North Carolina, allows turf areas to be designated as overflow parking areas for occasional use (maximum 10 uses per year) (City of Concord, 2004).

Baseball Fan Transport Management

About half of all fans traveling to the San Francisco Giants' baseball stadium use public transit, due to effective planning and promotion, significantly reducing the amount of parking required. "No matter how you interacted with the Giants, whether it was with our Web site, our broadcasts, whatever, it would have been hard not to have been touched by the message, which was that there were a number of ways to get to Pacific Bell Park and that you were encouraged to take transit," says Giants Ballpark Transit Director Alfonso Felder (San Francisco Municipal Railway, 2004).

Houston Rodeo Express Transit

The Houston Livestock Show and Rodeo in Houston, Texas, is the world's largest livestock exhibit. It attracts two to three million visitors and generates more than a quarter billion dollars in revenue during two weeks of operation at the Astrodome each February. To reduce the traffic and parking problems that it creates, the Houston Livestock Show and Rodeo and regional transportation agencies organize the Rodeo METRO Express, a Park & Ride shuttle bus service that averages 16,000 patrons per day, representing more than 15 percent of rodeo attendance. Buses are given priority access to the Astro-dome, resulting in significant time savings to those who use this service. Adults pay a $2 per round-trip fare and children are free. It has reduced traffic and parking problems, allowing the rodeo to expand and attract new patrons. The program is considered cost effective, with 77 percent of expenses paid by users, and the remainder funded by sponsorships and the Houston Livestock Show and Rodeo (Trout and Ullman, 1997).

CHAPTER 5 (ESTABLISH OVERFLOW PARKING PLANS) REFERENCES AND INFORMATION RESOURCES

American Public Transportation Association (2000), *A Winning Team: Transit and Sports Facilities*, American Public Transportation Association (www.apta.com).
City of Concord (2004) (www.ci.concord.nc.us).
Cronin, J. Joseph, Roscoe Hightower, and Michael Brady (2000), "Niche Market Strategies; The Role of Special Purpose Transportation Efforts in Attracting and Retaining Transit Users," *Journal of Public Transportation* (www.nctr.usf.edu/jpt/journal.htm), Vol. 3, No. 3, pp. 63-86.
Dunn Engineering (2002), *Transportation Management Strategies for Special Events: Synthesis of Practice*, Transportation Management Center, U.S. Department of Transportation, Federal Highway Administration (www.fhwa.dot.gov); available online (www.ops.fhwa.dot.gov/program_areas/sp-events-mgmt/handbook/index.htm).
Litman, Todd (1999), *First Resort; Resort Community Transportation Management*, Victoria Transport Policy Institute (www.vtpi.org); available online (www.vtpi.org/resort.pdf).
Mobility Management Strategies for the next Decades (2000), "Mobility Management for Temporary Sites," *MOST News*, No. 1 (http://mo.st).
Planned Special Events Traffic Management provides information on managing special event traffic (supported by the U.S. Department of Transportation, Federal Highway Administration, Office of Operations) (www.ops.fhwa.dot.gov/program_areas/sp-evnts-mgmt.htm).
San Francisco Municipal Railway (2004), "Routes & Schedules" (www.sfmuni.com/routes/pacbsvc.htm).
Trout, Nada D. and Gerald L. Ullman (1997), "A Special Event Park-and-Ride Shuttle Bus Success Story," *ITE Journal* (www.ite.org), December 1997, pp. 38-43.
Victoria Transport Policy Institute (VTPI) (2005), *Online TDM Encyclopedia*, VTPI (www.vtpi.org); available online ("Special Event Transport Management" (www.vtpi.org/tdm/tdm48.htm)).

ADDRESS SPILLOVER PROBLEMS

Description

"Spillover problems" refers to the undesirable use of off-site parking facilities, such as when business customers and employees park on nearby residential streets or use another businesses' parking lot. Concerns about spillover impacts are often used to justify excessive parking requirements and opposition to parking management strategies. Addressing spillover problems can directly increase parking management program acceptability and effectiveness.

There are several ways to address spillover parking problems:
- Provide information indicating where motorists may and may not park (see the section entitled "Improve User Information and Marketing" on page 171).
- Use regulations to control spillover impacts, such as time limits and permit programs on residential streets near activity centers (see the section entitled "Regulate Parking" on page 78).
- Use pricing to control spillover impacts, such as charging nonresidents to park on residential streets and charging noncustomers for using parking facilities at a business (see the section entitled "Price Parking" on page 129).
- Compensate people who bear spillover parking impacts. For example, a high school can send complementary sport event tickets to residents of nearby streets who experience spillover parking problems.
- Establish a monitoring program to identify when and where parking spillover problems occur. This may include parking utilization surveys to identify who is parking at what location, and hotlines for residents and businesses to report spillover problems.

Impacts on Parking Demand and Requirements

Addressing spillover problems can reduce a major objection to parking management and a common justification for excessive parking supply. Parking requirements can often be reduced significantly if this allows greater implementation of regulations, pricing, and other management strategies.

Benefits, Costs, and Consumer Impacts

Addressing spillover parking problems allows parking management programs to be implemented and expanded, increasing program effectiveness and benefits. Costs include additional planning, enforcement, and management activities. These costs may be offset by increased payment and fine revenues. Many consumers benefit if parking spillover problems are reduced, although some motorists may consider increased enforcement burdensome.

Suitable Applications

Parking management programs that reduce supply, increase regulation, or apply pricing often have spillover impacts that should be addressed. Spillover problems tend to be most significant in areas with limited parking supply and growing demand, such as busy commercial districts and popular residential neighborhoods. Parking spillover impacts are common around major activity centers (e.g., stores, schools, arenas, and parks) and during major events that attract crowds.

Implementation

Parking spillover management programs are generally implemented by local governments or by facility managers as part of an integrated parking plan. Below are recommended actions:

- Establish clear rules concerning where different types of motorists may or may not park.
- Use signs and brochures to inform motorists where they should and should not park.
- Establish effective parking enforcement systems.
- Provide information to neighbors concerning how to report parking violations.
- If necessary, provide compensation to neighbors negatively impacted by spillover parking.

Examples and Case Studies

Christchurch Parking Strategy

The parking strategy in Christchurch, New Zealand, includes several components to address spillover parking problems. Where such problems are significant, the city takes a zero-tolerance approach towards parking infringements, including monitoring, use of fines, and tow-aways. The city applies these measures in both commercial and residential areas and during special events that attract crowds. Where the demand for parking exceeds supply, the strategy gives priority for parking based on the adjoining land-use activity. For example, in residential areas, the priority is residential car parking, high-occupancy vehicles (particularly transit buses), visitor parking, and parking for people with disabilities. Permits are used to control on-street parking in residential areas. In the Central City area, the priority is high-occupancy vehicles (transit buses); tourism vehicles; loading zones; parking for people with disabilities; short-stay, private vehicles parking for business; and commuter parking (Christchurch City Council, 2004).

Houston Residential Parking Permits

The Residential Parking Permit Ordinance in Houston, Texas, provides for the establishment of parking permit areas in residential neighborhoods with documented problems of spillover parking from nearby nonresidential activity centers. If an area is designated a "decal-only" area, only residents with the proper decal on their vehicles are allowed to park along the street during the designated times. To be implemented, a neighborhood organization must submit a petition signed by area residents. Once the area is approved, residents are able to purchase parking permits for their vehicles and their visitors' vehicles to allow curbside parking. With a few exceptions, vehicles not displaying the permit are subject to ticketing (City of Houston Planning and Development Department, 2004).

CHAPTER 5 (ADDRESS SPILLOVER PROBLEMS) REFERENCES AND INFORMATION RESOURCES

Barr, Mary (1998), *Downtown Parking Made Easy*, Downtown Research & Development Center (New York) (www.downtowndevelopment.com).

Christchurch City Council (2004) (www.ccc.govt.nz).

City of Houston Planning and Development Department (2004) (www.ci.houston.tx.us/departme/planning/planning_dev_web/nbhd_svces/decal.htm).

Dunn Engineering (2002), *Transportation Management Strategies for Special Events: Synthesis of Practice*, Transportation Management Center, U.S. Department of Transportation, Federal Highway Administration (www.fhwa.dot.gov); available online (www.ops.fhwa.dot.gov/program_areas/sp-events-mgmt/handbook/index.htm).

Edwards, John D. (1994), *Parking: The Parking Handbook for Small Communities*, Institute of Transportation Engineers (Washington, DC) (www.ite.org) and National Main Street Center (Washington, DC) (www.mainstreet.org).

Heffron Transportation, Inc. (2002), *Parking Management Study*, City of Seattle (www.cityofseattle.net; available online (www.cityofseattle.net/td/plan_parkingtax_study.asp).

Parking Today often has articles concerning enforcement practices (www.parkingtoday.com).

Planned Special Events Traffic Management provides information on managing special event traffic (supported by the U.S. Department of Transportation, Federal Highway Administration, Office of Operations) (www.ops.fhwa.dot.gov/program_areas/sp-evnts-mgmt.htm).

IMPROVE PARKING FACILITY DESIGN AND OPERATION

Description

"Parking facility design and operation" refers to physical layout, construction, and day-to-day management of parking facilities. Parking facilities are a major land use and an important portion of the public realm, that is, public spaces where members of society meet and interact. Improved design and operation can better integrate parking facilities into communities, improve the quality of service experienced by users, support parking management, and help address various problems.

Current parking planning practices tend to emphasize *quantity* over *quality*, often resulting in large but unattractive and inconvenient facilities. Increasing emphasis on quality may mean fewer, larger spaces, with more resources devoted to landscaping, walkways, maintenance, and security. A well-designed parking facility incorporates attractive materials, and amenities such as benches, washrooms, and wayfinding signs. A well-planned parking facility can serve multiple functions, such as being a courtyard and walkway, a meeting and play area, and a flexible space available for festivals and markets.

Parking management both supports and is supported by improved facility design and operation. Parking management can reduce the number of parking spaces requird in an area, freeing up resources for design improvements. Design and operation improvements support management strategies, such as parking regulation and pricing, walkability, and improved user information.

Parking Facility Design Considerations

Below is a brief description of various parking design and operation issues. It is beyond the scope of this book to deal with these in detail. Specialized publications and parking planning experts should be consulted to ensure that current best practices are applied for each of these issues.

- *Access Management*

The term "access management" is used by transportation professionals to describe effective coordination between roadway design and land-use development ("Access Management," VTPI, 2005). This usually includes limits on the number of driveways on major roadways to reduce traffic congestion and accident risk, as well as encouragement for more compact land-use patterns. It supports parking management strategies, such as shared parking, improved walkability, and smart growth.

- *Accessibility or Universal Design*

"Accessibility" (also called "universal design") refers to accommodating people with disabilities and other special needs. Parking facilities should apply current best practices to determine the number and design of spaces reserved for people with disabilities, and design features to accommodate people using wheelchairs, strollers, and handcarts. Information on accessibility standards is available from The Access Board and the U.S. Department of Transportation's "Accessibility—Equal Access to Transportation" Web site.

- *Aesthetics*

Attention to landscaping, building materials, public art, and other design features can improve parking facility appearance, and therefore the overall aesthetics of a site, street, or city (Alexander et al., 1977; Smith, 1988; Childs, 1999). Some zoning regulations require that a portion of parking lots be devoted to landscaping (often 10 to 15 percent) and that visual screening and setbacks separate parking facilities from adjacent land uses (often 10 feet). Parking structures can be designed to enhance the streetscape, for example, by having ground-floor retail and using high-quality materials and maintenance practices. A public review process can be used to gain community input into parking facility design.

- *Asset Management*

"Asset management" refers to policies and programs designed to preserve the value of infrastructure. Parking facilities require adequate maintenance and repairs for long-term durability, safety, and aesthetics. Each facility should have an asset management plan that identifies inspection, cleaning, maintenance, repair, and reconstruction practices. Parking facilities require occasional repainting, sealing, and repaving, and major reconstruction after 20 to 30 years.

- *Flexibility*

Parking facilities can be designed to accommodate changing needs and temporary uses, including storage, recreation, and special events. For example, some condominium residents may want to use their parking spaces for bulk storage or as a work area. A parking lot may be used temporarily as a play area or market. The top floor of a parking structure could be used for an arts festival or café, particularly if it has an attractive view. The following actions can support this flexibility:

- Establish policies that allow temporary or permanent conversion of parking facilities to other uses, provided there is a management plan to address any problems that occur.
- Identify off-peak periods when excess parking can be used for other uses (e.g., operators may determine that parking facilities are less than half occupied during weekends or the off season).
- Publish rental rates for blocks of parking spaces during off-peak periods.

- Incorporate flexibility into parking facility design (e.g., a parking lot should have sufficiently large, flat areas for sports activities or for use as a market).
- Provide infrastructure needed for alternative uses, such as sufficient lighting, electrical connections, and water supply.

- *Heat Island Effect*

The "heat island effect" refers to higher local temperatures that result from sunlight on dark surfaces, such as parking lots, roads, and building roofs. This increases summer temperatures in urban areas (typically by 2° to 8° F), which is unpleasant for parking facility users, and increases air pollution and energy consumption. Such temperature gains can be reduced by limiting pavement area, shading pavement with trees and awnings, using light-colored materials (such as concrete rather than asphalt), and using turf surfaces for occasional-use parking facilities.

- *Preservation and Enrichment*

Parking facilities should be designed to protect and enhance historic, cultural, and natural resources. Parking facilities can incorporate design details and materials reflecting traditional building methods, and include information on unique features, such as a sign describing an event that occurred at that location, or buildings and their occupants previously located at the site. Artwork and design styles can celebrate cultural traditions. A parking lot can incorporate features of previous structures, such as an archway made from the building entrance or a portion of the foundation preserved as a border.

- *Lighting*

Adequate lighting is important for user comfort, safety, and security. Various standards have been established for minimum lighting in surface and structured parking lots (ULI, 2000). It is sometimes important to shield nearby residents from lighting glare.

- *Orientation*

"Parking facility orientation" refers to where parking lots are located with respect to streets, sidewalks, and buildings. It has been common to locate parking facilities in front of buildings, but many planners now recommend locating buildings close to the sidewalk to improve pedestrian access and create a more attractive streetscape, with some or all parking located behind or at the side of a building.

- *Security*

Security (safety of people, vehicles, and facilities) is an important design and operational issue, particularly for enclosed or isolated facilities. Parking facilities can be designed to increase security through natural surveillance (by providing maximum visibility from the street and nearby buildings), lighting, patrols, emergency alarms, and closed-circuit video observation. Special security measures may be needed at certain times (e.g., escort and shuttle services for employees using remote parking facilities).

- *Size and Scale*

In general, several smaller parking lots are more attractive than a single large lot. Large parking facilities can be divided into smaller units with landscaping. Individual bays should generally be less than 100 feet long with 10 to 12 spaces per side. In large parking facilities, zones can be designated by symbols and color codes to help users find their vehicles. Large, surface parking facilities should be located behind buildings and at the edge of business districts, rather than in front of buildings or on major commercial streets.

- *Stormwater Management*

Newer stormwater management and pollution control strategies can reduce environmental impacts and infrastructure costs (Center for Watershed Protection, 2005; NEMO, 2005; Booth and Leavitt, 1999). For example, stormwater runoff can drain into landscaped areas and bio-swales (ditches where water percolates into the ground). Grease traps may be needed to collect pollution. Total impervious surface area can be minimized and tree cover maximized. Permeable surfaces (such as pavement blocks) (see Figure 5-24) and Hollywood driveways (two narrow, paved lanes) (see Figure 5-25) can be used in some conditions, particularly for occasional-use parking facilities.

- *Traffic Calming*

"Traffic calming" refers to various design features intended to reduce vehicle traffic speeds and volumes on a particular roadway or within a parking facility (for information, see FHWA, 2004; "Traffic Calming," VTPI, 2005). A variety of traffic-calming strategies can be used to control traffic within parking lots. Speed platforms and speed humps (which have gradual, tapered profiles) are generally preferable to speed bumps (which have abrupt profiles).

- *Traffic Circulation*

Parking lots can be designed to facilitate traffic circulation. Dead-end lanes should be avoided and multiple entrances should be provided if possible. Traffic patterns should be clearly indicated with signs and arrows.

- *Traffic Safety*

Off-street parking facilities can be designed with features to control traffic speeds, improve visibility, minimize opportunities for crashes between vehicles, and protect pedestrians (Hamilton Associates, 1998). Safety features

Figure 5-24
Permeable Pavement Blocks

Permeable pavement blocks allow grass to grow and water to drain into the ground.

Figure 5-25
Hollywood Driveway

Hollywood driveways only pave two strips.

include adequate aisle and stall widths, clear sight lines, traffic controls (such as stop signs) at aisle intersections, speed controls (such as traffic calming), and separate walkways. Back-in angled parking (on-street, angled parking into which cars park by backing into a space rather than driving head in) tends to be safer than front-in angled or parallel curb parking, since drivers are better able to see as they exit into the traffic lane.

- *User Amenities*

Parking facilities can be designed with walkways, sheltered waiting areas, benches, drinking fountains, kiosks, telephones, bulletin boards, vending machines, and washrooms. Large parking structures can have enclosed lobbies, which are heated in winter and cooled in summer, where customers can wait and transact payments. Some commercial parking facilities offer services, such as washing and refueling, while a vehicle is parked. Parking facilities can have electrical hookups (in cold climate areas for engine block heaters and in other areas to recharge electric vehicles).

- *User Information*

Wayfinding information should be provided in parking facilities (see the section entitled "Improve User Information and Marketing" on page 171). These can include large-scale directional signs for motorists and detailed signs, maps, and brochures for pedestrians. They should be attractive, visible, easily understood and well maintained.

- *Weather Protection*

Parking lots can be shaded with trees and awnings to increase user comfort and reduce pollution emissions from cars. Awnings are important for shade in sunny climates and to protect vehicles from snow and hail in cold climates. A premium may be charged for parking in these covered areas.

Impacts on Parking Demand and Requirements

Design and operational improvements can support parking management programs, which can reduce demand and parking requirements. For example, access management supports shared parking, design changes can improve walkability, and signage can provide user information. Some design improvements, such as larger parking spaces, landscaping, walkways, and ancillary facilities such as washrooms, reduce parking supply. Parking management may be required to allow these improvements to be implemented.

Benefits, Costs, and Consumer Impacts

The benefits of improved parking facility design vary depending on specific conditions. They often include increased user convenience and safety, improved environmental and aesthetic qualities, and increased facility durability and long-term value. Costs can include additional operating expenses and reduced parking supply. Consumers often benefit from improved convenience, comfort, security, and aesthetics, although they may face higher prices or reduced supply.

Suitable Applications

Most parking facilities can benefit from improved design and operations.

Implementation

The first step for improving parking facility design and operation is to shift the emphasis of parking planning from quantity to quality. Parking standards should devote as much attention to parking facility design quality as to the number of spaces required and, where appropriate, allow reductions in supply in exchange for improved design and management.

Implementation requires that planners, developers, designers, and facility managers become familiar with specific parking facility design and operation issues. Best practices can be promoted through education and awards (e.g., an annual Best Parking Facility Design contest for developers and designers, and a Best Parking Facility Operations contest for facility managers). Local governments can apply best practices, innovative designs, and high standards to their own parking facilities and encourage property owners to apply them to private facilities. Design improvements can be required through regulations or encouraged through various incentives.

Childs (1999) recommends designating a steward responsible for the care and security of a parking lot, similar to the manager of a public park. This person can have several responsibilities, including collecting parking fees, enforcing regulations, selling goods from a kiosk, maintaining the facility and its landscaping, providing security, and providing support for alternative uses, such as games and markets.

Examples and Case Studies

Back-In Angled Parking

An increasing number of communities now use back-in rather than front-in angled parking, which provides a number of benefits, including increased user convenience and safety (since drivers can better see traffic, particularly cyclists, as they pull out of a space) and greater ease loading and unloading a trunk or the back of a truck or van.

Tucson, Arizona, has two blocks of reverse diagonal parking on University Boulevard. Prior to this design, the street had parallel parking and experienced two to three crashes each month; in the first two years after back-in diagonal parking was established, there were no crashes. Local traffic engineers attribute this safety improvement to the better view that drivers experience when pulling out of a parking space (Siegman, 2005).

Garage Door Limits

Portland, Oregon, restricts garage doors to 50 percent of the street-facing façade (City of Portland, 1999).

Restrictions on Parking in Front of Buildings

Gainesville, Florida, prohibits parking between the built-to line and the front property line in its Traditional City area (City of Gainesville, 2000).

CHAPTER 5 (IMPROVE PARKING FACILITY DESIGN AND OPERATION) REFERENCES AND INFORMATION RESOURCES

The Access Board is an independent Federal agency devoted to accessibility for people with disabilities (www.access-board.gov).

Access Management seeks to limit and consolidate access along major roadways, while promoting a supporting street system and unified access and circulation systems for development (www.accessmanagement.gov).

Alexander, Christopher et al. (1977), *A Pattern Language*, Oxford University Press (Oxford, UK) (www.oup.co.uk).

Booth, Derek and Jennifer Leavitt (1999), "Field Evaluation of Permeable Pavement Systems for Improved Stormwater Management," *Journal of the American Planning Association* (www.planning.org), Vol. 65, No. 3, Summer 1999, pp. 314-325.

Burden, Dan (1998), *Street Design Guidelines for Healthy Neighborhoods*, Center for Livable Communities (Sacramento, CA) (www.lgc.org/center).

Canadian Institute of Transportation Engineers (2005), *The Canadian Guide to Promoting Sustainable Transportation Through Site Design*, Canadian Institute of Transportation Engineers (www.cite7.org).

Center for Watershed Protection (2005) provides analysis and resources for minimizing hydrologic impacts and pollution (www.cwp.org).

Childs, Mark (1999), *Parking Spaces: A Design, Implementation and Use Manual for Architects, Planners, and Engineers*, The McGraw-Hill Companies (New York) (www.mcgraw-hill.com).

City of Gainesville (2000), "Gainesville Land Development Code" (Gainesville, FL) (www.cityofgainesville.org).

City of Portland (1999), "Special Standards for Garages," City of Portland Zoning Code Section 33.110.250.E., City of Portland Bureau of Planning (Portland, OR) (www.portlandonline.com/planning/index.cfm?c=31612).

Edwards, John D. (1994), *Parking: The Parking Handbook for Small Communities*, Institute of Transportation Engineers (Washington, DC) (www.ite.org) and National Main Street Center (Washington, DC) (www.mainstreet.org).

Federal Highway Administration (FHWA) (2004), U.S. Department of Transportation, "Traffic Calming" (www.fhwa.dot.gov/environment/tcalm/index.htm).

Hamilton Associates (1998), *Safety Design Guidelines for Parking Facilities*, Hamilton Associates (www.gdhamilton.com) for the Insurance Corporation of British Columbia (www.icbc.com).

Institute of Transportation Engineers (1994), *Guidelines for Parking Facility Location and Design*, Institute of Transportation Engineers (Washington, DC) (www.ite.org).

Institute of Transportation Engineers (1999), *Transportation Planning Handbook*, Institute of Transportation Engineers (Washington, DC) (www.ite.org).

Litman, Todd (2000), *Pavement Busters Guide: Why and How to Reduce the Amount of Land Paved for Roads and Parking Facilities*, Victoria Transport Policy Institute (www.vtpi.org); available online (www.vtpi.org/pav-bust.pdf).

National Parking Association (2003), *Security Design for a Parking Facility*, National Parking Association (Washington, DC) (www.npapark.org).

Nonpoint Education for Municipal Officials (NEMO) (2005) is a University of Connecticut educational program that addresses impervious surface impacts) (http://nemo.uconn.edu).

Seattle Department of Transportation (2001), *Parking Guide: Simple Ways to Improve Your Neighborhood's Parking*, City of Seattle (www.cityofseattle.net); available online (www.seattle.gov/transportation/parking/parkingguide.htm).

Siegman, Patrick (2005), *On-Street Bike Lanes Preferred Alternative*, Nelson/Nygaard. Memorandum to City of Lincoln, Nebraska (www.lincoln.ne.gov/city/plan/dt_plan/mtg/021105/bike1.pdf).

Smith, Thomas P. (1988), *The Aesthetics of Parking*, Planning Advisory Service, American Planning Association (Chicago, IL) (www.planning.org).

Stover, Vergil G. and Frank J. Koepke (2002), "Parking Design," *Transportation and Land Development, Second Edition*, Institute of Transportation Engineers (Washington, DC) (www.ite.org).

Traffic Calming provides information on roadway design strategies for controlling traffic speeds and volumes (supported by the U.S. Department of Transportation, Federal Highway Administration) (www.fhwa.dot.gov/environment/tcalm/index.htm).

Transportation Research Board, Access Management Web site provides information on access management resources (www.accessmanagement.gov).

Urban Land Institute (ULI) (2000), *The Dimensions of Parking*, ULI (Washington, DC) (www.uli.org) and the National Parking Association (Washington, DC) (www.npapark.org).

U.S. Department of Transportation's "Accessibility—Equal Access to Transportation" (www.dot.gov/accessibility)

Victoria Transport Policy Institute (VTPI) (2005), *Online TDM Encyclopedia*, VTPI (www.vtpi.org); available online ("Access Management" (www.vtpi.org/tdm/tdm1.htm) and "Traffic Calming" (www.vtpi.org/tdm/tdm4.htm)).

SUMMARY

Table 5-23 summarizes the parking management strategies in this book.

Table 5-23
Parking Management Strategies Included in This Book

Strategy	Description
I. Strategies That Increase Parking Facility Efficiency	
Share parking	Provide parking spaces that serve multiple users or destinations.
Regulate parking	Establish regulations that encourage more efficient use of parking facilities.
Establish more accurate and flexible standards	Adjust parking standards to more accurately reflect demand in a particular situation.
Establish parking maximums	Establish maximum parking supply regulations.
Provide remote parking and shuttle services	Provide off-site or urban fringe parking facilities and encourage their use.
Implement smart growth policies	Incorporate land-use policies that encourage more compact, mixed, multimodal development.
Improve walking and cycling conditions	Improve walking and cycling conditions to expand the range of destinations serviced by a parking facility and reduce vehicle trips.
Increase capacity of existing parking facilities	Increase the level of parking supply by using otherwise wasted space, smaller stalls, car stackers, and valet parking.
II. Strategies That Reduce Parking Demand	
Implement mobility management	Encourage more efficient travel patterns, including changes in mode, timing, destination, and vehicle trip frequency.
Price parking	Charge motorists directly for using parking facilities.
Improve pricing methods	Use better charging techniques to make pricing more convenient and cost effective.
Provide financial incentives	Provide financial incentives to shift mode, such as parking cash-out and transit benefits.
Unbundle parking	Rent or sell parking facilities separately from building space, so occupants only pay for parking they use.
Reform parking taxes	Implement various tax policy changes that support parking management objectives.
Provide bicycle facilities	Provide bicycle storage and changing facilities.
III. Support Strategies	
Improve user information and marketing	Provide convenient and accurate information on parking availability and price, using maps, signs, brochures, etc.
Improve enforcement and control	Ensure that parking regulation enforcement is efficient, considerate, and fair.

Table 5-23 (cont.)
Parking Management Strategies Included in This Book

Parking Management Strategy	Description
Establish transportation management associations and parking brokerage	Establish member-controlled organizations that provide transport and parking management services in a particular area.
Establish overflow parking plans	Establish plans to deal with periods of peak parking demand.
Address spillover problems	Use management, enforcement, and pricing to address spillover problems.
Improve parking facility design and operation	Improve parking facility design and operation to help solve problems and achieve parking management objectives.

Summary of the parking management strategies described in this book.

Table 5-24 indicates whether a strategy directly reduces total vehicle traffic (and therefore provides benefits such as reduced traffic congestion and pollution emissions) and the typical range of reductions it can provide in parking requirements (the amount of parking supply needed in a particular situation).

Actual impacts vary depending on how a strategy is implemented, the base case (what would happen without the proposed management strategies), and other specific factors. (See individual descriptions and Chapter 3 for more discussion of how to predict parking and travel demand impacts.) Below are some general guidelines:

- Impacts are higher where there are better parking and travel options. For example, parking pricing will have greater demand reduction impacts if implemented in conjunction with improvements in walking and cycling conditions and rideshare and public transit services.
- Financial incentives tend to have greater impacts on lower-income rather than higher-income consumers.
- Some strategies are complementary. For example, shared parking becomes more effective if implemented with suitable regulations, pricing, and walkability improvements.
- Impacts are generally smaller when a strategy is first implemented and increases as programs mature. A *low* value may be appropriate the first year, but this can increase to *medium* after two or three years, and *high* after five or 10 years.

Table 5-24
Typical Traffic Impacts and Parking Requirement Reductions

Strategy	Vehicle Traffic Impacts	Typical Reductions in the Amount of Parking Supply Required at a Destination		
		Low	Medium	High
Share parking		10%	20%	30%
Regulate parking		10%	20%	30%
Establish more accurate and flexible standards		10%	20%	30%
Establish parking maximums		10%	20%	30%
Provide remote parking and shuttle services		10%	20%	30%
Implement smart growth policies	Reduction	10%	20%	30%
Improve walking and cycling conditions	Reduction	10%	20%	30%
Increase capacity of existing parking facilities		5%	10%	15%
Implement mobility management	Reduction	10%	20%	30%
Price parking	Reduction	10%	20%	30%
Improve pricing methods	Reduction	NA	NA	NA
Provide financial incentives	Reduction	10%	20%	30%
Unbundle parking	Reduction	10%	20%	30%
Reform parking taxes	Reduction	5%	10%	15%
Provide bicycle facilities	Reduction	5%	10%	15%
Improve user information and marketing	Reduction	5%	10%	15%
Improve enforcement and control		NA	NA	NA
Establish transportation management associations and parking brokerage	Reduction	NA	NA	NA
Establish overflow parking plans		NA	NA	NA
Address spillover problems		NA	NA	NA
Improve parking facility design and operation		NA	NA	NA

NA = not appropriate, indicating strategies that do not directly affect parking requirements.

Indication of whether a parking management strategy tends to reduce vehicle traffic and the typical reductions in parking requirements it provides relative to conventional practices.

Evaluating Multiple Strategies

Special care is needed when predicting the impacts of a program that includes multiple parking management strategies. Be careful to count each impact only once. For example, transportation management associations provide an institutional framework for implementing strategies that directly affect parking requirements such as increased sharing, pricing, and regulation of parking facilities. While it would be true to say that a transportation management association can reduce parking requirements by 10 to 30 percent compared with the absence of such an organization, it would be incorrect to add the demand reductions of the transportation management association to the impacts of the individual strategies it helps implement, since those individual strategies are what actually affect parking requirements.

For example, without a transportation management association, parking sharing, pricing, and mobility management may each reduce parking requirements by 10 percent; with a transportation management association they become more effective, each providing 15 percent reductions. Table 5-25 illustrates the incremental gain that can be attributed to the transportation management association due to the increase in the effectiveness of these strategies. In this example, the transportation management association causes an addi-

Table 5-25
Transportation Management Association Parking Requirement Reductions

Parking Management Strategy	Without TMA	With TMA	Gain
Shared parking	10%	15%	5%
Parking pricing	10%	15%	5%
Mobility management	10%	15%	5%
Total impacts (calculated by multiplication)	**100% – (90% × 90% × 90%) = 27%**	**100% – (85% × 85% × 85%) = 39%**	**12%**

TMA = transportation management association.

Illustration of how a TMA increases implementation of individual parking management strategies such as shared parking, pricing parking, and mobility management programs. Their combined travel reduction impacts are calculated by multiplication, as described.

tional 12 percent reduction in parking requirements by enhancing the effects of other management strategies.

When calculating the effects of multiple strategies, total impacts are multiplicative and not additive (see Chapter 3). In the example in Table 5-25, shared parking initially reduces the parking requirements by 10 percent, to 90 percent of the original level. Parking pricing reduces this another 10 percent to 81 percent of the original level, and mobility management provides another 10 percent reduction, resulting in 73 percent of the original level—a 27 percent reduction, somewhat less than the 30 percent reduction that would be calculated by adding three 10 percent reductions. With a TMA, these three strategies become more effective, reducing parking requirements 15 percent each, or 39 percent in total, calculated by multiplying the level of demand that remains after each is implemented.

Some combinations of strategies have synergistic effects (that is, total impacts are greater than the sum of their individual impacts) and so become more effective if implemented together. For example, sharing parking and walkability improvements may each reduce parking requirements just 10 percent if implemented alone, but 25 percent if implemented together because they are complementary.

6

Developing an Integrated Parking Plan

This chapter provides guidance for developing an integrated parking plan that includes an optimal combination of complementary management strategies.

PLANNING PROCESS

An integrated parking plan requires a comprehensive planning process to identify the combination of strategies that provide the greatest overall benefits. Below are recommended steps for this process.

DEFINE SCOPE

Define the geographic scope of analysis. Parking planning can be performed at site, street, district/neighborhood, and regional scales. It is best to consider at least the area within walking distance from the study site, since this is the functional scale of parking impacts. For example, when planning parking for a building or mall, it is best to survey parking supply and demand within about four to eight blocks in each direction of the site to help identify opportunities for sharing parking and potential spillover problems. Similarly, when developing a downtown area parking management plan, include nearby residential neighborhoods in the analysis.

Some types of parking planning require larger, regional-scale planning in order to coordinate parking standards, regulations, pricing, and enforcement programs, and to integrate parking policies with other regional transport and land-use objectives. For example, parking policies should be coordinated between different commercial districts and neighborhoods to develop common parking pricing methods and standards.

INVOLVE STAKEHOLDERS

"Stakeholders" are people affected by a planning decision. Including diverse stakeholders in the planning process can help identify potential problems, identify creative solutions, and build support for program implementation. Special public outreach campaigns may be needed to involve the public and educate them about parking issues. People tend to oppose innovation until they learn enough about problems and new solutions, so they understand the benefits that can result from change (see the section entitled "Change Management" on page 220).

DEFINE PROBLEMS

Carefully define parking problems. For example, if people complain of parking shortages, it is important to determine exactly where, when, to whom, and for what types of trips (e.g., deliveries, commuting, shoppers, and tourists) this occurs. Be sure to consider all possible parking problems, not just peak-period congestion. Take into account user convenience, the costs of parking facilities, spillover effects, the adequacy of user information, the convenience of pricing methods, difficulties walking between parking facilities and destinations, and environmental impacts. A broader problem definition allows decision-makers to consider a wider range of objectives and avoid solutions to one problem that exacerbate others.

COORDINATE PARKING DECISIONS
WITH STRATEGIC OBJECTIVES

Parking planning should be coordinated with a community's overall strategic vision. This helps ensure that individual decisions reflect broader community objectives. There may be several possible solutions to a parking problem, some of which support strategic objectives while others contradict them. For example, there may be several ways to address parking congestion problems, but expanding parking supply will tend to increase vehicle traffic and urban sprawl, while more efficient management of existing parking supply tends to support other community planning objectives, such as encouraging use of alternative modes and creating more compact, walkable communities.

ESTABLISH EVALUATION FRAMEWORK

Develop a comprehensive evaluation framework (Litman, 2002). This framework should identify:
- Perspective and scope (the geographic range and time scale of impacts to consider).
- Goals (desired outcomes to be achieved) and objectives (ways to achieve goals).

- Evaluation criteria (impacts to be considered in the analysis), including various categories of costs, benefits, and equity impacts.
- Evaluation method (how impacts are to be evaluated), such as benefit/cost or cost-effectiveness analysis.
- Performance indicators (practical ways to measure progress toward objectives), such as increased availability of parking to customers or reduced complaints of spillover parking.
- Base case definition (conditions expected to occur if a proposed policy or program is not implemented).
- How results will be presented and compared. For example, results can be presented as annualized cost per parking space or net present value (the full value of an option over the analysis period reflected in one unit, with all costs and benefits depreciated to a base year). This facilitates comparisons between options with different impacts over time (e.g., when comparing an option with low capital and high operating costs with an alternative that has higher capital but lower operating costs).

SURVEY CONDITIONS

Survey parking supply and demand in the study area. (For information on parking survey methods, see Edwards, 1994; ITE, 1999; ITE, 2004; ULI, 2000.) Inventory all parking facilities in an area, including those that are currently unavailable to the general public, since some management strategies involve expanding the use of such spaces.

Collect the following information on each parking facility:
- Location and ownership.
- Type of facility (e.g., on-street, off-street surface, off-street structured, and underground).
- Number of spaces.
- Intended users (e.g., customers, employees, residents).
- Regulation (e.g., "1 Hour Maximum," "Delivery Vehicles Only").
- Prices (e.g., hourly, daily, weekly, and monthly fees).
- Utilization (portion of available parking spaces occupied at a particular location and time; also called "occupancy rate" or "load factor"), turnover (the number of different vehicles that park in a specific space or area during a particular time period, such as vehicles per hour or vehicles per day), and duration (length of time a vehicle remains in a specific parking space).
- Problems identified (e.g., parking congestion, spillover conflicts, poorly maintained facilities, inadequate enforcement, and inadequate security).

Use field surveys and stakeholder interviews to investigate the extent of the parking problems and identify where, when, and to whom such problems occur. Below are indicators of parking problems:
- Motorists frequently have difficulty finding a parking space.

- All spaces within view of a destination are frequently occupied.
- Vehicles frequently park illegally, such as parking in prohibited areas or double parking.
- Vehicles often cruise streets while searching for parking.
- Motorists are frequently cited for parking violations.
- There are often parking spillover problems.

Project future conditions and problems. For example, an area may currently have adequate parking supply, but planned development will reduce supply and increase demand. The base case for analysis would therefore be the projected future if no additional action is taken.

IDENTIFY OPTIONS

Develop a list of potential solutions using ideas from this book, stakeholders' suggestions, and other planning resources. This list may include a combination of capacity expansion and management strategies. Develop integrated programs that include a coordinated set of strategies. For example, one program might include a combination of regulations, remote parking, and pedestrian improvements, a second program might emphasize incentives to reduce automobile commuting, while another program might include building more on-site parking facilities.

EVALUATE OPTIONS

Identify impacts (benefits and costs) to consider in analysis, such as those in Table 6-1. This list can be adjusted to reflect specific planning requirements and stakeholder preferences. Evaluate each option with respect to these impacts.

At a minimum, provide a sentence or two that describes the impact of each strategy. As much as possible, impacts should be quantified (measured), monetized (measured in monetary units), and compared using standard reference units, such as total land required, annualized cost per parking space, or net present value (total costs and benefits depreciated to a base year).

Economic evaluation should reflect marginal analysis (the incremental impacts of an additional unit of consumption). For example, the costs of increasing parking capacity should be assigned only to peak-period users, if existing supply is adequate during off-peak periods. "Marginal analysis" also means that impacts are calculated for each category of mode, vehicle, location, and time. For example, larger vehicles impose somewhat higher parking costs than smaller vehicles.

Management strategies that reduce parking requirements should be evaluated based on avoided costs, the savings that result from reducing demand. For example, if a management strategy reduces the need for 25 parking spaces, its value is at least equivalent to the cost of building that many addi-

Table 6-1
Impacts to Consider

Impact Category	Description
Land costs	Value of land devoted to parking facilities
Construction costs	Project construction expenses
Operation and maintenance costs	Ongoing operation and maintenance expenses
Implementation requirements	Ease of implementation
User convenience	Relative ease of use
Consumer choice	Impacts on the range of parking, transport, and housing options available to consumers
User financial impacts	Additional consumer payments, savings, or benefits
Revenues	Additional revenue to facility owners
Spillover impacts	Undesired use of off-site parking spaces
Economic development impacts	Changes in employment and business activity
Travel impacts	Shifts in parking location, mode, destination, and time; some are considered desirable and others undesirable, depending on conditions and perspective
Traffic impacts	Changes in vehicle traffic volumes, including changes in total vehicle travel and vehicles cruising for parking spaces
Land-use impacts	Changes in land-use patterns (such as whether it increases or reduces sprawl), transit access, and walkability
Greenspace preservation	Changes in the amount of land that must be paved, and the amount of land that can be dedicated to greenspace, including farmland, parkland, and landscaping
Stormwater management and heat island effects	Changes in the amount of impervious surface, stormwater management costs, and solar heat gain
Equity and fairness	Impact on the distribution of impacts, particularly on people who are physically, economically, or socially disadvantaged

Impacts (costs and benefits) to consider when evaluating parking management programs.

Table 6-2
Evaluation Matrix Example

Option	Cost Effectiveness	Mobility for Nondrivers	Affordability	Impervious Surface	Discourages Sprawl	Total Points
Option 1	−2	4	4	3	4	14
Option 2	−1	4	−1	4	4	10
Option 3	−4	5	3	4	1	9
Option 4	−1	3	−4	5	3	6
Option 5	−3	2	4	−3	5	5

Each option is rated from −5 (negative) to 5 (positive) based on how well it helps achieve each objective.

tional parking spaces. Analysis of avoided costs should also include indirect savings, such as reduced traffic congestion and pollution emissions if parking management strategies reduce vehicle trips.

It is important to distinguish between economic transfers (resources shifted) and true costs (a total reduction in valued resources). For example, parking fees are economic transfers, not true resource costs, so it is important to account for both payments and revenues when evaluating pricing effects. The true resource costs of pricing parking consist of transaction costs (any additional time and inconvenience to motorists for paying for parking, and the administrative costs of collecting and enforcing payments). It is also important to identify the distribution of impacts, indicating who bears additional costs and who benefits from a particular policy.

Some impacts, such as equity and land-use effects, are unsuited for monetization. They can be evaluated using a multicriteria evaluation rating system (Spackman et al., 2001; Litman, 2002). For example, a community may have established equity objectives to improve mobility for nondrivers and provide affordable mobility for low-income people, and land-use objectives to reduce total impervious surface and discourage sprawl. A committee of experts or stakeholders rates each option according to these objectives. The results are presented in a matrix (see Table 6-2). More sophisticated rating systems can be developed with different weights assigned to different impacts.

Good analysis compares options in ways that help stakeholders understand and rank them. This means highlighting key differences, discussing implications in terms of strategic objectives, presenting results in nontechnical language suitable for the intended audience, and using visual images (e.g., maps, graphs, photographs, and drawings) to convey information.

PRIORITIZE OPTIONS

Options should be prioritized based on their cost effectiveness (their unit costs, such as dollars per space, or their benefit/cost ratio) and their support for overall planning objectives. Below are two examples.

Single Building Example

Conventional standards require 100 parking spaces (90 employee and 10 visitor spaces) for a 100-employee office. Each space has an annualized cost of $600. Various management strategies are considered and ranked by cost effectiveness (annualized dollars per space).

- By sharing parking rather than assigning reserved spaces, parking requirements can be reduced by 20 spaces, with an estimated annualized cost of $10 per space to deal with occasional problems.

- Arranging to use parking at a nearby church in exchange for their use of office parking on Sunday mornings, and improving the path to the church, reduces the need for 10 spaces at $50 annualized cost per space.
- Allowing more employees to telecommute and installing bicycle storage and changing facilities are estimated to reduce parking requirements by five spaces at $200 annually per space.
- A $15 per month cash-out incentive to 20 employees who use alternative modes (10 who currently walk, bicycle, rideshare, or use public transit, and 10 more who would give up driving if offered this incentive) is predicted to reduce parking requirements by 10 spaces at $360 per space (20 employees × $15 per month × 12 months = $3,600 ÷ 10).
- A $25 per month cash-out benefit is predicted to reduce parking requirements by 15 spaces at a cost of $500 per space (25 employees × $25 per month × 12 months = $7,500 ÷ 15).
- A $40 per month cash-out benefit is predicted to reduce parking requirements by 20 spaces at a cost of $720 per space (30 employees × $40 per month × 12 months = $14,400 ÷ 20).
- Additional spaces could be leased nearby at $65 per month.

Table 6-3 summarizes the results, ranked from lowest to highest unit costs.

Table 6-3
Office Parking Management Evaluation Example

Strategy	Unit Cost $/Space/ Year	Spaces Provided	Cumulative Increase Total Spaces	Cumulative Cost $/Year
Shared parking	$10	20	20	$200
Remote parking and improved walkability	$50	10	30	$700
Bicycle parking and telecommuting	$200	5	35	$1,700
Cash-out A ($15 per month to 20 employees)	$360	10	45	$5,300
Cash-out B ($25 per month to 25 employees)	$500	15	50	$9,200
Expanding parking facility	$600	No Limit		
Cash-out C ($40 per month to 30 employees)	$720	20	55	$16,100
Additional remote parking (leased at $65 per month)	$780	20	75	$31,700

Ranks various strategies by cost effectiveness. Management strategies should be implemented if they are cheaper than capacity expansion. Note that only one of the three cash-out options may be selected.

The developer should therefore implement all parking management strategies up to the $25 per month parking cash-out benefit and provide 50 rather than 100 parking spaces to minimize direct financial cost. Additional management strategies may be implemented to help achieve other objectives, for example, as a valued employee benefit, or to reduce traffic congestion and pollution emissions. For example, from society's perspective, the $40 per month cash-out option may be considered cost effective because employees consider it a valuable benefit and because of the resulting reduction in congestion and pollution.

Commercial District Example

A growing commercial district is experiencing parking congestion problems. The area has 10,000 parking spaces: 1,000 free, on-street spaces; 3,000 public, priced, off-street spaces; and 6,000 private, off-street spaces currently serving individual destinations and unavailable to the general public. Most on-street spaces are occupied during peak periods but many off-street spaces are vacant. Planners identify various parking management and capacity expansion options and rank them by increasing unit costs:

- Two hundred on-street parking spaces at the edge of the district are currently unregulated and used all day by commuters. These can have 2-hour limits to encourage turnover. This is estimated to cost $1,000 annually for additional signs and enforcement.
- Signs and maps can be provided to help motorists find parking. This is predicted to increase peak-period customer parking supply by an equivalent of 300 spaces (the number of spaces that are unused because customers don't know about them). This project is estimated to cost $6,000 per year for user information materials.
- A program can encourage employees to use remote parking. This is estimated to increase customer parking supply by 100 spaces. Costs are estimated to total $5,000 per year for program materials and administration.
- Free shuttle bus service could be provided during peak days (summer weekends and holiday shopping periods) among the commercial district, remote parking facilities, and a transit terminal. This is predicted to free up 500 additional parking spaces within the commercial district. Costs are estimated to total $35,000 per year. This would also increase user convenience and reduce some traffic congestion.
- A transportation management association could provide trip reduction services, help establish parking sharing arrangements, provide parking information and enforcement services, and support other parking management strategies. Three options are considered:
  - A minimal program costing $50,000 annually is predicted to increase peak-period parking supply available to the public by 500 spaces.

o A moderate program costing $150,000 annually is predicted to increase peak-period parking supply by 1,000 spaces.
o A maximum program costing $500,000 annually is predicted to increase peak-period parking supply by 2,000 spaces.

- Three hundred surface spaces could be built on otherwise unused city land for $200 annualized cost per space; beyond this, adding more spaces will require structured parking with annualized costs of $1,500 per space. Although the city could charge for this parking, existing parking structures are seldom filled, so net revenues from this additional capacity would be minimal.

Table 6-4 summarizes these options. The city can begin with the most cost-effective options (lowest unit cost) and work down to more costly strategies if needed. Although it may be difficult initially to predict the effectiveness of some management strategies, this becomes easier with experience. For example, the first year a parking management association is established, it may only free up 250 parking spaces, but this should increase over time as its services develop and as managers gain experience. Note that some of these strategies also reduce vehicle traffic and so may be implemented to help address both parking and traffic congestion problems.

Table 6-4
Community Parking Management Evaluation Example

Strategy	Unit Cost $/Space/ Year	Spaces Provided	Cumulative Increase Total Spaces	Cumulative Cost $/Year
Regulate currently unregulated parking	$5	200	200	$1,000
Provide user information	$20	300	500	$7,000
Encourage employees to use less convenient spaces	$50	100	600	$17,000
Provide free shuttle bus service	$70	500	1,100	$52,000
Option A. Parking management association, minimum	$100	500	1,600	$102,000
Option B. Parking management association, moderate	$150	1,000	2,100	$202,000
Add surface parking	$200	300	2,400	$262,000
Option C. Parking management association, maximum	$250	2,000	3,100	$552,000
Add structured parking	$1,500	No limit		

This table ranks various strategies from lowest to highest unit costs. Management strategies should be implemented if they are cheaper than building additional capacity. Note that only one of the three parking management association options may be selected.

ANALYZE EQUITY IMPACTS

Parking decisions can have a variety of equity impacts that should be considered in the planning process. There are three general categories of transportation equity issues:

1. Horizontal equity (also called "fairness") is concerned with whether each individual or group is treated equally, assuming that their needs and abilities are comparable. It suggests that people with comparable incomes and needs should receive an equal share of public resources and bear an equal burden of public costs. It also implies that the costs of providing a facility or service should be borne by its users unless a subsidy is specifically justified (the "User Pays principle").

2. Vertical equity with regard to income considers the allocation of costs between different income classes, assuming that public policies should favor people who are economically disadvantaged. Policies that provide proportionally greater benefits to lower-income groups are called "progressive," while those that make lower-income people relatively worse off are called "regressive."

3. Vertical equity with regard to mobility need and ability considers whether a transportation system provides adequate service to people who have special transportation needs (they are "transportation disadvantaged"). It justifies facility design features and services to accommodate people with disabilities.

Some common parking management equity issues are discussed below.

Administrative Consistency

People sometimes argue that it is most fair to apply regulations consistently, for example, to impose the same parking standards on every building of a particular type without variation. Similarly, they may consider it most fair to charge the same parking fee at all times and locations. However, such inflexibility tends to be inefficient and unfair since it prevents regulation adjustments to reflect the actual needs of a particular location, or differences in the cost of providing parking, and it fails to reward property owners who implement management strategies that reduce parking demand. For example, it would be consistent but wasteful and unfair to impose the same parking requirements on housing for rich and poor residents knowing that poor households tend to own fewer vehicles, or to impose the same requirements on businesses that share parking and have commute trip reduction programs as on those that do not.

Regulation of Public Parking

There are often conflicts over the regulation and allocation of parking. For example, residents often want exclusive use of on-street parking in front of their homes. They sometimes make long-term decisions, such as whether to choose a particular house or purchase a vehicle, based on the availability of free parking nearby. However, on-street parking is a public resource provided by a community, so fairness (horizontal equity) suggests that it should be available equally to all motorists. A compromise solution is often best, such as providing one residential parking permit per house and applying a time limit or fee to other vehicles. The exact regulations will depend on the situation and may require ongoing adjustments over time.

Parking Pricing: Horizontal Equity

Paying for parking facilities indirectly through taxes, rents, or the price of retail goods forces people who use a less-than-average amount of parking to subsidize others who use a more-than-average amount. Pricing parking tends to be more horizontally equitable; it reflects the principle that consumers should "get what they pay for and pay for what they get."

Parking Pricing: Vertical Equity

Parking pricing can have various impacts on people who are economically, socially, and physically disadvantaged. Charging for parking is often considered regressive (it imposes an excessive burden on lower-income people), since a particular fee represents a greater share of income for lower-income than for higher-income motorists. However, higher-income people tend to own more vehicles and take more trips and so tend to capture more parking subsidies.

Low-income people generally benefit more from subsidies that can be transferred to other modes, such as parking cash-out, or from unbundled parking because they tend to drive less than average, own fewer vehicles, and place more value on financial savings than people with higher incomes. Low-income people can benefit from priced parking if revenues are used to reduce their rents or taxes, or to fund transportation services they use. If parking pricing is implemented in areas that have good travel options, and revenues are used in ways that benefit lower-income people, it tends to be progressive with respect to income overall. Pricing can incorporate special features to benefit disadvantaged groups, such as need-based discounts (e.g., lower rates for people with disabilities, lower-income students and workers, and local residents), particularly during the transition period when it is first introduced.

DEVELOP AN IMPLEMENTATION PLAN

Once the general components of a parking management program are selected, the next step is to develop an implementation plan that identifies what, when, and how parking management strategies will be implemented.

This may include various phases and contingency-based options. For example, some strategies will be implemented the first year, others within three years, and a third set will only be implemented if necessary, based on performance indicators that identify parking congestion or spillover problems. Table 6-5 illustrates an example of such a plan.

Once the implementation plan is established, create a workplan that identifies specific tasks to be accomplished, who is responsible for them, and when they should be completed.

Table 6-5
Example of Contingency-Based Parking Management Plan

Phase	Indicator	Strategies
Phase 1	Implement within one year.	• Improve parking information with signs and maps. • Shift from reserved to shared parking spaces in each lot. • Impose 2-hour limits on the most convenient parking spaces. • Encourage employees to use less convenient parking spaces. • Improve enforcement of parking regulations and fees. • Establish an evaluation program to identify impacts and problems.
Phase 2	Implement within two years.	• Price the most convenient parking spaces. • Impose 2-hour limits on a larger portion of parking spaces. • Arrange shared parking agreements at a few sites, where facility managers are most cooperative, as pilot projects. • Install bicycle storage and changing facilities. • Establish a commute trip reduction program.
Phase 3	Implement if peak-period occupancy exceeds 85%.	• Gradually and predictably increase parking fees (e.g., 10% annual price increases). • Encourage more shared parking agreements, and change zoning codes to encourage shared parking. • Improve area walkability and address security concerns. • Provide real-time information on parking availability using changeable signs.
Phase 4	Implement as needed, based on peak-period occupancy rates.	• Address spillover parking problems. • Address barriers to walking between remote parking and destinations. • Develop overflow parking plans for special events and peak periods. • Provide incentives for shared parking in areas with parking shortages, including in-lieu fees to build public rather than private parking facilities.
Phase 5	Implement if problems continue.	• Expand the portion of parking spaces that are priced and regulated. • Increase support for commute trip reduction programs. • Provide shuttle van services to bus stops and remote parking during peak periods.

This table illustrates a multiphase parking management plan. Some strategies are implemented right away; others over a longer period; and some are only implemented if needed, based on specific indicators, such as excessive parking congestion or spillover problems.

Innovative strategies can initially be implemented as pilot projects. This helps overcome objections and uncertainties. For example, shared parking can initially be implemented in a relatively small area, and the program expanded after operators gain experience and the strategy proves its effectiveness.

ESTABLISH ADMINISTRATION RESPONSIBILITY

Parking management programs require an institutional home. An existing organization, such as a facilities department or local traffic agency, or a new organization such as a transportation management association, can be given administrative responsibility and necessary resources for implementing the parking plan. This typically includes the following tasks:

- Coordinate ongoing parking planning.
- Maintain an inventory of parking facilities.
- Perform regular parking utilization surveys.
- Monitor and respond to parking problems.
- Advise on parking facility design and management.
- Advise on regulations and enforcement policies.
- Provide parking brokerage.
- Coordinate shared parking and enforce sharing agreements.
- Provide parking user information.
- Provide enforcement services.
- Provide other parking and transportation management services as needed.

UPDATE PLANNING DOCUMENTS

It is often useful to review existing transportation and land-use plans, zoning codes, and development practices to identify any changes needed to make them consistent with parking management objectives. For example, it may be appropriate to add sections that specify analysis methods that may be used to adjust minimum parking requirements, establish guidelines for shared parking, and identify parking regulation enforcement practices.

COORDINATE WITH OTHER JURISDICTIONS

It may be important to coordinate parking plans with other nearby jurisdictions in order to avoid and address conflicts. For example, it can be helpful for adjacent cities to have similar parking standards, regulations, and prices, and to work together to develop a transportation management association that provides parking and transportation services throughout the area. For this reason, it is often helpful for regional planning agencies to provide leadership in developing parking policies and plans.

ESTABLISH PERFORMANCE INDICATORS

"Performance indicators" are practical ways to measure progress toward objectives. Below is a list of performance indicators that may be suitable for parking planning and program evaluation. This list can be modified as appropriate for a particular situation.

Planning Process

- Quality of parking planning process.
- Degree of agreement on the definition of problems, objectives, and evaluation criteria.
- How well parking planning integrates with strategic transportation and land-use planning objectives.
- Degree of stakeholder involvement.
- Ability of planning process to respond to changing needs and conditions (such as inclusion of contingency-based strategies that can be implemented quickly if needed in the future).
- Quality of data collection (e.g., inventories, utilization surveys, and user surveys).
- Clarity of plan (specifies exactly what needs to be done, by when, and by whom).

Transportation System Impacts

- Ease of finding a parking space, particularly for priority users, such as delivery vehicles, customers, and clients.
- Impacts on traffic congestion.
- Parking duration and turnover at a particular location.
- Mode split, and progress toward mode split objectives, such as increased use of public transit.
- Changes in total vehicle mileage, energy consumption, and pollution emissions.
- Walkability (quality of walking conditions) between parking facilities and the destinations they serve.

Fiscal Impacts

- Cost effectiveness (e.g., dollars per parking space or peak-period user).
- Cost recovery (portion of facility costs funded through user fees).
- Net revenue.
- Tax revenue.
- Impacts on development costs (parking facility costs as a portion of the costs of new development).

Local Community Perspective

- Parking facility design quality (e.g., aesthetics and environmental quality).
- Magnitude of spillover impacts.
- Responsiveness to concerns and complaints.
- Impacts with regard to community equity objectives.
- Impacts with regard to community land-use objectives.
- Impacts with regard to community transportation objectives.
- Impacts with regard to community economic development objectives.

User Perspective

- Diversity of parking and travel options.
- Quality of user information on parking availability and price.
- Parking availability, particularly for priority trips (e.g., emergencies, loading/drop-off and quick errands).
- Convenience (e.g., of using pricing methods).
- User and vehicle safety and security.

Equity Impacts

- Fairness (whether parking regulations and prices are considered reasonable).
- User pays (the degree to which users pay the full costs of parking facilities and services).
- Affordability (whether affordable transportation and vehicle parking options are available to low-income users).
- How well parking facilities accommodate people with special needs, such as people with disabilities and those who have difficulty reading the local language.

CHANGE MANAGEMENT

Innovative solutions often face resistance from stakeholders who fear change. Parking management implementation often requires change management, that is, special planning activities and resources to support innovations and reform. Proponents must be change agents (see the sidebar entitled "Being a Change Agent"). Although this may initially seem difficult, if a new program is fundamentally sound and advocates are persistent, it will usually succeed. Often, many of the people who originally opposed change will embrace it and claim it as their own!

For example, a new parking payment system can increase convenience and efficiency but, at first, some motorists may find it confusing to use and will complain loudly. When introduced into a community, it is important that new technologies are promoted with signs and brochures that describe their operation and emphasize their benefits. Over time, enough motorists will become familiar with the new system that such problems will disappear. Similarly, local planners accustomed to applying conventional parking standards may resist more flexible practices. However, by demonstrating that flexible standards are endorsed by transportation professional organizations and are widely used, and by working with staff to understand and use new, flexible standards, objections should decline over time.

It is important to listen to concerns and negotiate with stakeholders. It can be helpful to present different justifications for change to different interest groups:

- To transportation professionals and business managers, emphasize potential cost savings and traffic congestion reductions.
- To community groups, emphasize local environmental benefits and improved travel options for nondrivers.
- To designers and planners, emphasize increased flexibility and support for strategic planning objectives.

Being a Change Agent

"Change agents" are people who provide leadership for innovation. This is not a role for people who are easily discouraged, since innovations often face criticism and numerous minor difficulties. However, over time, worthwhile reforms are accepted and embraced.

Change agents must:

- Look at the big picture. Pay attention to context and long-term goals.
- Expand the range of solutions to be considered.
- Use comprehensive evaluation. Objections to justified reform often reflect a narrow, short-term analysis perspective.
- Make change more attractive than continuing with current practices. Ask, "Are current trends desirable?" and "What could be better?"
- Use positive statements. Emphasize benefits of change.
- Listen to stakeholders. Acknowledge their concerns and work with them to find acceptable solutions.
- Don't be afraid to say "no" to bad ideas, but try to offer an alternative that better balances overall objectives.
- Don't give up! Change may require several attempts before success occurs.

RESPONDING TO COMMON CONCERNS AND OBJECTIONS

Common concerns to parking management strategies and possible responses are discussed below.

Parking Management Programs Reduce User Service Quality

- *Concern:* Motorists will have difficulty finding a parking space, will find paying for parking inconvenient, and will dislike efforts forcing them to change their travel habits.
- *Response:* If properly planned and implemented, parking management programs can increase overall quality of service experienced by users. Parking management programs include strategies that increase the supply of parking available to users (through shared parking), prioritize use (through regulations and pricing), improve user information, increase travel options (e.g., walking, cycling, and public transit), create more accessible land-use patterns (by clustering activities), and improve facility design—all of which tend to benefit users.

A Generous Parking Supply is Necessary for Economic Development

- *Concern:* Some businesses fear that reduced parking supply, regulations, and pricing will discourage customers and reduce economic activity.
- *Response:* Parking management strategies can improve overall accessibility, parking availability, and user convenience, create a more attractive local environment, and provide cost savings. This can make an area more attractive to customers, increase productivity, and free up funds

Treasure Hidden in Your Parking Lot

What would you do if somebody told you that a valuable treasure is hidden in your parking lot? Would you search for it? Would you work hard to recover it? Would you be willing to dig for it?

Not all treasure is hidden underground. Sometimes, valuable resources sit undiscovered right before our eyes. With better management, most parking facilities can provide additional income, cost savings, and increased benefits to users and the community. These benefits can be substantial, often totaling hundreds of dollars in annual value per parking space.

Of course, like any treasure hunt, there are obstacles to overcome, but that is part of the fun. Management solutions require changing the way we think about problems and expanding the range of solutions that are considered in the planning process. There is often resistance to such changes, but don't give up. Victory belongs to the persistent. With a little effort, you'll find that your parking lot is paved with gold.

for other marketing activities. If an area is attractive, if short-term parking is convenient, and if businesses offer good value and services, customers are usually willing to pay for parking. Businesses can encourage their employees to use alternative modes and parking locations and offer parking fee discounts to customers.

Reduced Parking Supply Will Cause Spillover Parking Problems

- *Concern:* Reducing parking supply and additional regulations or pricing will cause spillover parking problems on adjacent streets or in nearby parking lots.
- *Response:* Parking management programs can include activities to address spillover parking problems by providing appropriate regulations and enforcement, or compensation for people who are impacted.

Traffic Will Be Delayed

- *Concern:* Traffic congestion may increase if motorists cruise around while searching for a space.
- *Response:* Parking management can reduce the need to cruise for parking by improving user information, increasing turnover of on-street parking, increasing the amount of parking that serves each destination (e.g., by improving walking conditions), and by reducing total vehicle trips (e.g., by encouraging shifts to alternative modes).

Management Program Effectiveness Will Decline Over Time

- *Concern:* Local officials may be reluctant to rely on parking management programs due to difficulties insuring that sharing agreements, transportation services, and other support activities will continue in the future. They may also be concerned that parking demand will increase sometime in the future due to changes in land use or other factors.
- *Response:* There are many ways to ensure that obligations are fulfilled, including performance bonds and special assessments imposed on violators, with revenues used to finance public parking facilities and services. Contingency-based planning can be used to identify what measures can be implemented if needed in the future.

Motorists Won't Know Where to Park

- *Concern:* Relying on off-site parking is confusing, inconvenient, and unsafe.
- *Response:* With good user information (e.g., maps, brochures, and signs), motorists can find off-site parking facilities and destinations. Walking conditions and security may need improvement to facilitate off-site parking.

Is Parking Management Effective?

Skeptics sometimes argue that parking management is ineffective, citing examples of a particular program that failed. However, in most cases, failures result from inadequate or inappropriate implementation rather than ineffectiveness of the strategies themselves. For example, parking regulations and pricing are generally effective where they are applied, but are often implemented in just a few areas with excessive exemptions and inadequate enforcement. It is wrong to conclude that these strategies are ineffective or wasteful. On the contrary, greater implementation is justified to maximize their effectiveness and benefits.

Liability and Insurance Costs Will Increase

- *Concern:* Shared parking will increase liability and insurance costs.
- *Response:* There are usually no significant impacts on liability or insurance costs. Investigate risks and risk-management strategies.

Planning Costs Will Increase

- *Concern:* Parking management requires more public staff time for planning, analysis, and negotiation.
- *Response:* Once parking management programs and practices are established, staffing requirements tend to decline. Administrative costs can be offset by increased parking fee revenues, additional tax revenues from increased development, and facility cost savings.

Projects Will Not Receive Financing with Inadequate Parking

- *Concern:* Developers will have difficultly obtaining financing if they have inadequate parking supply.
- *Response:* Properly planned parking management can increase economic feasibility and profitability. Even large chains (e.g., 7–11, McDonalds, and Fred Meyers) are often willing to accept innovative parking arrangements as long as they provide a high level of customer service. Lenders and developers may need information concerning the potential economic benefits of parking management. Contingency-based planning can be used to provide flexibility and respond to future needs.

CHAPTER 6 REFERENCES AND INFORMATION RESOURCES

Edwards, John D. (1994), *Parking: The Parking Handbook for Small Communities*, Institute of Transportation Engineers (Washington, DC) (www.ite.org) and National Main Street Center (New York) (www.mainstreet.org).

Howard/Stein-Hudson Associates, Inc. and Parsons Brinckerhoff Quade and Douglas (1996), *Public Involvement Techniques for Transportation Decision-making*, U.S. Department of Transportation, Federal Highway Administration (www.fhwa.dot.gov); available online (www.fhwa.dot.gov/reports/pittd/cover.htm).

Institute of Transportation Engineers (ITE) (1999), *Transportation Planning Handbook*, ITE (Washington, DC) (www.ite.org).

Institute of Transportation Engineers (ITE) (2004), *Parking Generation, Third Edition*, ITE (Washington, DC) (www.ite.org).

Litman, Todd (2002), *What's It Worth? Economic Evaluation For Transportation Decision-Making*, originally presented at the Internet Symposium on Benefit-Cost Analysis, Transportation Association of Canada; available online (www.vtpi.org/worth.pdf).

Litman, Todd (2004a), *Evaluating Transportation Equity*, Victoria Transport Policy Institute; available online (www.vtpi.org/equity.pdf).

Litman, Todd (2004b), *Transportation Cost and Benefit Analysis; Techniques, Estimates and Implications*, Victoria Transport Policy Institute (www.vtpi.org); available online (www.vtpi.org/tca).

Office of Transportation Management, *Transportation Performance Measures*, Office of Operations, U.S. Department of Transportation, Federal Highway Administration (www.ops.fhwa.dot.gov); available online (www.ops.fhwa.dot.gov/travel/deployment_task_force/perf_measures.htm).

Puget Sound Regional Council (2003), *Parking Management Plan Checklist: Planning for Your Regional Growth Center*, Puget Sound Regional Council (www.psrc.org), Summer 2003; available online (www.psrc.org/projects/growth/parking.pdf).

Seattle Department of Transportation (2004), *Parking In Seattle*, City of Seattle (www.seattle.gov); available online (www.seattle.gov/transportation/parking).

Spackman, Michael, Alan Pearman, and Larry Phillips (2001), *Multi-criteria Analysis Manual*, Office of the Deputy Prime Minister (www.odpm.gov.uk), January 2001; available online (www.odpm.gov.uk/stellent/groups/odpm_about/documents/page/odpm_about_608524.hcsp).

Toolbox for Regional Policy Analysis describes methods for evaluating transportation and land-use policies (supported by the U.S. Department of Transportation, Federal Highway Administration) (www.fhwa.dot.gov/planning/toolbox).

Transportation Research Board (2001), *Performance Measures to Improve Transportation Systems and Agency Operations*, Transportation Research Board (www.trb.org); available online (http://gulliver.trb.org/publications/conf/reports/cp_26.pdf).

Urban Land Institute (ULI) (2000), *The Dimensions of Parking*, ULI (Washington, DC) (www.uli.org) and the National Parking Association (Washington, DC) (www.npapark.org).

Victoria Transport Policy Institute (VTPI) (2005), *Online TDM Encyclopedia*, VTPI (www.vtpi.org); available online ("Parking Evaluation" (www.vtpi.org/tdm/tdm73.htm) and "Planning and Implementation" (www.vtpi.org/tdm/tdm50.htm)).

7

Evaluating Individual Parking Facilities

This chapter describes how to evaluate specific parking facilities in terms of various parking performance indicators and management strategies. This illustrates many of the concepts discussed in this book and helps readers develop an appreciation of well-managed parking facilities.

EXAMPLES

Figure 7-1 shows a well-designed and managed parking facility: a 50-space lot in a mini-mall with a variety of shops, including a pharmacy, a sports shop, clothing stores, cafés, and restaurants. Additional priced parking is available on adjacent streets. Table 7-1 describes various features that indicate good management and potential ways to improve management.

Figure 7-2 illustrates another example of an efficiently managed parking facility: a 40-space lot located adjacent to a restaurant and shops. Parking is free to restaurant and shop patrons and to certain employees, and available to others for a fee. This lot has most of the positive attributes of the previous example plus priced parking available to motorists who do not quality for free parking (see Table 7-2).

Figure 7-3 illustrates an example of a poorly managed parking facility: a 50-space lot located behind a large computer store with free parking available to customers and employees. It is excessively large, with most parking spaces unoccupied on most days. It has minimal landscaping and no pedestrian amenities. Due to its excessive size (it occupies about a quarter of a city block) and poor condition, it is unattractive and unpleasant for pedestrian use (see Table 7-3).

Figure 7-1
Well-Managed Shopping Center Parking Facility

Example of a well-designed, efficiently managed parking facility in a commercial center.

Table 7-1
Shopping Center Parking Facility Evaluation

Good Management Features	Potential Improvements
• Multiple destinations served with diverse demand cycles, allowing efficient sharing. • Relatively small and efficiently used; most spaces occupied on most days. • Overflow parking available nearby; motorists can park on nearby streets and commercial lots if this lot is full. • Located in an area with diverse transportation and parking options with good sidewalks, bike lanes, and transit service, making it convenient to park a block or two away and walk to various shops, and allowing many customers and employees to use alternative modes. • Attractive lot with abundant landscaping and quality street furniture (e.g., lighting standards, benches, and signs). • Traffic flow logical and clearly indicated with signs and pavement markings. • Multiple access points for vehicles and pedestrians, including a pedestrian shortcut through the middle of the block. • Traffic speeds minimized, making the lot safe for motorists and pedestrians. • Secure and covered bicycle parking available near store entrances. • Clean and well maintained.	• Improve enforcement to control use and encourage turnover. • Add more signs indicating the location of overflow parking options. • Provide information on alternative transportation options, including transit and taxi services. • Price the most convenient parking spaces. • Implement a program to encourage employees to use alternative modes.

Summary of good features and potential improvements for parking management at an urban shopping center.

Figure 7-2
Well-Managed Commercial Parking Facility

Example of an efficiently managed commercial parking facility serving multiple destinations.

Table 7-2
Multidestination Parking Facility Evaluation

Good Management Features	Potential Improvements
• Multiple destinations served with diverse demand cycles. • Priced parking, for users who do not qualify for free parking. • Efficiently used; most spaces are used most days. • Relatively small, which is an appropriate scale for the area. • Good signage that indicates who may use which spaces. • Clean and well maintained.	• Improve pricing methods. Convert to a system that accommodates credit cards and charges for just the amount of time a motorist is parked. • Add more landscaping and amenities.

Summary of good features and potential improvements for parking management at a multidestination facility.

Figure 7-3
Poorly Managed Parking Facility

Example of a poorly managed parking facility.

Table 7-3
Poorly Managed Parking Facility Evaluation

Undesirable Management Features	Potential Improvements
• Serves only two destinations and is not available to other users. • Has a low utilization rate; most spaces are not used most days. • Unpriced. • Too large. • Poor lighting and visibility, creating security problems. • Unattractive and unpleasant for pedestrians. • Limited access points for pedestrians and motorists. • Poorly maintained.	• Convert it to paid, commercial parking so other motorists may use the lot. • Convert part of the lot to other uses, such as a new building. • Divide the lot into smaller sections or bays. • Improve the lighting and eliminate any parking spaces that are not clearly visible to nearby building occupants, to increase security. • Increase the number of access points for pedestrians. • Improve aesthetics and maintenance.

Summary of the undesirable features and potential improvements for a parking facility that is currently inefficiently managed.

Figure 7-4 illustrates an attractive driveway shared by two houses, built with paver blocks that allow rainwater to percolate and grass to grow. This design minimizes total pavement area and increases aesthetics.

Figure 7-5 illustrates parking in a multifamily complex. Parking spaces are located in the building courtyard, providing a high level of security and allowing the facility to serve as a meeting space and children's play area. The facility is well maintained (see Table 7-4).

Figure 7-4
Paver Block Residential Driveway

Example of a shared residential driveway made of paver blocks.

Figure 7-5
Multifamily Housing Parking Lot

Example of a well-managed parking lot in a multifamily development.

Table 7-4
Multifamily Housing Parking Lot Evaluation

Good Management Features	Potential Improvements
• Appropriate scale and size. • High utilization rate; most parking spaces used most days. • Creates a central courtyard, providing a high level of security and allowing the space to serve other uses. • Well maintained.	• Unbundle parking from housing so residents only pay for the parking spaces they use. • Rent any excess spaces to nonresidents. • Use paver blocks for a portion of parking spaces (any that are seldom used).

Summary of good management features and potential improvements to a multifamily parking lot.

Figure 7-6 illustrates an example of a poorly managed parking lot serving an apartment building. It is far larger than necessary. Most spaces are unoccupied most of the time and it is never more than a third full. There are no provisions to make excess capacity available to other uses (e.g., by renting unoccupied spaces). It is unattractive and poorly maintained and contains several nonoperating vehicles and piles of garbage. Due to its large size and poor condition, it degrades the neighborhood environment (see Table 7-5).

Figure 7-7 illustrates an attractive, 20-space parking lot located at a large, downtown church. There are several nice features, including its relatively small size, beautiful landscaping, attractive design and materials, and clear signage, which make it fit well into the site (see Table 7-6).

Figure 7-8 shows a well-maintained downtown parking structure with ground-floor retail, creating an attractive, lively, and secure street. In contrast, Figure 7-9 shows a parking structure with a large, unattractive façade covering about a third of a city block, creating a dead spot in the city. Some cities now require that parking structures incorporate ground-floor retail and other design details to enhance the streetscape.

Figure 7-6
Poorly Managed Residential Parking Facility

Example of a poorly managed residential parking facility.

Table 7-5
Poorly Managed Multifamily Parking Lot Evaluation

Undesirable Management Features	Potential Improvements
• Serves a single destination. • Too large. • Unpriced. • Unattractive and unpleasant for pedestrians. • Poorly maintained.	• Convert to paid, commercial parking so other motorists may use the lot. • Reduce size and convert a portion of the lot to other uses, such as additional housing or greenspace. • Improve aesthetics and maintenance.

Summary of undesirable features and potential improvements at a multifamily parking lot.

Figure 7-7
Church Parking Facility

Example of a well-designed church parking facility.

Table 7-6
Church Parking Facility Evaluation

Good Management Features	Potential Improvements
• Appropriate scale and size. • High utilization rate; most spaces used most days. • Attractive design and materials. • Use of paver blocks with grass growing on lightly used spaces. • Clear signing indicating who may use the facility. • Designated spaces for people with disabilities. • Well maintained.	• Make excess capacity available for rent during off-peak periods.

Summary of good management features and potential improvements for a small church parking lot.

Figure 7-8
Parking Structure with Ground-Floor Retail

Example of a parking structure that includes ground-floor retail.

Figure 7-9
Unattractive Parking Structure

Example of a parking structure that lacks ground-floor retail, which presents an unattractive face to the street.

8

Examples

This chapter contains examples to illustrate various types of parking management programs. Each example includes a description of the situation, a discussion of how parking management can be applied, and a checklist of potential management strategies suitable for that situation. Note that many of the parking management strategies described here provide a variety of benefits, including increased user convenience, cost savings, reduced traffic congestion, reduced environmental impacts, and improved travel options, which can help justify more implementation of management solutions than would be justified by parking facility cost savings alone.

INCREASE OFFICE BUILDING INCOME

Reducing parking requirements can increase commercial building profitability. Because more land is often devoted to parking than to the building footprint, a small reduction in parking requirements allows a large increase in the amount of building space that can be developed on a given parcel of land.

In a case study by Willson (1995), a four-story office building on a 190,000-square-foot site can either accommodate a 95,000-square-foot gross floor area building with 3.8 parking spaces per 1,000 square feet, or 135,000 square feet gross floor area if parking requirements are reduced to 2.5 per 1,000 square feet (see Table 8-1). With the lower (but generally sufficient) parking requirements, building space and the number of employees can increase 42 percent. As a result, annual net rental income increases 38 percent, increasing profitability and tax revenue.

Of course, it is possible that this reduced parking supply may be insufficient some time in the future. In that case, various parking management strategies can be deployed. The exact combination will depend on specific circumstances. This may include sharing rather than assigning individual parking spaces to employees, encouraging the use of alternative commute

Table 8-1
Fiscal Impacts of Reducing Parking Requirements

Factor	Conventional Requirements	Reduced Requirements	Difference
Parking requirements per 1,000 square feet GFA	3.8	2.5	−34%
Building GFA (square feet)	95,000	135,000	42%
Number of parking spaces	361	338	−6%
Parking lot area (square feet)	133,570	125,060	−6%
Floor area ratio	0.50	0.71	42%
Project cost	$10.6 million	$14.5 million	37%
Annual net income	$1,042,000	$1,440,000	38%
Property tax revenue	$117,030	$160,050	37%

GFA = gross floor area.

Effects of reducing parking requirements for an office building. In this case, a reasonable reduction in parking allows a 42 percent increase in building space and a 38 percent increase in annual income.

Sources: Willson, 1995; cited in Shoup, 2005.

Figure 8-1
Sharing Parking

A typical commercial building devotes far more land to parking than to the building footprint. Providing individual reserved spaces for each employee results in low utilization rates.

modes (e.g., walking, cycling, ridesharing, public transit, and telecommuting), arranging to share parking facilities with other nearby buildings, and creating an overflow parking plan.

Improved management can allow parking supply to be reduced in existing buildings, as described in the following example: An office building has 100 employees and 120 surface parking spaces, providing one space for each employee plus 20 spaces for visitors. The building earns $1,000,000 annually in rent, of which $900,000 is spent on debt servicing and operating expenses, leaving $100,000 annual net profit.

Parking management begins when a nearby restaurant arranges to use 20 spaces for staff parking during evenings and weekends for $50 per month per space, providing $12,000 in additional annual revenue. After subtracting $2,000 for walkway improvements between the sites and additional operating costs, this increases profits 10 percent. Later, a nearby church arranges to use 50 parking spaces on Sunday mornings for $500 per month, providing $6,000 in annual revenue. After subtracting $1,000 for additional operating costs, this increases profits by another 5 percent. Next, a commercial parking operator arranges to rent the parking to the general public during evenings and weekends. This provides $10,000 in net annual revenue, providing an additional 10 percent profit.

Inspired, the building manager develops a comprehensive management plan to take full advantage of the parking facility value. Rather than giving each employee a reserved space, employees share spaces, which reduces their parking requirements by 20 percent, to 80 spaces. A commute trip reduction program is implemented with a $40 per month cash-out option, which reduces parking requirements by another 20 spaces. As a result, employees only need 60 parking spaces. The extra 40 parking spaces are leased to nearby businesses for $80 per month, providing $32,000 in annual revenue, $9,600 of which is used to fund cash-out payments and $2,000 of which is used to cover additional operating costs, leaving about $20,000 net profit. Total building profits increase approximately 45 percent.

Because their business is growing, the building tenant wants to accommodate 30 additional employees. Purchasing land for another building would cost approximately $1 million and result in two separate work locations—an undesirable arrangement. Instead, the building manager stops leasing out daytime parking and raises the cash-out rate to $50 per month, which reduces employee parking demand by another 10 percentage points. With these management strategies, 87 parking spaces are adequate to serve 130 employees plus visitors, leaving the land currently used by 33 parking spaces available for a building site. (Figure 8-2 summarizes these changes.)

To address concerns that this parking supply may be insufficient some time in the future, a contingency plan is developed that identifies what will be done if more parking is needed, which might involve providing additional

Figure 8-2
Parking Demand Reductions

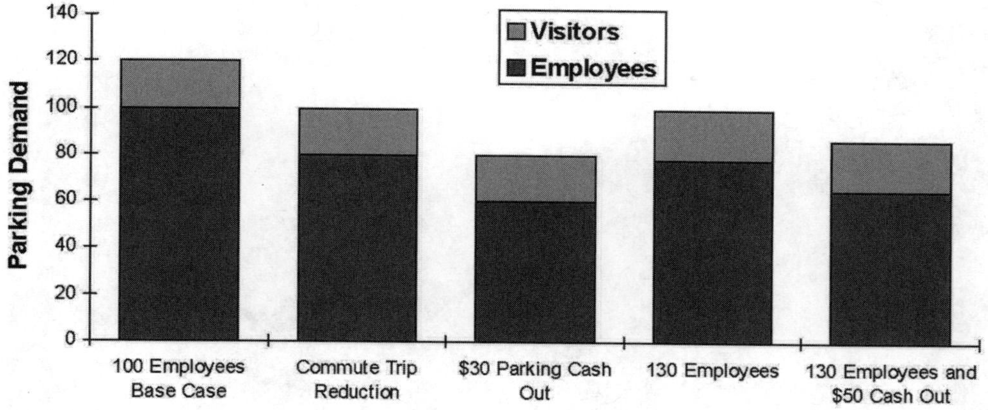

Various strategies can reduce the amount of parking required at a worksite. The unused parking spaces can be leased or rented, or the land can be used for new buildings or other activities.

commuter services and incentives during peak periods, leasing nearby parking, or building structured parking.

This parking management plan saves $1 million in land costs—a $50,000 annualized value. Parking spaces can still be rented on weekends and evenings, bringing in an additional $10,000. These parking management strategies increase total profits approximately 75 percent, allow the business to locate entirely at one location, and provide parking to other motorists during off-peak periods. Other benefits include increased travel options and parking cash-out benefits for employees, reduced traffic congestion and air pollution, and reduced stormwater runoff due to reductions in total pavement area.

Local governments can facilitate these strategies by allowing flexible minimum parking requirements and supporting development of a transportation management association in the area to provide parking brokerage and commute trip reduction services.

DOWNTOWN PARKING MANAGEMENT

Parking management is common in large cities. Good examples include Portland, Oregon, and Seattle, Washington (Kuzmyak et al., 2003), but some smaller cities and towns are also implementing creative programs as part of their efforts to redevelop their downtowns and older neighborhoods.

A good example is Ashland, Oregon (see Figure 8-3)—a small but rapidly growing city in central Oregon, famous for its Shakespeare Festival that attracts tens of thousands of visitors each year (City of Ashland, 2001). The

Figure 8-3
Downtown Ashland

Downtown Ashland, Oregon, is a commercial center and tourist attraction.

Source: City of Ashland Planning Department.

city's downtown is a major destination and activity center, particularly during the summer tourist season. Motorists often complain about parking problems there. A number of studies have examined ways to improve downtown traffic and parking conditions. The most recent study, performed in 1999/2000, began with a stakeholder consultation, which identified the following issues:

- Concern that existing parking supply is at capacity for customers and visitors during peak periods, leading to user inconvenience and limiting downtown economic activity.
- Concern that pricing parking would have a negative effect on customer traffic.
- Desire to balance customer, visitor, theater patron, and employee parking demand.
- Desire to use existing parking supply more efficiently, particularly by shifting downtown, on-street use to off-street lots and peripheral locations.
- Desire for better user information (e.g., signs and maps).
- Concern that regulations are enforced ineffectively, resulting in some employees occupying parking spaces intended for customer use.

Guiding Principles

CORE ZONE

- The purpose of, and priority for, parking in the core of downtown is to support and enhance the vitality of the retail/theater core.
- Parking will be provided to assure convenient, economical, and user-friendly access for customers, clients, and visitors to downtown.
- Priority will be given to short-term visitor parking (both on and off street) in this zone.

INTERMEDIATE ZONE

- Parking is established to provide opportunities for longer-term stays.
- It is the city's goal to further support the long-term development of this zone as an expansion of the retail/theater core.
- Parking is intended to be convenient, supportive of business activities, and user friendly.

PERIPHERY ZONE

- Parking is unregulated. As such, no time limits are in effect. Future management strategies assumed for this area will be contingent on the parking activity, capacity, and utilization of all other parking zones.

Source: City of Ashland, 2001.

A survey found 92 percent parking utilization in the downtown core at peak periods during the summer, and over 80 percent utilization during the fall. However, even during peak periods, parking is available on streets just outside the downtown (City of Ashland, 2001).

To address concerns that parking pricing would discourage customers and visitors, planners examined the experience of five comparable cities that have recently implemented priced parking. Their research indicated that pricing did not adversely affect visitor demand or use, that it increased turnover, that it generates net revenue, and that newer multispace meters work well.

Using this information, the planners developed a parking management plan. They divided the downtown into three zones (Core, Intermediate, and Periphery). For each of these zones, they developed overall guiding principles, parking management strategies, and an implementation plan that identifies near-, mid-, and long-term actions (see the sidebar entitled "Guiding Principles").

Based on these principles, consultants developed specific recommended strategies and actions for each zone. For example, in the Core zone, the plan determines that, over time, an increasing portion of on-street parking will be limited to 2 hours. The city will conduct regular parking surveys to determine the peak hour utilization and turnover rates. If utilization exceeds 85 percent and turnover rates are below a designated level, the city will begin one or more of the following actions:

- Increase level of enforcement of time limits.
- Encourage employees to park outside the Core zone.
- Reduce on-street time limits (e.g., 2 hours to 90 minutes and 4 hours to 2 hours) to increase turnover.
- Expand the Core zone boundaries to increase the number of on-street visitor spaces.
- Price parking (on and/or off street).
- Encourage use of alternative modes.
- Create new parking supply.
- Develop special regulations as needed, such as for disabled access, delivery, and loading areas, or to accommodate other particular land uses.

Similar, detailed implementation plans were developed for the two other zones, identifying planning objectives, implementation criteria, and specific actions. The plan recommends that the city consider pricing publicly owned parking facilities to increase turnover, shift employee parking to less convenient locations, encourage use of alternative modes, and provide funding to increase parking supply and support alternative modes. The plan recommends that the city apply the following policies when pricing publicly owned, off-street facilities:

- The short-term rate is comparable to rates for on-street parking.
- Special evening rates are applied to serve appropriate uses.
- Long-term, daily/monthly rates reflect the objectives of each zone.
- Rates are adjusted as needed to maintain optional utilization (85 percent peak occupancy).
- Rates are set to shift long-term parkers to locations outside the Core zone.

The plan recommends that parking revenues be deposited into a Downtown Parking Fund to pay for parking facility debt repayment and operating costs, downtown parking enforcement, marketing, mobility management programs, and building of additional parking supply. The plan recommends that the city:

- Develop user information resources, including signs and maps directing motorists to appropriate parking facilities, and promotion of alternative modes (e.g., walking, cycling, and transit).
- Establish high design standards for any new parking structures, including ground-level retail, convenient pedestrian access, and appropriate landscaping, signs, and lighting.
- Consider developing a downtown circulation bus service.
- Implement a residential parking permit program if needed to address spillover problems in nearby residential areas.

MAJOR DOWNTOWN REDEVELOPMENT

Kolozsvari and Shoup (2003) describe how parking management helped redevelop Pasadena, an older suburb in southern California. Its downtown declined between 1930 and 1980, leaving many derelict and abandoned buildings, in part due to the limited amount of parking available to customers. Curb parking was restricted to a 2-hour duration, but many employees used the most convenient, on-street spaces and moved their vehicles several times each day to avoid citations. In 1983, Old Pasadena was listed in the National Register of Historic Places and concerted efforts were made to redevelop it as a unique commercial district.

To address parking problems, the city proposed pricing on-street spaces to increase turnover and make more parking available to customers. Many local merchants initially opposed this idea. As a compromise, city officials agreed to dedicate all revenues to improving downtown public facilities and services. In 1993, a parking meter zone was established within which parking was priced and revenues were invested. With this proviso, the merchants supported the proposal. They began to see parking meters as a way to fund projects and services that directly benefit their customers and businesses. Because parking had previously been unpriced, the city lost no general fund revenue; in fact, the city gained overtime fine revenue.

The city formed a parking meter zone advisory board consisting of business and property owners, which recommended parking policies and set spending priorities for the meter revenues. This approach of connecting parking revenues directly to additional public services and keeping it under local control helped guarantee the program's success. Investments included new street furniture and trees, more police patrols, better street lighting, more street and sidewalk cleaning, pedestrian facility improvements, and marketing, such as the production of area maps showing local attractions and parking facilities. To highlight these benefits to motorists, each parking meter has a small sticker that reads, "Your Meter Money Will Make a Difference: Signage, Lighting, Benches, Paving."

This created a virtuous cycle: parking revenue funded community improvements, which attracted more visitors, which increased the parking revenue, which allowed further improvements. This resulted in extensive redevelopment of downtown buildings, which attracted more business and residents (see Figure 8-4). Parking is no longer a problem for customers. Local sales tax revenues have increased much faster than in other shopping districts with cheaper parking and nearby malls that offer free parking. This indicates that charging market rate parking (prices that result in 85 to 90 percent peak-period utilization rates), with revenues dedicated to local improvements, can be an effective way to support urban redevelopment and benefit local customers, businesses, and residents overall.

Below are examples of parking management strategies used in Old Pasadena, which can be applied in other commercial centers:

- Establish a community vision that identifies strategic goals and objectives.
- Inventory public and private, on- and off-street parking supply. Establish an ongoing evaluation program to track parking utilization rates and investigate problems such as times and locations where customers cannot find parking, and spillover impacts.
- Regulate on-street parking to favor higher-value users. Dedicate special parking spaces to loading, taxis, and disabled motorists. Limit the most convenient spaces (those most suitable for customer parking) to 2 hours or less.
- Encourage employees to use less convenient parking spaces, including spaces behind buildings or those located a few blocks from the main commercial core.

Figure 8-4
Downtown Old Pasadena

Old Pasadena merchants supported pricing downtown parking if the revenues were used to improve local services. This increased economic development and downtown livability.

Source: Pasadena Convention and Visitors Bureau.

- Price parking and use revenues to improve local public services, with guidance from stakeholders concerning how the money will be spent. Charge higher fees for central locations and peak periods.
- Use convenient pricing methods. Choose one system for use by both public and private operators.
- Improve user information, including signs, maps, brochures, and Web sites, indicating parking availability and price for both public and commercial parking facilities.
- Provide effective enforcement. Establish friendly enforcement policies, such as "first violation free," backed with adequate fines and apprehension for repeat violators.
- Develop an overflow parking plan for busy periods, such as peak tourist and holiday shopping periods. Consider use of shuttle services between remote parking and destinations during periods of high demand.
- Implement a commute trip reduction program that encourages downtown employees to walk, bicycle, carpool, or ride transit to work.
- Improve walking connections between parking facilities and destinations.
- If nearby residential streets experience spillover parking problems, implement a residential parking permit system.
- Establish a transportation management association to provide transportation and parking management services in the area.
- Encourage unbundling of parking from building space.
- Establish parking facility design guidelines and standards to improve facility quality, safety, aesthetics, and environmental performance.
- Provide bicycle parking and changing facilities and, where appropriate, allow bicycle parking to substitute for a portion of automobile parking.
- Create more accurate and flexible parking standards. Reduce parking requirements where developers implement parking management programs.
- Train local planning professionals in parking management concepts and practices. Provide technical assistance to private developers, designers, and facility managers to help implement parking management programs. Support ongoing professional development concerning parking management.
- Identify and change any municipal laws or policies that discourage sharing, unbundling, and pricing of parking facilities and other parking management strategies.
- To demonstrate leadership, apply progressive parking practices to municipal buildings.

URBAN VILLAGE

An urban village is a walkable, mixed-use neighborhood center. An example is the Cook Street Village in Victoria, British Columbia, which has about 50 businesses along eight blocks of a minor arterial, surrounded by medium-density apartments and single-family housing (see Figure 8-5). It is a hub of neighborhood activity. Parking is considered a problem and a constraint on further commercial and residential growth; recent proposals for new development were rejected, largely due to concerns over increased vehicle traffic and parking problems.

Although the most convenient on-street spaces are well used, and most parking lots fill at some point during a typical week, there are always plenty of unoccupied parking spaces somewhere in the village. For example, during weekdays, the retirement home parking lot is often full, but there are plenty of unoccupied spaces nearby behind the pub, beauty parlor, and coffee shop. On weekend evenings, the pub's parking lot fills, but there is plenty of parking at the retirement home and bakery. On weekend mornings, the coffee shop parking lot is well used, but there are plenty of spaces at the pub and bakery. Several parking utilization surveys performed at various times of the week never found more than 55 percent of the total parking spaces occupied (see Figures 8-6, 8-7, and 8-8). However, much of this parking is unavailable to the motorists who need it. Coffee shop patrons risk a fine if they park in the

Figure 8-5
Cook Street Village

The Cook Street Village in Victoria, British Columbia, is a typical, small commercial center with various shops along a minor arterial. Shoppers often complain of insufficient parking, which results from poor management of area parking rather than an actual shortage of supply.

empty pub parking lot during weekdays, and pub patrons face a fine if they park in the empty coffee shop lot on weekend evenings.

A parking management program can address parking problems in the area by allowing more efficient use of existing parking supply. Such a program can be implemented by the city or a local business organization, or by creating a local transportation management association. It begins with a survey to identify all parking facilities in the area, both public and private, and their utilization patterns. Based on this information, property owners are encouraged to share or rent out parking spaces during their off-peak periods, so motorists have access to the maximum number of spaces. The most convenient spaces are regulated and priced to favor priority users (e.g., delivery vehicles, people with disabilities, and customers), and employees and other long-term users are encouraged to use more remote spaces or alternative modes.

Below are parking management strategies suitable for application in an urban village:

- Encourage businesses to share parking, so, for example, the coffee shop allows its parking spaces to be used by pub employees and patrons weekend evenings in exchange for using pub parking on weekdays and weekend mornings.
- Provide signs and maps showing where customers may park.

Figure 8-6
Weekday Noon

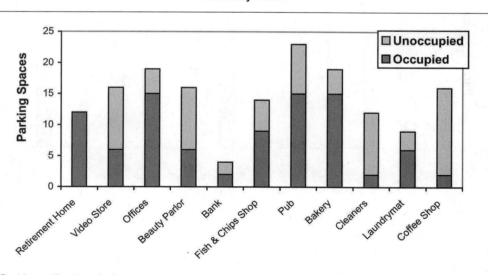

Parking utilization during the middle of a typical weekday.

Figure 8-7
Weekend Evening

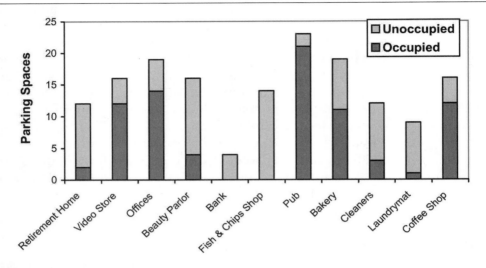

Parking utilization during a typical weekend evening.

Figure 8-8
Weekend Morning

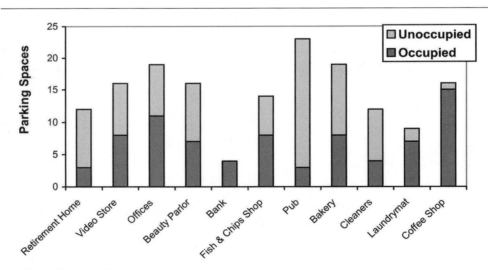

Parking utilization during a typical weekend morning.

- Use parking regulations, pricing, and incentives to make the most convenient spaces available to customers and delivery vehicles. Encourage employees and residents to use less convenient spaces, including parking hidden behind buildings or located a few blocks away.
- Allow and encourage nearby apartments and condominiums to lease extra spaces to village businesses and employees.
- Provide adequate enforcement of parking regulations, particularly during busy periods, but ensure that enforcement is considered friendly and fair.
- Implement a commute trip reduction program that encourages village employees to walk, bicycle, carpool, or ride transit to work.
- Have an overflow parking plan for occasional special events that attract crowds to the village.
- Install suitable bicycle parking and clothes-changing facilities; one facility can serve several worksites.
- Apply more accurate and flexible parking requirements. Allow developers to reduce the parking supply at their buildings if they implement a parking management program.
- Allow or require in-lieu fees to fund new public parking facilities instead of single-destination private parking.
- Establish high standards for parking facility design, including aesthetic and safety features, to reflect the high quality of the village environment.
- If necessary, implement a residential parking permit system, but only restrict nonresidential use of on-street parking as much as necessary. For example, allow 1-hour parking or price parking on nearby streets, so shop patrons can use it, but turnover is high.

URBAN NEIGHBORHOOD PARKING MANAGEMENT

Seattle, Washington, has a proactive parking planning and management program. The program Web site (see Figure 8-9) sets a positive tone by beginning with the question, "How May We Serve You?" It discusses parking management concepts, identifies various parking management strategies suitable for different conditions and problems (e.g., business districts and residential areas), identifies how residents and business owners can initiate changes (including specific people to contact within city agencies), and answers common questions concerning parking issues. The Web site contains specific information on parking regulations and enforcement practices, instructions on using new parking payment systems, and various parking planning documents, including *Parking Guide: Simple Ways to Improve Your Neighborhood's Parking* (Seattle DOT, 2001). This helps stakeholders identify a broad range of possible solutions to parking problems and allows neighborhoods to develop parking plans that best meet their specific needs.

Figure 8-9
Seattle Parking Information Web Site

Seattle's official city Web site has extensive information on parking issues.

Source: Seattle DOT, 2001.

For example, the Capitol Hill neighborhood experiences significant parking congestion. A survey found that, although there is plenty of parking available in the neighborhood overall (even during peak periods, 30 percent of spaces are vacant), parking demand was concentrated on certain streets. Much of the on-street parking is unregulated and used by commuters, many of whom park in the area and ride transit downtown. Although commercial off-street parking prices are low ($3 to $6 per day), these lots are only half filled because so many motorists can park for free. Some on-street parking is regulated, but this is often abused. For example, surveys found that, in areas with 1-hour maximum parking, vehicles actually averaged 2.7 hours per stay (Seattle DOT, 1999).

In this situation, parking management consists largely of incentives to prevent commuters from using on-street parking spaces. The city worked with neighborhood organizations to develop appropriate regulations, pricing, user information, and enforcement.

Below are strategies suitable for managing parking in urban neighborhoods:
- Work with local residents and businesses to develop a parking management program that responds to the specific needs of the neighborhood.
- Improve user information, indicating where motorists should and should not park, including information for commuters on the availability and price of off-street parking and alternative travel modes.
- Encourage businesses to share parking facilities and rent their parking to the public during off hours, to allow maximum use of each space.
- Encourage nearby residential buildings to rent unused parking for employee and overflow use.
- Improve parking enforcement.
- Regulate on-street parking to favor short-term customer use on commercial streets.
- If necessary, implement a residential parking permit system, but only restrict nonresidential use as much as necessary.
- Allow or require in-lieu fees to fund public parking instead of single-destination private parking facilities.

RESORT HOTEL DEVELOPMENT

Parking management can help address parking problems and support economic development in resort communities (USEPA, 1999). Long Beach, California, is experiencing significant redevelopment in its downtown core, supported by a convention center, a rail transit station, a pedestrian walkway, commercial development, and tourist activities. The four-star D'Orsay Hotel was proposed for one prime site. It would include 162 rooms and 35,000 square feet of retail space. To accommodate the site, and due to high land values in the area, costly underground parking will be needed. According to the city's parking standards, this development would normally require one parking space per room, plus four spaces per 1,000 square feet of retail space, totaling 302 spaces. With construction costs of at least $16,000 per space, this would have added $4.8 million, making the project financially infeasible.

After conducting a traffic study to assess parking demand at comparable hotels, the city planning department decided that parking requirements could be reduced to three spaces per 1,000 square feet of retail, and 0.7 spaces per room, reflecting the fact that many guests do not bring a vehicle. This reduced total parking requirements from 288 to 218 spaces, saving $1.3 million, but even this reduction was insufficient to make the project profitable. As a result, the city agreed to offer in-lieu fees of $3,000 per space in capital costs plus $50 per month in operating costs for 56 of the 218 spaces. This reduced the developer's parking construction costs by a total of $2 million, which made the project financially more feasible.

Below are strategies suitable for managing parking in a resort area:

- Ensure that parking policies and planning practices are consistent with strategic economic development and land-use objectives. In particular, policies should support parking management strategies and discourage paving land for more parking facilities, in order to preserve environmental quality and walkability.
- Encourage mixed-use, infill development with shared parking facilities.
- Use flexible, lower-bound parking requirements (such as 50 percent rather than 80 percent demand curves), adjusted to reflect factors that reduce parking demand, such as shared parking or use of alternative modes.
- Provide off-site parking facilities to accommodate overflow parking.
- Improve walkability and transit services to reduce parking demand and expand the range of parking facilities that serve a destination.
- Price and regulate parking to prioritize use and reduce demand.
- Provide adequate regulation and enforcement to address concerns about spillover parking in nearby areas.
- Create a local organization, such as a transportation management association, to coordinate parking planning, construction of public parking facilities, user information, and other parking management services.
- Allow in-lieu fees to fund municipal parking facilities and programs that substitute for a portion of on-site spaces.
- Monitor parking problems and evaluate parking management programs to determine what additional changes might be needed in the future.

URBAN RESIDENTIAL DEVELOPMENT

Parking management is important for urban redevelopment (City of Victoria, 1997). Harris Green is a mixed neighborhood at the edge of downtown Victoria, British Columbia. As a result of a local design charrette (a community planning exercise involving residents, developers, and public officials), the city eliminated minimum parking requirements in the area, allowing developers to decide how much parking to provide based on market demand. Between 1999 and 2004, about a dozen medium- and high-density residential developments were approved for this area, mostly condominiums and townhouses containing 25 to 75 units. Parking is unbundled in many of these buildings, so occupants only pay for the amount of parking they want, rather than a certain number of spaces being included automatically with their unit. In these conditions, residents typically demand just 0.5 to 0.8 spaces per unit, compared with 1.0 to 2.0 spaces per unit required by conventional standards.

A typical example is a five-story condominium at 1030 Yates Street, with 47 units containing 75 total bedrooms and dens (see Figure 8-10). Prices range from $170,000 for a 786 square-foot, one-bedroom unit, up to $355,000 for a 1,618-square-foot, two-bedroom, two-story penthouse. This location has excellent access to numerous nearby shops and public services, good walking

Figure 8-10
Urban Residential

Example of a new condominium with unbundled parking, where parking spaces are rented separately from the housing unit.

and cycling facilities, and excellent transit service. Many residents in this area do not own an automobile. Parking lots at older apartment complexes nearby, constructed when generous parking requirements were still in place, are often half empty.

By conventional parking standards, this development would require 59 to 72 parking spaces (1.5 per unit or 1.0 per bedroom), but the developers only built 27. Each of the 12 penthouses is sold with a parking space included, and the remaining 15 spaces are managed by the condominium council, to be rented according to demand, with prices expected to be about $100 per month for each space, or about 10 percent of apartment rents.

Below are strategies suitable for managing parking in growing medium- and high-density residential areas:

- Encourage mixed-use (commercial on the ground floor, with residential above) development in accessible, multimodal locations, so residents do not need to own as many vehicles.

- Use more accurate and flexible parking standards, or eliminate parking requirements altogether and let the market determine how much parking to supply.
- Unbundle parking. Allow residents to rent just the number of parking spaces they need.
- Establish a carsharing program within or near residential buildings, so residents can conveniently rent a vehicle by the hour or day.
- Provide information to residents on travel options in the area, including bus, taxi, and vehicle rental services, and cycling programs.
- Provide information to residents and guests on nearby public parking rental options.
- Provide convenient, secure, covered bicycle parking for residents and their visitors.
- Support development of commercial parking facilities nearby to provide off-site parking if needed.

TRANSPORTATION TERMINALS

Parking management is important at transportation terminals, such as airports, trains, bus stations, and ferry docks. Careful planning is needed to provide adequate parking supply while supporting other planning objectives, such as the ability to accommodate residential and commercial development around transit stations and future facility expansion. Improved management can help reconcile these objectives (see Figure 8-11).

For example, when planning the new Hiawatha and Northstar rail transit stations in Minneapolis, Minnesota, the planning agency performed a detailed study to identify parking needs and potential management strategies (Metropolitan Council, 2003). Experts recommended the following strategies:

- Create a Parking Management Action Team with residents, elected officials, and government staff to provide ongoing planning and program development.
- Implement neighborhood-based parking management and enforcement.
- Increase regulations where needed to increase turnover of convenient, on-street spaces.
- Improve pedestrian and bicycle access to each station (e.g., improved and new sidewalks, paths, and bike lanes, and bike lockers/racks).
- Couple parking and transit fare collection and enforcement.
- Privatize parking management.
- Provide connecting bus service, so residents along the corridor will never be more than four blocks from a bus route that connects to a station.
- Use additional revenue from parking pricing and enforcement for neighborhood improvements, such as streetscape and transit improvements.
- Build new parking facilities to be shared with other users, such as nearby shops, offices, and gyms.

Figure 8-11
Parking Management at Transportation Terminals

Parking management is important around transportation terminals, including train and bus stations, airport, and ferry terminals to accommodate parking for travelers, plus business activity and residents.

- Create "kiss-and-ride" drop-off areas where appropriate.
- Encourage people to bicycle by having bike lockers at the stations.
- Launch a comprehensive marketing and education program prior to and after opening transit lines (e.g., create a transit trip planner, provide parking availability information indicating how to reach stations and where to park, and distribute parking user information rather than issuing citations to first-time violators of parking regulations).
- Address real and perceived security concerns of pedestrians and transit users.
- Collect data to quantify parking problems and establish an ongoing evaluation program.
- Establish transit overlay districts around each station (e.g., apply reduced and more flexible parking requirements, require mobility management plans, and allow developments to buy and sell parking credits).
- Expand and modify residential parking permit programs around transit stations as needed.
- Encourage transit commuting to central business districts, and limit future increases in parking supply there.
- Encourage increased housing density around stations without increasing parking supply.
- Improve parking facility pricing systems to increase user convenience.

CAMPUS PARKING MANAGEMENT

Parking management can help college, university, and industrial campuses address parking problems and accommodate growth. The University of Victoria is located in a suburban neighborhood about 5 miles from downtown (UVIC, 2003). Many students live off campus. Parking is currently relatively plentiful (approximately 4,500 spaces) and cheap. Users pay just $142 for an annual pass or $5 per day, and there are few restrictions on the use of parking passes (e.g., a pass can be used on multiple vehicles, and unlimited-use complementary passes are distributed to various volunteers and donors). Although motorists often complain about inadequate parking, utilization surveys show that there is adequate supply; however, during peak periods, the most convenient lots (those closest to the campus center) often fill.

The 25-year strategic campus development plan anticipates 2 percent annual growth in campus population (students, staff, and researchers), and includes plans to construct new buildings on some existing parking lots and a commitment to preserve existing campus greenspace. Any additional parking supply will require costly multistory structures.

In 2000, students voted to establish the UPass program: students pay an additional $45 per term fee, which gives them unlimited local transit service (their student body card becomes a transit pass). In addition, campus walking

Figure 8-12
University of Victoria Parking

Improved parking management at the University of Victoria accommodates growth without increasing campus parking supply. Like many campuses, motorists often have difficultly finding a parking space, although unoccupied parking spaces are available elsewhere on campus. Better user information, regulations, and pricing can result in more efficient use of parking resources.

and cycling facilities have been improved. As a result, parking demand on campus has declined. Consultants recommended a contingency-based plan that includes a variety of additional management strategies, some of which should be implemented immediately; others would be implemented only if conditions require.

Below are some recommended strategies:

- Expand the mandate of the campus parking services department to include a wide range of parking and transportation management services. Provide the new department with the resources needed for effective management and enforcement.

- Gradually increase the number of parking passes that may be sold per available parking space. Monitor utilization rates and complaints, and implement additional management strategies as needed to respond to any problems that develop.

- Raise parking fees, particularly unlimited-use, long-term fees. Increases should be gradual and predictable, such as a 10 percent annual increase for the next five years.

- Restructure fees to reduce or eliminate unlimited-use, long-term (weekly, monthly, and annual) parking passes, and replace them with daily and hourly fees. Increase prices for long-term passes so there is less financial incentive to use them rather than daily tickets. Unlimited-use, long-term passes can be eliminated altogether so motorists pay always by the day or hour (daily tickets can be sold with bulk discounts, such as 20 for the price of 15, but users will still save each day they avoid using a campus parking space).

- Improve pricing methods to make daily and hourly passes more convenient to use. Use pricing systems that accommodate credit cards, debit cards, and cellular telephone payments, and only charge for the amount of time a vehicle is actually parked.

- Regulate the most convenient parking spaces to favor higher-priority uses (e.g., by putting shorter time limits and short-term meters on spaces near building entrances).

- Offer discounted passes that may only be used at less convenient parking lots (those at the edge of campus) during peak periods. This could be implemented when parking pass rates increase, allowing motorists to avoid rate increases if they accept restrictions on their peak-period parking location.

- Establish a commute trip reduction program that encourages campus commuters to use alternative modes. In particular, extend the UPass program to staff, establish rideshare programs (e.g., carpool and vanpool), provide guaranteed ride home services, and address barriers to the use of alternative modes identified by commuters.

- Increase enforcement of parking regulations, particularly during busy periods, but ensure that enforcement is considered friendly and fair.
- Limit parking passes to a particular vehicle (they are currently transferable).
- Make sure that campus officials are aware of the cost of the complementary parking passes they distribute, and set limits on when and where they may be used and by whom.
- Develop special parking management programs during peak periods, such as the first week of the school year and during major sports events. These might include information encouraging visitors to use alternative modes, information on available parking facilities, arrangements to use off-campus overflow parking facilities, and shuttle van services to those facilities.
- Improve user information about parking and transportation options. Provide signs and maps indicating the location of parking facilities.
- Ensure that parking facility design and operations reflect best current practices in terms of aesthetics, convenience, safety, environmental impact reduction, and asset management.
- Establish a transportation management association with nearby businesses to facilitate sharing and commute trip reduction programs.
- Improve campus walkability, particularly connections to outer parking lots. Provide signs and maps to help visitors walk from parking facilities to destinations.

REGIONAL PARK

Goldstream Regional Park, located a few miles from Victoria, British Columbia, currently has about 100 parking spaces. This is adequate most times but insufficient during autumn weekends, when many visitors come to view the salmon runs (see Figure 8-13). At various times, park administrators have considered adding additional parking spaces, but expanding the parking lots will cost thousands of dollars per space, increase annual maintenance and operating expenses, and have negative environmental impacts. This is not justified for capacity that is only needed a few days each year.

Instead of expanding parking supply to accommodate occasional peaks, park officials could implement a parking and mobility management program. This will preserve parkland, reduce roadway traffic congestion and crash risk, and improve travel options for nondrivers.

Below are strategies suitable for addressing regional park parking problems:

- Produce park maps and brochures describing transportation and parking options, with information on recommended overflow parking locations (e.g., "If the main parking lot is full, you can park south of the main entrance on the highway shoulder.").
- Produce signs displayed on the highway to the park, indicating parking conditions and the location of alternative parking facilities.

Figure 8-13
Regional Park Parking

A regional park occasionally experiences parking congestion. Rather than adding additional parking, this situation can be addressed with parking and mobility management strategies.

- Charge a higher parking fee during peak periods.
- Provide subsidized shuttle service from downtown during peak periods. Offer family discounts, and equip shuttle vehicles to carry recreational equipment, such as roof racks for canoes and bike racks.
- Improve walking and cycling connections to the park.
- Encourage park staff to use alternative modes for commuting, or park at remote parking lots during busy periods.
- During peak periods, have staff direct traffic and increase enforcement of parking regulations.
- Rather than paving land to provide additional parking that is needed occasionally, use pavement blocks and stabilized lawns for overflow parking.

SPORTS ARENA

A new, 7,000-seat sports arena and entertainment center is being built at the edge of downtown Victoria, British Columbia (see Figure 8-14). During the planning process, some residents argued that it would have been cheaper to locate the facility in a nearby suburban community where land costs are lower. Although this would have reduced parking costs per space, it would have required many more parking spaces, thus increasing total parking costs.

According to conventional standards (one space per two seats plus one space per employee), the arena would require about 4,000 parking spaces, cov-

Figure 8-14
Victoria Arena

Locating an arena in a downtown area allows patrons and employees to use nearby, existing parking facilities. If located in a suburban area, many acres of land would need to be paved for parking.

ering about 32 acres of land, at a cost of approximately $20 million. By locating near downtown, most of the arena's transportation requirements can be met with existing facilities and services. Patrons can use the thousands of existing downtown parking spaces. Since most major events occur during evenings or weekends, there is generally plenty of parking available. In addition, the downtown location is accessible to people who arrive by transit or bicycle, and is near numerous restaurants and bars to enjoy before or after an event.

A number of management strategies can improve parking and travel at sports and cultural centers. Many of these strategies can also be applied to facilities in suburban locations, although they would be less effective due to fewer parking and travel options.

Below are strategies suitable for managing parking at a major sport and cultural activity center:

- Provide information to event attendees on parking location and cost, and transportation options, such as public transit services. Include information with event publicity and tickets, on directional signs, and in maps and brochures about the facility.
- Negotiate with nearby businesses to maximize the amount of parking that is available to arena patrons. For example, encourage nearby office buildings to rent their parking spaces during evenings and weekends.

- Regulate and price parking to make the most convenient spaces available to priority users. For example, ensure that there are an adequate number of parking spaces for people with disabilities and for rideshare vehicles close to the arena entrance.
- Implement parking regulation and enforcement programs on nearby residential streets to minimize parking spillover problems.
- Price on-street parking nearby, with exemptions for residents if necessary, and use a portion of the revenue to benefit neighborhood residents with street improvements, school programs, or other special services.
- Have special plans to deal with parking problems during especially large events, which may include shuttle bus services to remote parking lots, and special publicity to encourage patrons to use more distant spaces or to arrive by alternative modes.
- Offer valet service during particularly busy periods so that motorists' cars will be parked at an off-site lot.
- Implement travel and parking management programs for arena staff to minimize the number of spaces they use during major events.

AFFORDABLE RESIDENTIAL DEVELOPMENT

Parking management can increase housing affordability, as illustrated by the following example. Imagine that a developer plans to construct four-story apartment buildings on a 3-acre parcel to provide affordable housing. Parking is a major cost. As the number of surface parking spaces increases, the number of housing units declines and the cost per unit increases (see Table 8-2). Using underground parking reduces land requirements but significantly increases construction costs. As a result, it is impossible to provide affordable rents while meeting conventional parking requirements. Developers' most common response is to build less affordable urban housing.

Parking requirements also impose costs on nonprofit developments (Nelson/Nygaard Consulting, 2002). To provide housing priced at $80,000 per unit (for a monthly rent of about $500), a subsidy of only $4,000 would be

Table 8-2
Residential Development Options

	Option 1	Option 2	Option 3	Option 4
Parking ratios	0.5	1.0	1.33	1.0
Housing units	50	40	30	50
Parking spaces	25 (surface)	40 (surface)	40 (surface)	50 (underground)
Cost per unit	$50,000	$60,000	$75,000	$80,000
Monthly rent	$312	$375	$468	$500

As the number of parking spaces per unit increases, so do housing costs.

needed if no parking is required, a $12,792 subsidy would be required for one parking space per unit, and a $26,251 subsidy would be required for two parking spaces. In this case, a given housing subsidy fund can benefit about 6.5 times as many households with no parking spaces compared with two spaces per unit.

Residents of affordable urban housing tend to own fewer than the average number of vehicles, tend to respond to financial incentives, and are often willing to use alternative travel modes. It therefore makes sense to reduce parking requirements and rely more on management strategies for such housing (see Figure 8-15).

Below are parking management strategies that can help reduce residential parking requirements and increase housing affordability:

- As much as possible, locate affordable housing in accessible, multimodal neighborhoods (those with good walking, cycling, and public transit).
- Apply more flexible and accurate parking requirements, reflecting the lower parking demand for lower-income residents in accessible, multi-

Figure 8-15
Affordable Housing Requires Less Parking

Housing occupied by people with lower incomes, people with disabilities, students, and retired people generally needs less off-street parking than required by conventional standards, particularly if parking is unbundled (rented separately rather than automatically included with each housing unit) and suitable options are available nearby to accommodate overflow. For example, this five-unit condominium probably needs just three or four off-street parking spaces, rather than the five to eight typically required by zoning codes. Visitors can use on-street spaces.

modal locations. This typically allows 25 to 50 percent reductions compared with conventional parking standards.

- Unbundle parking from housing, so residents only pay for the parking spaces they need. For example, rather than charging $500 per month for an apartment with a "free" parking space, charge $450 per month for the apartment and $50 per month for each parking space used.
- Incorporate a carshare service in the building so residents can easily rent a car by the hour or day.
- Provide secure and convenient bicycle storage for residents and their visitors.
- Implement a plan to deal with any spillover parking problems that occur, such as restrictions on overnight, on-street parking.
- Use contingency-based planning to deal with uncertainty.

SMALL BUSINESS

Parking management can help small businesses reduce costs and address parking problems. For example, imagine that a hair stylist wants to develop a new five-chair hair salon. Convenient parking is important for customers and employees. During peak periods, a stand-alone, five-chair hair salon requires 14 to 16 parking spaces (five hair stylists, one receptionist, five customers being served, and three to five customers waiting their turn). There are a number of ways that a small business like this can encourage more efficient use of parking facilities.

Below are parking management strategies suitable for small commercial development:

- Rather than developing a stand-alone shop, locate businesses in a mini-mall. Because different types of businesses have different peak periods, they can efficiently share parking, thus reducing total parking requirements (see Figure 8-16).
- Offer employees incentives to use alternative commute modes and remote parking spaces during busy periods.
- Work with local traffic officials to maximize the supply and turnover of on-street parking, for example, by imposing time limits or pricing, and by increasing enforcement of regulations.
- Post signs indicating the location of overflow parking options (e.g., "If this lot is full, additional parking is available on Oak Street.")
- Improve walking conditions in the area to help customers and employees walk to the shop from homes, worksites, and nearby parking facilities.
- Provide bicycle parking for employees and customers.
- Price parking, and offer discounts or exemptions to customers.
- Work with other nearby businesses and local governments to create a transportation management association, which provides services to support more efficient use of parking facilities, including sharing and bro-

Figure 8-16
Cluster of Shops

A cluster of shops requires about half the number of parking spaces that would be needed if each business was located alone and supplied all of its own peak-period parking.

kerage services, better regulation of public parking facilities, promotion of alternative modes, pedestrian improvements, and even shuttle services during busy periods.

- Ensure that parking facility design and operation reflect best current practices in terms of aesthetics, convenience, safety, environmental protection, and asset management.

COMMUNITY EVENT PARKING

Community organizations such as schools and recreation centers occasionally sponsor events that attract large numbers of visitors, such as football games and concerts, which cause traffic and parking problems on nearby residential streets. As a result, event sponsors may receive complaints from neighbors.

In response, these organizations should develop special-event transportation and parking management plans. Below are strategies for managing major events at schools and other community facilities. Not all of these strategies need to be applied to every event but can be implemented as needed based on circumstances.

- Clearly indicate to event participants where they should and should not park. Provide user information (e.g., signs and maps) showing where parking is available.

- Find off-site parking that can be used when needed. For example, a nearby church may have parking available during weekday evenings, and an office or factory may have parking available during weekends. Arrange to borrow, share, or rent these parking spaces for occasional use.
- Encourage participants to share rides and use alternative travel modes to events.
- Identify areas on campuses, in community centers, and in parks that can be used for occasional overflow parking, such as reinforced lawns and industrial areas.
- Implement ongoing commute trip reduction programs that encourage staff to use alternative modes for commuting.
- Improve walking and cycling access to school and community centers, and provide secure and convenient bicycle parking.
- Use school buses and volunteer vans to help transport event participants and, if necessary, to provide shuttle service to off-site parking spaces.
- If necessary, provide valet service during particularly busy periods, with motorists leaving their car to be parked at an off-site lot.
- If necessary, arrange for traffic police to direct traffic and enforce parking regulations.
- Meet with the local neighborhood association to discuss local traffic and parking problems, and provide a small gift, such as free event tickets, to nearby residents as compensation for enduring occasional traffic and parking problems.

CHAPTER 8 REFERENCES AND INFORMATION RESOURCES

Baker, David (2002), *Why it's a good idea to unbundle new urban housing and parking*, David Baker + Partners Architects, (www.dbarchitect.com); available online (www.dbarchitect.com/firm/writing/writing_pdfs/parking_and_housing.pdf).

City of Ashland (2001), "Parking Plan," *Ashland Downtown Plan: Phase II* (Ashland, OR) (www.ashland.or.us); available online (www.ashland.or.us/Files/Downtown%20Plan%20Phase%20II.pdf).

City of Victoria (1997), *Harris Green Charrette* (Victoria, BC) (www.city.victoria.bc.ca).

Jia, Wenyu and Martin Wachs (1998), *Parking Requirements and Housing Affordability: A Case Study of San Francisco*, Research Paper 380, The University of California Transportation Center (www.uctc.net); available online (www.uctc.net/scripts/countdown.pl?380.pdf).

Kolozsvari, Douglas and Donald Shoup (2003), *Turning Small Change Into Big Changes*, ACCESS No. 23, University of California Transportation Center (www.uctc.net), Fall 2003, pp. 2-7; available online (www.uctc.net/access/23/Access%2023%20-%2002%20-%20Small%20Change%20into%20Big%20Change.pdf).

Kuzmyak, J. Richard, Rachel Weinberger, Richard H. Pratt, and Herbert S. Levinson (2003), *Parking Management and Supply: Traveler Response to Transport System Changes*, Chapter 18, Report 95, Transit Cooperative Research Program; Transportation Research Board (www.trb.org); available online (http://gulliver.trb.org/publications/tcrp/tcrp_rpt_95c18.pdf).

Metropolitan Council (2003), *Preliminary Findings of Expert Panel on Parking Management Strategies Around Hiawatha LRT and Minneapolis' Northstar Stations*, Twin Cities Metropolitan Council (www.metrocouncil.org); available online (www.metrocouncil.org/transportation/lrt/ParkingRecs.htm).

Nelson/Nygaard Consulting (2002), *Housing Shortage/Parking Surplus*, Transportation and Land Use Coalition (www.transcoalition.org); available online (www.transcoalition.org/reports/housing_s/housing_shortage_home.html).

Raphael, David and Charles Rutkowski (2000), *Enhancing Public and Visitor Transportation in the Greater Sedona Area: A Strategic Partnership Between the City of Sedona, Arizona and the Coconino National Forest*, Community Transportation Association of America (Washington, DC) (www.ctaa.org), presented at the Transportation Research Board Annual Meeting.

Seattle Department of Transportation (Seattle DOT) (1999), *Comprehensive Neighborhood Parking Study*, City of Seattle (www.cityofseattle.net); available online (www.seattle.gov/transportation/parking/parkingstudy.htm).

Seattle Department of Transportation (Seattle DOT) (2001), *Parking Guide: Simple Ways to Improve Your Neighborhood's Parking*, City of Seattle (www.cityofseattle.net); available online (www.seattle.gov/transportation/parking/parkingguide.htm).

Seattle Department of Transportation (Seattle DOT) (2004), *Parking In Seattle*, City of Seattle (www.seattle.gov); available online (www.seattle.gov/transportation/parking).

Shoup, Donald (2005), *The High Cost of Free Parking*, American Planning Association (Chicago, IL) (www.planning.org).

University of Victoria (UVIC) (2003), *University of Victoria Campus Plan*, UVIC (www.uvic.ca); available online (http://web.uvic.ca/vpfin/campusplan/5.html).

U.S. Environmental Protection Agency (USEPA) (1999), *Parking Alternatives: Making Way for Urban Infill and Brownfield Redevelopment*, Urban and Economic Development Division, USEPA (www.epa.gov) , EPA 231-K-99-001; available online (www.smartgrowth.org/pdf/PRKGDE04.pdf).

Willson, Richard (1995), "Suburban Parking Requirements; A Tacit Policy for Automobile Use and Sprawl," *Journal of the American Planning Association*, Vol. 61, No. 1, Winter 1995, pp. 29-42.

9

Glossary

Access guide: Document that provides concise, customized information on various ways to reach a particular destination, such as a hospital, campus, or business district, including information on parking options.

Accessibility: The ability to reach desired goals, activities, and destinations.

Accessible design: The accommodation of people with disabilities and other special needs. Also called *inclusive design* and *universal design*.

Access management: Term used by transportation professionals to describe effective coordination between roadway design and land-use development.

Accumulation: Total number of vehicles parked, or the portion of available parking spaces occupied, in a specific area at a particular time.

Active transportation: Includes walking, cycling, and their variants, such as wheelchair use. Also called *nonmotorized transport*.

Adjusted parking ratio: Value used to calculate the amount of parking that should be provided at a particular location, taking into account specific geographic, demographic, economic, and management factors.

Annualized cost per parking space: Total capital and operating costs converted into a single annualized value.

Asset management: Policies and programs designed to preserve the value of infrastructure, such as parking facilities and equipment.

Attendant parking: The practice of having attendants park vehicles, as opposed to self-park, in which drivers park their own vehicles. Also called *valet parking*.

Auto mode split: Percentage of travelers to a destination that drive and park a vehicle at that location. Also called *driving ratio*.

Avoided costs: Incremental cost savings that result from a particular decision.

Back-in angled parking: On-street, angled parking into which cars park by backing into a space rather than driving head in.

Base case: Conditions expected to occur if a proposed policy or program is not implemented.

Bio-swale: Ditch where water percolates into the ground.

Boot: Wheel clamp that immobilizes a vehicle.

Bundled good: Term used by economists for additional goods automatically included and at no extra cost with a purchase.

Bundled parking: Parking spaces automatically included with purchased or leased building space, with costs automatically incorporated into mortgages and rents (as opposed to unbundling, which means that parking and parking costs are a consumer option).

Car-free tax discount: Property tax discount provided to households that do not own an automobile, reflecting the lower roadway and traffic service costs that they impose.

Carsharing: Automobile rental services intended to substitute for private vehicle ownership, with vehicles located in residential areas and rented by the hour and day.

Cash-out: Allowing commuters to choose cash instead of a parking subsidy (e.g., a commuter who is offered a parking space might be able to choose to receive $50 per month in cash if they use an alternative mode).

Central business district: Major commercial center of a city, which usually contains a significant portion of high-value business activity, including banking, insurance, real estate, and related services.

Chain parking: Using a parking space multiple time periods.

Change agents: People within existing institutions that provide leadership for innovation and reform.

Change management: Activities that support organizational innovation and reform.

Charrette: A community planning exercise, which involves stakeholders meeting together for one or two days.

Clustering: Trip generators located close together, such as locating shops and offices in a business district rather than sprawled along a highway.

Commercial parking: Parking provided by a for-profit business for which users pay a direct fee.

Commercial parking operator: A person or organization that provides day-to-day parking facility management. Many operators are for-profit businesses that manage parking for property owners on contract, often based on revenue-sharing. Also called *operator*.

Commercial parking tax: Special tax on commercial parking transactions.

Commute mode split: Portion of commuters who use a particular travel mode.

Context-sensitive design: Planning and design practices that are flexible and responsive to local conditions.

Contingency-based planning: A planning strategy that deals with uncertainty by implementing appropriate strategies on an as-needed basis.

Contingency-based standards: Minimum parking requirements that are flexible and adjusted over time based on performance indicators. For example, a contingency-based standard may allow half of the parking ratio published in the Institute of Transportation Engineers' *Trip Generation* (2003), provided that the developer implement a specified parking management program and be required to expand the program or add parking supply if needed.

Cost-based pricing: Prices set to recover the full costs of providing a good or service.

Cost-recovery parking: Parking facilities that are priced to recover their full costs.

Credits: Specified reductions in parking requirements allowed for factors that increase efficiency or reduce parking demand.

Curb parking: Parking spaces provided in the curb lane of a street. Also called *on-street parking*.

Deck: Multistory parking facility. Also called *garage, parkade, ramp* or *structured parking*.

Demand ratio: Number of parking spaces required, based on a reference unit (e.g., per 1,000 square feet of floor space, bed, employee, or housing unit).

Density: Number of people or jobs in an area.

Design-based code: Building code that defines the type of development desired and provides maximum flexibility for achieving it. Also called *form-based code*.

Design hour: Number of annual hours that parking demand is allowed to exceed supply at a particular location. Parking requirements are often designated for the 10th or 20th design hour.

Design review: Process used to gain community input into facility design.

District parking: Parking supplied and managed by a central authority to serve an area, rather than each site supplying its own parking (common in commercial centers, campuses, and malls).

Double dividend: Additional benefits that result from a policy or management strategy.

Driving ratio: Percentage of travelers to a destination that drive and park a vehicle at that location. Also called *auto mode split.*

Duration: Length of time a vehicle remains in a specific parking space.

Economic transfers: Economic resources shifted from one person or group to another.

Efficiency-based standard: Standard that sizes facilities for optimal utilization, which means that parking supply decisions are based on the specific needs and conditions of each location, as opposed to generic and inflexible standards.

Elasticities: The percentage of change in consumption of a good in response to a percentage change in its price.

End-of-trip facilities: Bicycle parking, storage, and shower/changing rooms.

E-purse: Internet payment system.

Evaluation framework: The basic structure for analyzing and comparing planning options.

Fairness: Concerned with whether each individual or group is treated equally, assuming that their needs and abilities are comparable. Also called *horizontal equity.*

Financial incentives: Fees, discounts, and financial benefits intended to encourage a change in consumer behavior.

Footprint: Outline of a structure viewed from above.

Form-based code: Building code that defines the type of development desired and provides maximum flexibility for achieving it. Also called *design-based code.*

Free parking levy: Special tax imposed on unpriced parking, such as a $50 annual tax per space provided free to employees.

Garage: Multistory parking facility. Also called *deck, parkade, ramp* or *structured parking.*

Geographic Information System (GIS): Computer-based system for storing and analyzing geographic information, such as maps and building location data.

Greenspace: Biologically active land uses such as parks, lawns, gardens, farms, forests, and wetlands.

Gross floor area (GFA): Total floor area of a building, including exterior walls and other building space that is not usually used by occupants, such as utility spaces.

Gross leasable area (GLA): Portion of gross floor area that is available for leasing to a tenant; excludes common areas that are not leased to tenants (e.g., lobbies, elevator cores, stairs, corridors, and atriums), utility spaces, and parking areas.

Heat island effect: Higher local temperatures due to solar gain from dark-colored surfaces, such as pavement and building roofs.

Horizontal equity: Concerned with whether each individual or group is treated equally, assuming that their needs and abilities are comparable. Also called *fairness.*

Impervious surface: Land covered by pavement or buildings through which rainwater cannot seep into the ground.

Impervious surface fee: One-time or annual fee imposed on property owners based on the amount of impervious surfaces on their property.

Inclusive design: The accommodation of people with disabilities and other special needs. Also called *accessible design* and *universal design.*

In-lieu fees: Fees paid by developers to fund public parking facilities as a substitute for private, off-street parking serving a single destination.

Index: Reference value used to calculate the number of parking spaces required at a particular location (e.g., spaces per 1,000 square feet or per housing unit). Also called *parking ratio.*

Intelligent Transportation System (ITS): Various communication technologies used to improve transportation services.

Inventory: Survey of the number and type of parking spaces in a particular area. Also called *supply inventory.*

Land banking: Land set aside to be used for parking facilities if needed in the future.

Land-use accessibility: The ease of reaching activities and destinations.

Land-use mix: Different land-use types, such as residential and commercial, located close together.

Least-cost planning: Planning process that considers efficiency improvements equally with capacity expansion, taking into account all costs.

Level of service: Qualitative measure describing the performance of a facility or service; often rated A (best) through F (worst).

Load factor: Portion of available parking spaces used at a particular location and time. Also called *occupancy rate* or *utilization.*

Loading zones: Curb or parking area regulated for short-term use for vehicle loading and unloading.

Long-term parking: Parking spaces intended for 4 hours or more duration, for use by commuters and residents.

Lot-sharing agreement: Agreement that specifies how parking facilities are to be shared by multiple users.

Marginal analysis: Analysis of the incremental impacts (costs and benefits) of an additional unit of consumption, production, or capacity.

Marketing: Activities to determine consumer needs and preferences, produce goods and services that meet those needs, and promote the use of specific products.

Mass transit: Transportation services using shared vehicles (e.g., shuttle vans, buses, or rail systems) that provide local or regional mobility to the general public. Also called *public transport* or *transit.*

Mobility: The movement of people or goods.

Mobility management: General term for various strategies and programs that result in more efficient use of transportation resources, by changing travel timing, route, mode, destination, and frequency. Also called *transportation demand management.*

Mode split: Portion of trips made by each mode (e.g., walking, cycling, ridesharing, automobile, and public transit).

Multimodalism: Transportation system or facility designed for and used by multiple modes, which can include walking, cycling, ridesharing, automobile, and public transit.

Multistop pedestrian trip: The practice of motorists parking in one location and walking to various nearby destinations, rather than driving to and parking at each destination. Also called *park-once trip.*

Net floor area: Usable building floor area, excluding exterior building walls and utility spaces.

Net leasable area: Portion of net floor area that is rentable to a tenant. Also called *net rental area.*

Net rental area: Portion of net floor area that is rentable to a tenant. Also called *net leasable area.*

Net present value: The full value of an option over the analysis period, with all costs and benefits depreciated to a base year.

New urbanism: General term for development practices that result in more compact and walkable communities with mixed land use.

Nonmotorized transport: Includes walking, cycling, and their variants, such as wheelchair use. Also called *active transportation.*

Occupancy rate: Portion of available parking spaces used at a particular location and time. Also called *utilization* or *load factor.*

Off-street parking: Parking spaces on a separate piece of land, not on the street.

On-street parking: Parking spaces included in the curb land of a street. Also called *curb parking.*

Operator: A person or organization that provides day-to-day parking facility operations. Many operators are for-profit businesses that manage parking for property owners on contract, often based on revenue-sharing. Also called *commercial parking operator.*

Overflow parking: Parking spaces available for occasional use during periods of high demand, which are often less convenient or less durable than regular parking facilities. Also called *remote parking* or *satellite parking.*

Overflow parking plan: Plan that identifies the responses that will be applied when parking demand exceeds the available supply at a location.

Overlay planning district: Area where special zoning codes and development practices apply, such as a downtown area or transit-oriented development.

Paradigm shift: A fundamental change in how a problem is perceived and how solutions are evaluated.

Parallel parking: Parking alongside or parallel to the curb; a common type of on-street parking.

Park & Ride: Parking facility intended for use by commuters when they use transit or carpool.

Parkability: Ease with which motorists can park.

Parkade: Multistory parking facility. Also called *deck, garage, ramp,* or *structured parking.*

Parker: Motorist who uses a parking facility.

Parking authority: An agency that manages the public parking facilities in an area.

Parking bank: A service provided by a local organization that involves helping businesses share, trade, lease, rent, and sell parking facilities. Also called *parking brokerage* or *parking exchange.*

Parking bay: A defined group of parking spaces.

Parking benefit district: Designated area in which on-street parking is priced, with revenues used to provide local services.

Parking brokerage: A service provided by a local organization that involves helping businesses share, trade, lease, rent, and sell parking facilities. Also called *parking bank* or *parking exchange.*

Parking caps: Limit to the amount of parking that may be supplied in an area.

Parking demand: Number of parking spaces that could be occupied at a particular location, time, and price. Also called *parking generation.*

Parking exchange: A service provided by a local organization that involves helping businesses share, trade, lease, rent, and sell parking facilities. Also called *parking bank* or *parking brokerage.*

Parking facility orientation: Where parking lots are located with respect to streets, sidewalks, and buildings.

Parking generation: Number of parking spaces that could be occupied at a particular location, time, and price. Also called *parking demand.*

Parking impact fee: One-time or annual fee imposed on parking spaces in a particular area used to fund transportation services and stormwater management programs.

Parking management: Any policy, program, or technique that results in a more efficient use of parking resources.

Parking management association: A business organization that provides parking management services in a particular area.

Parking maximums: An upper limit placed on supply of parking allowed, either at individual sites or throughout an area, such as a commercial district.

Parking meter zone: The area within which public parking is priced by meters.

Parking planning: Process for determining the location, quantity, price, management, design, enforcement, and administration of parking facilities.

Parking ratio: Reference value used to calculate the number of parking spaces required at a particular location (e.g., spaces per 1,000 square feet or per housing unit). Also called *index*.

Parking regulations: Regulations that control who, when, and how long vehicles may park at a particular location in order to prioritize parking facility use.

Parking requirement: Number of parking spaces that must be supplied at a particular location, which is often mandated in zoning codes or development requirements based on published standards.

Parking requirement reduction credits: Specified reductions in parking requirements allowed for factors such as shared parking facilities, proximity to transit, and other parking management strategies.

Parking space: Single parking stall, typically a 10 × 20-foot paved area connected to a roadway, suitable for motor vehicle storage.

Parking standard: Reference value (called a *parking ratio* or *index*) used to calculate the number of parking spaces that should be provided at a particular location, often established by professional organizations (e.g., the Institute of Transportation Engineers or the American Planning Association), and incorporated into zoning codes, planning regulations, and development requirements. Also called *unadjusted parking ratio*.

Parking supply: Number of parking spaces available at a particular location.

Park-once trip: The practice of motorists parking in one location and walking to various nearby destinations, rather than driving to and parking at each destination. Also called *multistop pedestrian trip*.

Peak: Time period when parking demand is greatest.

Performance indicators: Practical ways to measure progress toward objectives.

Per-space levy: Special tax or fee imposed on parking facilities, such as a $30 annual tax on each nonresidential parking space.

Planning overlay district: Area where special zoning codes and development practices apply, such as a downtown or transit-oriented neighborhood.

Priced parking: Parking for which users must pay a fee.

Pricing parking: The practice of requiring motorists to pay directly for using parking facilities.

Progressive: With respect to income, policies that provide proportionally greater benefits to lower-income groups.

Public parking: Parking facilities that may be used by the general public.

Public realm: Public spaces where members of society meet and interact, including streets, sidewalks, parks, plazas, and other public facilities.

Public transport: Transportation services using shared vehicles (e.g., shuttle vans, buses, or rail systems) that provide local or regional mobility to the general public. Also called *mass transit* or *transit*.

Quality of service: Convenience, comfort, and safety of a facility or service as perceived by users. Also called *service quality*.

Ramp: Multistory parking facility. Also called *deck, garage, parkade,* or *structured parking*.

Real-time information: Information reflecting actual current conditions, such as signs and Web sites that indicate the actual number of parking spaces available in a parking facility based on automated tracking systems.

Regressive: With respect to income, policies that make lower-income people relatively worse off.

Remote parking: Use of off-site parking facilities. Also called *overflow parking* or *satellite parking*.

Reserved space: Parking space that may only be used by a particular motorist (as opposed to a shared space).

Residential parking zone: Area where on-street parking is regulated to favor residents, often using residential parking permits or other enforcement mechanisms.

Satellite parking: Use of off-site parking facilities. Also called *overflow parking* or *remote parking*.

Self-park: The practice of drivers parking their own vehicles, as opposed to valet parking in which attendants park each vehicle.

Service quality: Convenience, comfort, and safety of a facility or service as perceived by users. Also called *quality of service*.

Shared parking: A parking lot that serves multiple destinations, and parking spaces shared by more than one user (as opposed to a reserved space).

Short-term parking: Parking spaces intended for 2 hours or less duration, for use by delivery vehicles, customers, and other visitors.

Single-destination parking: A parking facility that only serves one destination and may not be used by motorists going elsewhere or by the general public.

Site: A particular parcel of land, building, or other facility.

Smart growth: General term for development practices that result in more compact mixed and accessible land-use development.

Speed bump: Traffic speed reduction device (with abrupt profiles), often used to control traffic within parking lots.

Speed hump: Traffic-calming device (with gradual, tapered profiles), often used to control traffic within parking lots. Also called *speed platform*.

Speed platform: Traffic-calming device (with gradual, tapered profiles), often used to control traffic within parking lots. Also called *speed hump*.

Spillover parking: Undesired use of off-site parking spaces, such as when one business's customers park at another nearby business, or when employees park on residential streets near their worksite.

Stall: Single parking space.

Stormwater management fee: Utility fee based on a property's impervious surface area to fund stormwater management services, such as a $15 annual fee per 1,000 square feet of pavement or a $5 annual fee per parking space.

Structured parking: Multistory parking facility. Also called *deck, garage, parkade* or *ramp*.

Subsidy: A payment by another party that reduces the price to consumers of a particular product.

Sunk costs: Costs incurred in the past that are irretrievable and therefore do not affect current decisions.

Supply inventory: Survey of the number and type of parking spaces in a particular area. Also called *inventory*.

Surface parking: Parking facilities built directly on the ground.

Swale: Ditch into which stormwater drains and percolates into the ground.

Tandem parking: One vehicle parked behind another on a driveway.

Time-variable rates: Prices that vary over time, with higher rates during peak periods.

Traffic calming: Various design features intended to reduce vehicle traffic speeds and volumes on a particular roadway or within a parking facility.

Transaction cost: Any incremental cost required for regulations and pricing, including costs for equipment (e.g., signs, parking meters, ticket printers, and access gates), attendants, land (such as sidewalk space used by parking meters), administration, and enforcement.

Transit: Transportation services using shared vehicles (e.g., shuttle vans, buses, or rail systems) that provide local or regional transportation services to the general public. Also called *mass transit* or *public transport*.

Transit benefit: Free or discounted transit fares, usually provided by employers to employees as an alternative to subsidized parking.

Transit-oriented development: General term for development policies that result in more compact and accessible land-use development around transit stations and lines.

Transportation demand management: General term for various strategies and programs that result in more efficient use of transportation resources, by changing travel timing, route, mode, destination, and frequency. Also called *mobility management.*

Transportation disadvantaged: People who have special transportation needs due to economic, physical, or social constraints.

Transportation diversity: Range of transportation options available.

Transportation management association: Private, nonprofit, member-controlled organization that provides transportation and parking services in a particular area (e.g., a commercial district, a mall, a medical center, or an industrial park).

Turnover: Number of different vehicles that park in a specific space or area during a particular time period, such as vehicles per hour or vehicles per day.

Unadjusted parking ratio: Reference value used to calculate the amount of parking that should be provided at a particular location that has not been adjusted to account for specific geographic, demographic, economic, and management factors. Also called *parking standard* and *unconstrained values.*

Unbundle parking: Parking rented and sold separately from building space, so occupants only pay for the amount of parking they want.

Unconstrained values: Generous minimum parking ratios set without concern to the costs of providing parking facilities or adjusted to account for specific geographic, demographic, economic, or management factors that reduce parking demand. Also called *unadjusted parking ratio.*

Underground parking: Parking facilities located under a building.

Universal design: The accommodation of people with disabilities and other special needs. Also called *accessible design* and *inclusive design.*

Universal transit passes: Bulk purchase of discounted transit passes for all members of a group, such as all students at a college or all employees at a worksite.

Urban village: Walkable, mixed-use neighborhood center.

User information: Information provided to users of a facility or service, such as information about parking availability, regulations, price, and alternative travel options, provided to people traveling to a particular destination.

User Pays principle: The economic principle that the costs of providing a good or service should be borne by users unless a subsidy is specifically justified.

Utilization: Portion of available parking spaces used at a particular location and time. Also called *occupancy rate* or *load factor.*

Valet parking: The practice of having attendants park vehicles, as opposed to self-park where drivers park their own vehicles. Also called *attendant parking.*

Walkability: Quality of walking conditions.

Workplace parking levy: Per-space tax or fee applied specifically to employee parking.

10

References

Barr, Mary (1998), *Downtown Parking Made Easy,* Downtown Research & Development Center (New York) (www.downtowndevelopment.com).

Childs, Mark (1999), *Parking Spaces: A Design, Implementation and Use Manual for Architects, Planners, and Engineers,* The McGraw-Hill Companies (New York) (www.mcgraw-hill.com).

Community Research & Development Information Service (2001), *COST 342: Parking Policy Measures and their Effects on Mobility and the Economy,* European Commission; available online (www.cordis.lu/cost-transport/src/cost-342.htm).

Congress for the New Urbanism, *Narrow Streets Database,* Congress for the New Urbanism (www.cnu.org); available online (www.sonic.net/abcaia/narrow.htm).

de Cerreño, Allison L.C. (2002), *The Dynamics of On-Street Parking In Large Central Cities,* Rudin Center for Transportation Policy & Management (New York) (www.nyu.edu/wagner/rudincenter).

Davidson, Michael and Fay Dolnick (2002), *Parking Standards,* Planning Advisory Service Report 510/511, American Planning Association (Chicago, IL) (www.planning.org).

Edwards, John D. (1994), *Parking: The Parking Handbook for Small Communities,* Institute of Transportation Engineers (Washington, DC) (www.ite.org) and National Main Street Center (Washington, DC) (www.mainstreet.org).

Everett-Lee, Reed (1999), *Parking Management,* Transportation Tech Sheet, Congress for the New Urbanism (www.cnu.org); available online (www.cnu.org/cnu_reports/CNU_Parking_Management.pdf).

Ewing, Reid (1996), *Best Development Practices; Doing the Right Thing and Making Money at the Same Time,* American Planning Association (Chicago, IL) (www.planning.org).

Institute of Transportation Engineers (2003), *Trip Generation,* Institute of Transportation Engineers (Washington, DC) (www.ite.org).

Institute of Transportation Engineers (2003), *Smart Growth Transportation Guidelines,* Smart Growth Task Force, Institute of Transportation Engineers (Washington, DC) (www.ite.org).

Institute of Transportation Engineers (2004), *Parking Generation, Third Edition*, Institute of Transportation Engineers (Washington, DC) (www.ite.org).

Institution of Civil Engineers (2002), *Recommendations for the Inspection, Maintenance and Management of Car Park Structures*, Institution of Civil Engineers (London) (www.ice.org.uk).

International Association of Public Transport (1999), *Parking Policy: State of the Art*, International Association of Public Transport (Paris) (www.uitp.com).

International Parking Institute (2002), *Parking 101: A Parking Primer*, International Parking Institute (Fredericksburg, VA) (www.parking.org).

K.T. Analytics, Inc. (1992), *TDM Status Report: Parking Pricing*, U.S. Department of Transportation, Federal Transit Administration (www.fta.dot.gov); available online (www.fta.dot.gov/library/planning/tdmstatus/tdm.htm).

K.T. Analytics, Inc. (1995), *TDM Status Report: Parking Supply Management*, U.S. Department of Transportation, Federal Transit Administration (www.fta.dot.gov); available online (www.fta.dot.gov/library/planning/tdmstatus/tdm.htm).

Kuzmyak, J. Richard and Richard H. Pratt (2003), *Land Use and Site Design: Traveler Response to Transportation System Changes*, Chapter 15, Report 95, Transit Cooperative Research Program; Transportation Research Board (www.trb.org); available online (http://gulliver.trb.org/publications/tcrp/tcrp_rpt_95c15.pdf).

Kuzmyak, J. Richard, Rachel Weinberger, Richard H. Pratt, and Herbert S. Levinson (2003), *Parking Management and Supply: Traveler Response to Transport System Changes*, Chapter 18, Report 95, Transit Cooperative Research Program; Transportation Research Board (www.trb.org); available online (http://gulliver.trb.org/publications/tcrp/tcrp_rpt_95c18.pdf).

Litman, Todd (2000), *Transportation Land Valuation; Evaluating Policies and Practices that Affect the Amount of Land Devoted to Transportation Facilities*, Victoria Transport Policy Institute (www.vtpi.org); available online (www.vtpi.org/land.pdf).

Litman, Todd (2004), "Parking Costs," *Transportation Cost and Benefit Analysis: Techniques, Estimates and Implications*, Victoria Transport Policy Institute (www.vtpi.org); available online (www.vtpi.org/tca/tca0504.pdf).

McClintock, Hugh (2004), *Parking Policy, Pricing, Management & Provision—Planning Bibliography*, School of the Built Environment, The University of Nottingham (www.nottingham.ac.uk); available online (www.nottingham.ac.uk/sbe/planbiblios/bibs/sustrav/refs/0x80f3d2fe_0x000a1b57.html).

Millard-Ball, Adam (2002), "Putting on Their Parking Caps," *Planning* (www.planning.org), April 2002, pp. 16-21.

National Parking Association is an organization of the parking industry (www.npapark.org).

Nelson/Nygaard Consulting (2002), *Housing Shortage/Parking Surplus*, Transportation and Land Use Coalition (www.transcoalition.org); available online (www.transcoalition.org/reports/housing_s/housing_shortage_home.html).

Nonpoint Education for Municipal Officials is a University of Connecticut educational program that works to encourage local policies that reduce impervious surface impacts (http://nemo.uconn.edu).

Oregon Downtown Development Association (2001), *Parking Management Made Easy: A guide to taming the downtown parking beast*, Transportation and Growth Management Program, Oregon Department of Transportation and the Oregon

Department of Land Conservation and Development (www.lcd.state.or.us); available online (http://egov.oregon.gov/LCD/docs/publications/parkingguide.pdf).

Puget Sound Regional Council (2003), *Parking Management Plan Checklist: Planning for Your Regional Growth Center*, Puget Sound Regional Council (www.psrc.org), Summer 2003; available online (www.psrc.org/projects/growth/parking.pdf).

Robertson, Kent A. (2001), "Parking and Pedestrians: Balancing Two Key Elements in Downtown Development," *Transportation Quarterly*, Vol. 55, No. 2, Spring 2001, pp. 29-42.

Russo, Ryan (2001), *Planning for Residential Parking: A Guide For Housing Developers and Planners*, The Non-Profit Housing Association of Northern California (www.nonprofithousing.org) and the Berkeley Program on Housing and Urban Policy (http://urbanpolicy.berkeley.edu); available online (www.nonprofithousing.org/actioncenter/toolbox/parking/index.atomic).

Seattle Department of Transportation (2001), *Parking Guide: Simple Ways to Improve Your Neighborhood's Parking*, City of Seattle (www.cityofseattle.net); available online (www.seattle.gov/transportation/parking/parkingguide.htm).

Shoup, Donald (1995), "An Opportunity to Reduce Minimum Parking Requirements," *Journal of the American Planning Association*, Vol. 61, No. 1, Winter 1995, pp. 14-28.

Shoup, Donald (1999), *Instead of Free Parking*, ACCESS No. 15, University of California Transportation Center (www.uctc.net), Fall 1999, pp. 6-9; available online (www.uctc.net/access/access15lite.pdf).

Shoup, Donald (2005), *The High Cost of Free Parking*, American Planning Association (Chicago, IL) (www.planning.org).

Shoup, Donald C. (1999), "In Lieu of Required Parking," *Journal of Planning Education and Research*, Vol. 18, pp. 307-320; available online (www.sppsr.ucla.edu/dup/people/faculty/Shoup%20Pub%202.pdf).

Shoup, Donald C. (1997), *The High Cost of Free Parking*, ACCESS No. 10, Department of Urban Planning, The University of California Transportation Center (www.uctc.net), Spring 1997; available online (www.uctc.net/scripts/countdown.pl?351.pdf).

Smith, Mary (1999), "Parking," Chapter 14, *Transportation Planning Handbook*, Institute of Transportation Engineers (Washington, DC) (www.ite.org).

Smith, Thomas P. (1988), *The Aesthetics of Parking*, Planning Advisory Service, American Planning Association (Chicago, IL) (www.planning.org).

Urban Land Institute (2000), *The Dimensions of Parking*, ULI (Washington, DC) (www.uli.org) and the National Parking Association (Washington, DC) (www.npapark.org).

U.S. Environmental Protection Agency (1998), *Parking Management*, Transportation and Air Quality TCM Technical Overviews, U.S. Environmental Protection Agency (www.epa.gov); available online (www.epa.gov/oms/transp/publicat/pub_tech.htm).

U.S. Environmental Protection Agency (1999), *Parking Alternatives: Making Way for Urban Infill and Brownfield Redevelopment*, Urban and Economic Development Division, U.S. Environmental Protection Agency (www.epa.gov) , EPA 231-K-99-001; available online (www.smartgrowth.org/pdf/PRKGDE04.pdf).

U.S. Environmental Protection Agency (2004), *Smart Growth Policies Data Base*, U.S. Environmental Protection Agency (www.epa.gov); available online (http://cfpub.epa.gov/sgpdb/sgdb.cfm).

Valleley, Mark (1997), *Parking Perspectives: A Sourcebook for the Development of Parking Policy*, Landor Publishing Ltd. (London) (www.landor.co.uk).

Victoria Transport Policy Institute (2005), *Online TDM Encyclopedia*, Victoria Transport Policy Institute (www.vtpi.org); available online (www.vtpi.org/tdm).

Voith, Richard (1998), "The Downtown Parking Syndrome: Does Curing the Illness Kill the Patient?" *Business Review* (www.phil.frb.org/econ/br/index.html), Vol. 1, 1998, pp 3-14; available online (www.phil.frb.org/files/br/brjf98dv.pdf).

Washington State Department of Transportation (1999), *Local Government Parking Policy and Commute Trip Reduction: 1999 Review*, Commute Trip Reduction Office, Washington State Department of Transportation (www.wsdot.wa.gov); available online (www.wsdot.wa.gov/tdm/tripreduction/parking_policy.cfm).

Willson, Richard (1997), "Parking Pricing Without Tears: Trip Reduction Programs," *Transportation Quarterly*, Vol. 51, No. 1, Winter 1997, pp. 79-90.

Index